China Goes Green

China Goes Green

Coercive Environmentalism for a Troubled Planet

Yifei Li and Judith Shapiro

polity

First published in 2020 by Polity Press

Polity Press
65 Bridge Street
Cambridge CB2 1UR, UK

Polity Press
101 Station Landing
Suite 300
Medford, MA 02155, USA

ISBN-13: 978-1-5095-4311-3
ISBN-13: 978-1-5095-4312-0 (pb)

A catalogue record for this book is available from the British Library.

Library of Congress Cataloging-in-Publication Data

Names: Li, Yifei, 1978- author. | Shapiro, Judith, author.
Title: China goes green : coercive environmentalism for a troubled planet /
    Yifei Li and Judith Shapiro.
Description: Cambridge, UK ; Medford, MA : Polity, 2020. | Includes
    bibliographical references and index. | Summary: "Can China's
    eco-authoritarianism save the planet?"-- Provided by publisher.
Identifiers: LCCN 2020002554 (print) | LCCN 2020002555 (ebook) | ISBN
    9781509543113 (hardback) | ISBN 9781509543120 (paperback) | ISBN
    9781509543137 (epub)
Subjects: LCSH: Environmental policy--China. | Environmentalism--China. |
    Authoritarianism--China. | China--Environmental conditions--21st century.
Classification: LCC GE190.C6 L54 2020 (print) | LCC GE190.C6 (ebook) |
    DDC 363.700951--dc23
LC record available at https://lccn.loc.gov/2020002554
LC ebook record available at https://lccn.loc.gov/2020002555

Typeset in 11 on 13pt Sabon
by Fakenham Prepress Solutions, Fakenham, Norfolk NR21 8NL
Printed and bound in Great Britain by CPI Group (UK) Ltd, Croydon

For further information on Polity, visit our website:
politybooks.com

Contents

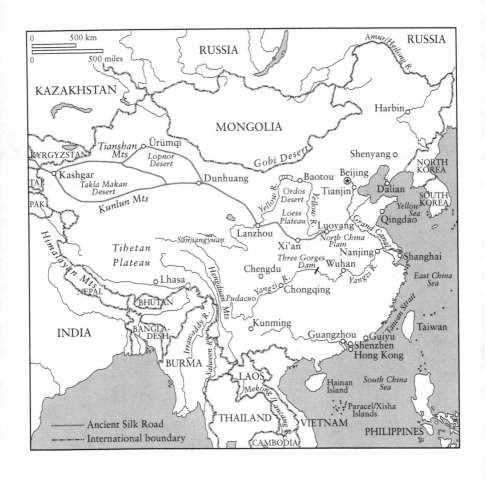

RUSSIA

RUSSIA

KAZAKHSTAN

MONGOLIA

Amur/Heilong R.

Harbin

0   500 km

0   500 miles

Tianshan Mts   Ürümqi
KYRGYZSTAN   *Lopnor Desert*   *Gobi Desert*   Shenyang   NORTH KOREA

Kashgar   *Takla Makan Desert*   Dunhuang   Baotou   Beijing   Dalian
TAJ.   *Yellow R.*   *Ordos Desert*   Tianjin   SOUTH KOREA
PAK.   *Kunlun Mts*   *Loess Plateau*   *Yellow R.*   Yellow Sea   Qingdao

Himalayan Mts   *Tibetan Plateau*   *Sanjiangyuan*   Lanzhou   Luoyang   *North China Plain*   *Grand Canal*
                                                                    Xi'an   Nanjing   Shanghai
NEPAL   Lhasa   *Hengduan Mts*   Chengdu   *Three Gorges Dam*   Wuhan   *East China Sea*
BHUTAN   *Pudacuo*   *Yangzi R.*   Chongqing   *Yangzi R.*
INDIA   BANGLA-DESH   *Irrawaddy R.*   Kunming   *Taiwan Strait*   Taiwan
            Salween R.   Guangzhou   Guiyu
        BURMA   Shenzhen
                                                Hong Kong
                    LAOS   Hainan Island   *South China Sea*
            Mekong/Lancang
        THAILAND   VIETNAM   *Paracel/Xisha Islands*   PHILIPPINES
        CAMBODIA

——— Ancient Silk Road
‑‑‑‑‑ International boundary

Acknowledgments

We are most grateful to two anonymous readers who helped us strengthen this book and to Isabella Baranyk, who provided exceptionally thoughtful and comprehensive feedback on drafts. We also acknowledge insightful comments and contributions from colleagues, friends, and relatives, including Jisho Warner, Elska Lennox, Rosa Shapiro-Thompson, Ivan Willis Rasmussen, Simon Nicholson, Jesse Ribot, Ken Conca, Craig Simons, and Bo Donners. Chen Qihang and Yuan Qianchun provided helpful research. Marcela Godoy generously shared her artwork. Tian Tian Wedgwood Young assembled the index. We are also grateful to our experienced editors at Polity, Louise Knight and Inès Boxman. Steve Leard designed an interesting cover, Neil de Cort expertly managed the production, and Ian Tuttle performed masterful copy edits. We are also immensely grateful to each other, for seamlessly building on the other's strengths to create a much better book than either of us could have written on our own.

Introduction: The Rise of Authoritarian Environmentalism

A decade or so after the start of the twenty-first century, China's policy makers appeared poised to assume global leadership on environmental protection. Where just a few years before, Chinese negotiators in global forums had argued vociferously for the primacy of international legal principles that protected developing country interests, China began to moderate its use of these arguments. Instead of focusing on the right to development, technology transfer from developed to developing countries, financing for mitigation and adaptation, absolute sovereignty over natural resources, and common but differentiated responsibilities, China's leaders began to speak about climate change and other environmental challenges as shared global threats. Where at one time the country was seen as a primary obstacle to achieving consensus on these issues, China seemed to some observers as the last best hope for efforts to save the planet.

At around the same time, environmental governance was changing dramatically within China. Once seen as having weak environmental institutions with poor enforcement capabilities, China renamed and elevated the environment ministry to become the Ministry of Ecology and Environment, expanding and centralizing its portfolio of responsibilities to cover a broad range of pollutants including carbon emissions and water contaminants. Once seen as unable to control local officials who exploited lax enforcement to profit from pollution, China's leaders changed criteria for performance evaluation to emphasize environmental protection and implemented severe punishments for local officials' failures to fulfill environmental goals. Once seen as unable to enforce its assortment of environmental laws, China strengthened them, got rid of loopholes, created a system of dedicated environmental courts, and opened up the judicial process to environmental advocacy groups. Once seen as bent on destroying its own biodiversity, China reorganized the administration of protected areas and embarked on an ambitious program to conserve vast swaths of its West, under the authority of a new Ministry of Natural Resources. Once seen as holding open its door to some of the world's most polluting industries and waste products, China banned them. The list could go on.

In 2009, at the Conference of the Parties to the UN climate negotiations in Denmark, observers excoriated China for undermining the talks. "How Do I Know China Wrecked the Copenhagen Deal? I Was in the Room," wrote the *Guardian*'s Mark Lynas (2009) in a typical account. Widely seen as the villain for snubbing heads of state, blocking transparent public negotiations, and rejecting hard targets even for developed countries, China managed to weaken the talks and make it appear that rich countries had failed developing ones. China's official position was characterized as wanting to "have it all," leveraging its developing country status for reduced responsibilities, seeking to mitigate the adverse impacts of climate change, and trying to achieve global recognition for domestic environmental efforts (Conrad 2012).

But by November 2014, everything appeared to have changed. At the Asia-Pacific Economic Cooperation (APEC) summit in Beijing, President Xi Jinping and President Barack Obama jointly announced that each country would take ambitious steps to reduce carbon emissions. In a landmark agreement, President Obama used his executive power to commit the US to stop building coal-fired power plants; he promised that by 2025 the US would emit 26–28 percent less carbon dioxide than in 2005. United States action may have allowed President Xi to claim that the developed world was going first, as required under widely accepted international principles of common but differentiated responsibilities. For his part, Xi announced that China's carbon emissions would stop growing by around 2030 and that clean energy sources would amount to 20 percent of China's energy mix by that year. Some have argued that these commitments were likely a reflection of the path China had set for itself regardless of multilateral negotiations, given that reducing coal use would also achieve the "double win" of reducing ground-level air pollution and improving public health in addition to mitigating climate change. Nevertheless, the joint declaration was greeted with fanfare (Hilton and Kerr 2017). Cooperation between the US and China, which together represented 40 percent of global emissions, brought new life to the 2015 Paris negotiations, which did indeed result in tangible, albeit voluntary, commitments from almost all parties. When, in 2017, President Donald Trump announced that the US would withdraw from the treaty, observers feared China might feel released from its own responsibilities. Instead, President

Xi Jinping reasserted China's commitment to fulfill its obligations and to uphold multilateralism, signing a pact with French president Emmanuel Macron recommitting to the agreement. In so doing, China assumed the moral high ground as compared with the United States and spurred even more hope that China would become the new global leader on climate change.

This has not yet come to fruition. During the December 2019 Madrid negotiations, China joined other big carbon emitters such as India and Brazil in resisting more ambitious targets. Together with members of the bloc called the G77 plus China, it insisted that developed countries had to uphold their 2015 Paris commitments before developing countries could commit to new ones. When the US and other wealthy countries balked, talks came to a stalemate. While there was plenty of blame to go around for the failure of the talks, especially with respect to the destructive role of the US, China was singled out for once again being unwilling to assume the kind of global leadership it had flirted with four years before.

Nonetheless, on the face of it the Chinese state appears indeed to be offering the world a green vision. After an astounding period of economic growth since the 1980s, during which the country became both the world's manufacturing hub and also one of the most intensely polluted places on the planet, the central leadership has issued hard-nosed policy changes intended to resolve China's environmental crisis. Green China boasts solid achievements, especially in the clean technology industry. China in 2012 surpassed the US to become the world's top wind energy user as measured by installed capacity (Lam et al. 2017). The growth of its solar sector helped drop world prices by 80 percent from 2008 to 2013 (Fialka 2016). The Chinese State Council has committed national support for hydrogen fuel-cell and battery-powered electric cars, with the eventual goal of totally eliminating gas-powered internal combustion engine vehicles (K. Wang 2018). China is the world's largest manufacturer and buyer of electric vehicles, including 99 percent of the world's electric buses. China has built tens of thousands of miles of new high-speed rail, using cutting-edge technology to shrink distances among cities and integrate the country into a vast, energy-efficient transit network. China has shut down the import of low-grade recyclables and hazardous e-wastes, switched heating systems from coal to natural gas, and outlawed ivory sales. Rhetoric about low-carbon lifestyles, the circular economy, sustainable development, ecological civilization, resilient growth, and green development is inescapable. By these measures, it seems indeed that China has gone green. This book will deconstruct and challenge that assertion.

Ecological Civilization as Political Philosophy

These rhetorical and regulatory shifts toward "green" China may be traced to a rethinking of the country's guiding political philosophy. For a struggling developing country emerging from Mao-era chaos in 1979, economic growth seemed the most important national goal. Ideological work to define and introduce "socialism with Chinese characteristics" – a formula that promoted the free market in a nominally Marxist society – was required. This formula helped make China the manufacturing hub of the world. But the explosive growth came at an unacceptable environmental cost, one that risked social upheaval and loss of legitimacy for the Communist Party. The country's core ideological principles needed revision and updating so as to provide guidance to address deepening post-Mao social and economic contradictions like inequality, unemployment, and consumerism, all exacerbated by the befoulment of China's air, water, soil, and food.

In China, to a degree unheard of in the West, major policy shifts must be justified through debate and agreement over underlying political philosophy. Supported by an extensive network of government think tanks, Party schools, and Marxism research centers at universities, the one-party system relies on ideological consensus for the country's overarching direction. In 2007, under Xi Jinping's predecessor Hu Jintao, "ecological civilization," or *shengtai wenming* 生态文明, became an explicit goal of the Chinese Communist Party. In 2012, the phrase was enshrined within the Party Constitution, and six years later within the Constitution of the People's Republic of China. With the successful elevation of this phrase to the level of official political philosophy, the latest iteration of the Party's ideological work came to fruition. Xi Jinping's ubiquitously quoted line encapsulates this: "Clear waters, green mountains are in fact gold mountains, silver mountains" (*lüshui qingshan jiushi jinshan yinshan* 绿水青山就是金山银山).

"Ecological civilization" garners widespread support across China's broad and sprawling state apparatus because it projects the Party's rule as both historical and visionary. Ecological civilization is described first and foremost as a continuation of China's developmental path under the leadership of the Communist Party – transforming from agricultural civilization to industrial civilization under Mao Zedong, then to material civilization under Deng Xiaoping, and now to ecological civilization under Xi Jinping – a faithful reincarnation of Marx's theory of the stages of development with Chinese characteristics. At the same time, on the world stage the phrase frames the Chinese nation as a leader of a rejuvenated civilization, reviving nationalistic fervor in a nation that has emerged out of its "century of humiliation" under Western and Japanese imperialism. Thus, in light of the tremendous political appeal of ecological civilization, China's go-green efforts are inextricably linked to the political and ideological ambitions of the state.

As a political philosophy, ecological civilization builds on two schools of thought, both with Western roots. These are ecological Marxism and constructive postmodernism. The former understands the commodification of nature as lying at the heart of contradictions that may spell the eventual demise of capitalism. The latter attempts to integrate the best characteristics of tradition and modernity, both as a philosophical thought experiment and as a practical path toward harmony between humans and non-human ecology. More than 20 Chinese government research centers are dedicated to debating and refining these concepts for the Chinese context, including, for example, the Center for Ecological Civilization at the Chinese Academy of Governance. Such centers spearhead domestic philosophical debates and provide the underpinnings for constitutional changes, legal initiatives, and broad policy directions like five-year plans and national directives. Within Chinese think tanks, analysis of China's environmental problems in the context of achieving ecological civilization often focuses on the negative influence of interest groups and capital, on the unhealthy "worship" of economic growth and development, and on the risks of an overly anthropocentric worldview (Z. Wang et al. 2014). In recent years, the discursive appeal of the phrase has enabled Chinese top leaders to institute governance reforms and reorganization and to promote technological innovations for environmental protection.

Alongside China's domestic efforts, international forums and publications laud China's newly articulated guiding philosophy. The world's environmental advocates have expressed admiration and even envy that ecological considerations have received such high levels of official endorsement. Ecological civilization is widely interpreted as China's effort to resolve tensions between environmental protection and economic development through concrete initiatives such as renewable energy promotion, carbon reduction, and reforestation. The phrase has become a focus of international optimism that China may be offering the world a visionary set of guiding principles, a sort of "sustainable development with Chinese characteristics" that both preserves China's distinctive traditions and governance system and confronts the problem of capitalist overexploitation of global resources (Zinda et al. 2018). Some have speculated that ecological civilization embodies "the potential for a more assertive and confident China to assume a stronger leadership role in global environmental debates" (Geall and Ely 2018). Excitement around China's prominent adoption of the concept has sparked conferences sponsored by the Yale School of Forestry and the Pulitzer Center on Crisis Reporting (Sawyer 2015). Typical scholarly work includes such titles as Barbara Finamore's *Will China Save the Planet?* (2018), Arran Gare's *The Philosophical Foundations of Ecological Civilization: A Manifesto for the Future* (2016), and Joanna Lewis's *Green Innovation in China: China's Wind Power Industry and the Global Transition to a Low-Carbon Economy* (2013). Ecological civilization thus figures both as China's self-proclaimed solution for a troubled planet and as a potential beacon of hope for some international observers.

A Global Call to Action

At least some of this international scrutiny must be traced to an awakening to the crisis of the Anthropocene, the idea that the outsized human impact on global ecosystems has created an entirely new geologic epoch unlike anything in the planet's long history. From this perspective, our planet is on the brink of becoming unlivable. Atmospheric scientists from the United Nations Intergovernmental Panel on Climate Change predict that climate change will be more severe than even some pessimists anticipated; activists are calling for an immediate end to fossil fuel extraction and use in order to avert catastrophe. A similarly authoritative UN panel, the Intergovernmental Science-Policy Platform on Biodiversity and Ecosystem Services, sees a biodiversity emergency with more than one million species on the brink of extinction. With his "Half Earth" call to action, biologist E. O. Wilson argues that no less than 50 percent of the earth's land and sea must be protected from development. Swedish teenager Greta Thunberg, who has become a voice for the younger generation's rage, denounces her elders at climate change conferences and demands to know why they have failed to act on the "existential crisis" that threatens humanity. Complicated and interconnected environmental challenges comprise what philosopher Stephen Gardiner (2011) calls "a perfect moral storm" confronting humanity. At a deep ethical level, our existing political, scientific, and social institutions are ill-prepared for the current ecological crisis.

For many scholars and activists, the urgency and gravity of the planetary situation justify decisive state interventions. Authoritarian environmentalism – the use of authoritarian methods to accomplish environmental goals – has a particular appeal at this historical moment. At a time when liberal democratic states repeatedly fail to address environmental problems, it is tempting to feel that draconian measures are needed, or at least worthy of serious consideration. Authoritarian environmentalism seems like a logical alternative to messy, gridlock-prone democracies that require unacceptable compromises with special interest groups. In autocracies, by contrast, policies that in democracies are subject to drawn-out political debates have been instituted almost overnight. In 2018, for example, Filipino president Rodrigo Duterte ordered a six-month closure of the tourism-dependent island of Boracay for its failure to meet environmental standards. During the rehabilitation period, hundreds of hotels and restaurants were shut down for environmental violations and the island's shoreline easement zone was fully restored. In stark contrast to environmental inaction in liberal democracies, illiberal political regimes have often demonstrated impressive decisiveness in combating environmental problems, from bans on plastics to mandated increases in renewable energy use.

In that context, enter China, which has one of the world's longest-lasting authoritarian governance systems and also one of the most explicit commitments to environmental protection. This is despite its well-deserved reputation for being one of the smoggiest places on the planet. China exemplifies a model of state-led, authoritarian environmentalism which concentrates political, economic, and discursive power within the parameters of the state under the centralized leadership of the Communist Party. Rather than sharing and balancing environmental tasks with independent scientists, entrepreneurs, and citizens' groups, the state aims to monopolize the production of environmental knowledge and policies, the innovation of environmental technologies and their deployment, and the implementation and practice of environmental protection.

State-led environmentalism is accomplished through concrete mechanisms: centralized and targeted disbursement of research funding, channeling of industrial subsidies and support for state-owned enterprises, and guided media programming about the environment that is censored if it challenges state authority. Environmental NGOs and scientists are forced to cooperate with the state if they wish to survive, playing a delicate game of testing boundaries and carefully monitoring the prevailing political winds. By simultaneously expanding the regulatory scope of the state to encompass a growing range of environmental issues and co-opting non-state actors into the state's environmental agenda, the Chinese state goes green.

China seems, on the face of it, to embody hope for a radically new approach to governing the planet, and given the limited time we have left to slow the pace of climate change and protect more than a million species from extinction, we need to consider whether a "green" authoritarian China can show us the way. In *The Collapse of Western Civilization*, a semi-fictional narrative of a post-apocalypse world of climate collapse, historians Naomi Oreskes and Erik Conway describe the rise of a "Second People's Republic of China" because of the supposedly superior model of state-led environmentalism that China practices. They conjecture that, from the perspective of an apocalypse survivor looking back, "China's ability to weather disastrous climate change vindicated the necessity of centralized government … inspiring similar structures in other, reformulated nations" (Oreskes and Conway 2014, p. 52).

The imagined scenario is not without basis. China's clean energy revolution has led some observers to view China's approach as "developmental environmentalism" – industrial development of the sustainability sector that follows national priorities dictated by the state (Kim et al. 2019). This concept draws from the extensive scholarly literature on the East Asian "miracle" of economic growth from the 1970s to the 1990s. The secret recipe, many have argued, was the East Asian "developmental state" that played a central role in shaping and implementing national industrial priorities. China's success in green technologies is also due to favorable state policies. However, as we will see in the examples and cases presented in this book, the developmental environmentalism framework is insufficient to explain China's environmental ambitions, which encompass many aspects of economic, political, and social life beyond clean technology.

As we look more closely, we see that China's track record of environmental success has often been accomplished through top-down, non-consultative coercive measures at the cost of citizen rights and livelihoods. China's state-led environmental action needs to be understood in a broader context: China is also the world's largest repressive state. For evidence, one need look no farther than the state's intrusions in Xinjiang and Tibet, its harassment of unauthorized Christian house churches, its internet Great Firewall that filters out whatever the state deems "unhealthy," and its introduction of facial recognition technologies that track and assign "social credit scores" to every resident.

We may also consider the state's handling of the 2020 coronavirus outbreak as evidence of the limits of the authoritarian governance model. While the state displayed apparent decisiveness in restricting travel from the hot zone, the lockdown came only after a lengthy delay that allowed five million people to leave for Spring Festival holidays. Record-time, ten-day construction of quarantine hospitals was admirable and would likely have been impossible in a non-authoritarian context, but this feat must be balanced by the fact that the state initially censored the findings of medical personnel and even detained doctors who attempted to share their concerns about an emerging SARS-like virus on a medical chat group. Other weaknesses in China's style of authoritarian governance show in the poor regulation of the wildlife markets that allowed the virus to jump the species barrier, as well as chaos in the provision of testing kits, masks, and medical care. Mistrust and anger resulted.

The admirable green policy developments under China's authoritarian system must similarly be set against the egregious pollution of water, soil, and air, unremitting environmental burden on the disadvantaged, globalizing appetite for resources, and export of carbon-intensive production (Power et al. 2012; Simons 2013; Shapiro 2015; Lora-Wainwright 2017). As *Financial Times* journalist Leslie Hook (2019) writes, China "is both the greenest in the world, but also the most polluting." Domestically, China is plagued by entrenched environmental challenges such as soil and water contamination, cancer villages, airpocalypses, and unabating pollution from rare-earth mining and other ecologically destructive undertakings. Even with respect to coal mining and consumption, actual trends countermand the promises made at APEC and in Paris. (China blames the US trade war for making it increase the percentage of "cheap" coal in its energy mix.) Internationally, China's export of coal-fired power plants, construction of roads and ports in ecologically sensitive areas, and extraction of natural resources have also undermined the country's self-proclaimed leadership in planetary ecological civilization. In this book, we seek to untangle these seemingly contradictory observations about China's green politics and ecological conditions.

What is State-led Environmentalism?

Almost every course on environmental politics includes discussion of the "Tragedy of the Commons," the classic 1968 *Science* magazine essay in which Garrett Hardin articulates a core metaphor describing how human beings deplete shared resources (Hardin 1968). We professors often organize students around tables with goldfish crackers and straws and instruct them to go fishing – before long, there are no fish left in the "sea." Hardin argued that rational individuals will necessarily and inevitably over-extract resources from shared spaces because their self-interests, collectively, outweigh the good of the group. In the essay, he describes townspeople who added so many sheep to an English common pasture that the fields could not sustain them. But the metaphor can be extended to other common "goods" – fisheries, forests, and water – as well as common "bads" – factory smoke-stack emissions, discharges into shared watercourses, "space junk," and noise pollution. Hardin's position is that "mutually agreed-upon coercion" is the only way to avoid the inevitable overexploitation of the shared resource; he lauds "the greater candor of the word coercion" and problematizes the ideal of individual freedom.

During the 1970s the essay was much discussed, and refuted, by scholars who objected to the authoritarian tenor of Hardin's approach. They showed that "open access" resources like the fisheries of the high seas were very different from "common pool" resources like coastal fisheries where communities could agree through consultation to be bound by measures to assure sustainable use such as catch size, technology restrictions, permit issuance, and seasonal limits. Elinor Ostrom is best known for writing on this but many others have used combinations of economic game theory and sociological research to show that communities who know each other and expect to work together for the foreseeable future are more likely to create workable community-based resource management systems (Ostrom 1990; Petrzelka and Bell 2000). For transnational and planet-level environmental issues, the challenge is to create a "global community" that can cooperate to manage shared resources without succumbing to self-interest.

International environmental treaties provide a form of coercion established collaboratively through the consent of the governed, and at times they have offered great promise. In 1992, with the Rio Earth Summit (United Nations Conference on Environment and Development), it appeared that such global cooperation might work. There were high hopes that countries would overcome the barriers of sovereignty to manage trans-boundary environmental problems like climate change, biodiversity loss, desertification, and so on. Along with 169 other countries, China signed the Rio Declaration and ratified many of the treaties that emerged from that historic meeting. By then, socialism was on the wane with the dissolution of the Soviet Union, and the debate over the need for coercive measures to resolve environmental problems had abated. Many Western scholars took it as a given that public participation, rule of law, and guarantees of access to information were necessary for robust environmental governance (Schnaiberg 1980; Young 1994). Unfortunately, since then environmental governance has struggled to find broad consensus and legitimacy at local, regional, international, and global levels.

In recent decades, it has become increasingly clear that the promise of the Rio Earth Summit has not been realized apart from isolated successes with phasing out a short list of ozone-depleting chemicals like CFCs and controlling obvious neurotoxins like mercury. The democratic elections of Donald Trump in the US and Jair Bolsonaro in Brazil, both of whom actively undermined principles and protections for the natural world, have further challenged assumptions about liberal market systems' environmental virtues. Can the planet afford a messy liberal democratic process when the threats are so urgent?

In this context, then, eco-authoritarianism seems to some observers and scholars to offer a possible solution when other measures have failed. Among those who have revived the conversation is Mark Beeson, who writes, in "The Coming of Environmental Authoritarianism," that "good" authoritarianism, where unsustainable behaviors are outright banned, by fiat, is essential for the long-term survival of humanity (Beeson 2010). Predictably, the essay sparked refutations. For example, Dan Coby Shahar writes that even though liberal market democracy does not seem to offer much hope for the environment, eco-authoritarianism is "not an attractive alternative" because the ruling class may not be capable of producing or implementing pro-environmental policies over the long run (Shahar 2015). During the revived debate, many environmentalists continue to argue instead for cooperative global governance of environmental problems through better multilateral treaties and institutions, on the grounds of shared interests and the findings of scientists. Others seek to reform global trade by internalizing the environmental costs of production and making them more transparent, and by changing the mindsets of consumers. Still others see hope in empowering local communities and restricting the extractive power of international corporations (Clapp and Dauvergne 2011).

Scholars of coercive state-led environmentalism have turned their focus to China to flesh out the implications of managing the environment through authoritarian means. The empirical literature has generated valuable insights into three main dimensions of Chinese environmental governance. First, research has uncovered a range of governmental tools that characterize the state's efforts to manage the environment. Often, technocratic elites take a dominant position in defining environmental problems in purely technical terms (Gilley 2012; Kostka and Zhang 2018). With these mechanistic approaches, officials set quantitative goals and targets for the ostensible purposes of monitoring environmental conditions and enforcing environmental standards (Kostka 2016; Yifei Li 2019). However, these targets give rise to "blunt force regulations" that over-enforce environmental mandates to the detriment of the livelihoods of ordinary citizens (van der Kamp 2017). Moreover, state-led environmental programs tend to orient toward outcomes but forgo transparency and justice (Johnson 2001; Chen and Lees 2018). On a positive note, in some cases the outcome orientation gives the local state a high level of flexibility and adaptability in enforcing environmental regulations (Ahlers and Shen 2017; Zhu and Chertow 2019). This first aspect of state-led environmentalism features a constellation of routine governmental tools used by state officials and bureaucrats in their exercise of environmental power. Some of these tools prove effective in advancing environmental goals, but others have mixed environmental, as well as political, consequences.

Second, the extensive use of state-centric governmental tools gives rise to changes in state–society relations. As the state increasingly intervenes into the environmental realm, it becomes commonplace for the state to regulate everyday citizen behaviors through coercive means (Eaton and Kostka 2014). From recycling to driving vehicles, environmental regulations are often instituted without meaningful public participation or grassroots input, giving the state sweeping power in its pursuit of environmental ends, with only limited access to feedback that might correct any missteps (Mao and Zhang 2018). With no threat that power holders will be removed from office via ballot or other electoral device, the state is unaccountable for its coercive dictates. Yet, the state has to come to terms with an increasingly diverse range of non-state environmental actors, from citizens to independent scientists, which the state needs but also fears (van Rooij et al. 2016; Guttman et al. 2018). Within its ambivalent relationship with society, the Chinese state casts a changeable shadow over the full range of environmental affairs. It narrows the space for non-state engagement in some cases (Wilson 2016), but also inadvertently creates opportunities in others (Geall 2018). In recent years, for example, domestic civil society organizations have seen some measure of success in their pursuit of environmental accountability, but international organizations are subject to increasing scrutiny and pressure (Tilt 2019). Taken together, China's state–society relations are in flux. In this constantly shifting landscape of power, growing non-state interests in environmental affairs are met with escalating state efforts to contain and co-opt the space for public participation.

Third, the rise of China's state-led environmentalism reflects a broad trend toward power centralization under the leadership of President Xi Jinping. For example, measures to tackle "airpocalypses" in urban areas have followed a top-down model that excludes even lower-level officials from the political process, making environmental programs part of a much larger authoritarian agenda of state control and power centralization (Ahlers and Shen 2018; Kosta and Zhang 2018). Although centralization is often assumed to produce better environmental results (Gilley 2012), it is not a panacea when the central government lacks adequate information about complex local realities (Kostka and Nahm 2017). Moreover, in an increasingly authoritarian era, the state has embarked on aggressive initiatives to use emerging technologies and big data analytics to buttress the centralization of environmental power (Kostka and Zhang 2018). Existing research on China points to the emergence of a highly centralized "hard" authoritarian model of government (Shambaugh 2016), under which environmental policies become a vehicle for the consolidation and centralization of state power (Yeh 2013). The state profits from the environmental crisis by projecting itself as the sole legitimate steward of the environment.

Such dynamics are not limited to authoritarian regimes, although they find their starkest expression there. As Naomi Klein and others have argued, natural disasters can sometimes provide opportunities for capitalist societies to impose neo-liberal policies that might otherwise have been resisted (Klein 2010). This problem is related to what some scholars identify as the "environmental fix" for the capitalist crises of our time. David Harvey's classic analysis of late capitalism points to its tendency to "fix" or deal with overaccumulation and underconsumption through global expansion into new spaces, temporarily displacing the crisis that results from such contradictions by finding new resources and markets (Harvey 1985; Bakker 2004; Castree 2008). State-led environmentalism can, and often does, serve non-environmental ends to strengthen the authority and reach of the state.

In sum, the debate over coercive state-led environmentalism may be one of the most pressing conversations of our time. Many people find themselves longing for radical solutions, as it appears time is running out. Even those who treasure liberal values and respect for human rights and public participation find themselves wondering if non-democratic measures may be necessary to protect the planet. They wonder if the earth may be in need of an autocrat to protect it from the abuses of people. Science and ecological necessity, rather than deliberative public processes, goes the argument, may be the most responsible ways to structure the governance systems of the future. This book will challenge this line of reasoning.

Here, we take stock of this rich body of past scholarship in order to evaluate China's approach to environmental protection. Building on previous research, we conceptualize coercive state-led environmentalism as a three-dimensional enterprise:

- State-led environmentalism materializes through a range of top-down governmental tools, techniques, and technologies that have the ostensible goal of environmental protection.
- The state manages its relations with the society by incorporating some non-state environmental interests while maintaining and consolidating its dominant position.
- The practice of state-led environmentalism has non-environmental spillover effects, most notably on the centralization of political power and the suppression of individual rights and public participation.

In each of the following four empirical chapters, we begin by identifying the primary governmental tools employed in the name of protecting, improving, or rehabilitating the environment. Examples include pollution crackdowns, centrally administered campaign-style inspections, target-setting, behavior modification, forcible relocations, big data monitoring, manipulating global trade, and geoengineering. Then, through a review of cases and examples where these tools are used, we evaluate the different mechanisms and discuss their social and political implications.

As the reader may have noticed, we use the terms "coercive environmentalism" and "state-led environmentalism" interchangeably with authoritarian environmentalism or eco-authoritarianism derived from past scholarship. We should also note that there are a host of other related terms – including eco-fascism, eco-totalitarianism, and eco-terrorism, as well as environmental fascism, environmental totalitarianism, and environmental terrorism – expressing the concept of coercion from both the political Right and Left. We agree with Anna Ahlers and Yongdong Shen (2018) that the notion of authoritarian environmentalism is a useful heuristic device, but it does not fully capture the nuances of how policies, practices, and social relations unfold on the ground. In an effort to investigate the practice of non-democratic approaches to environmental protection, then, we highlight the centrality of the state and its coercive power under the leadership of the Communist Party.

A note on the relationship between state and Party is in order as well. Beginning in 1987, under ongoing reforms first instituted by Premier Deng Xiaoping, a policy called "Separation of Party and State" – *dangzheng fenjia* 党政分家 – was enshrined into the main political report of the 13th Party Congress. Under this policy, the Communist Party was to yield day-to-day government operations to institutions like the National People's Congress and State Council, leaving the Party to provide overarching guidance and to intervene only in major decisions. To avoid overconcentration of power, the passage of laws, implementation, and administration was to belong to the state rather than the Party (Chamberlain 1987; Zheng 2009). Since the rise of Xi Jinping, however, the supreme power of the Party has been reasserted in almost all critical governance institutions (Wang and Zeng 2016). For this reason, when we refer to the Chinese state in this book, we almost always mean the Chinese state under the leadership of the Chinese Communist Party. Boundaries are so blurred that the institutions are all but inseparable.

China Goes Green follows the trajectory of the Chinese state under the leadership of the Chinese Communist Party (CCP) as it wields environmental power at home and abroad. We also engage the debate over the nature and scope of China's "consultative authoritarianism" in an effort to shed light on the particular governance style that the CCP has developed to maintain power for so many decades. The mobilization of grassroots neighborhood-level actors and volunteers, the co-optation of citizens' groups to further state goals, and the system of social rewards and punishments all have roles to play in the environmental realm, even as they fall short of a participatory governance system that would allow truly independent citizen organizations and supervision from below.

Authoritarianism in Green Clothing

Our analysis seeks to articulate not only the environmental implications of the Chinese green state, but also many of the non-environmental consequences of authoritarian environmentalism. Given that China is now one of the world's superpowers, this is a matter of enormous significance. The non-environmental spillover effects of Chinese environmental governance have been recognized: there are human rights consequences of big dam construction; nomads are sedentarized in the name of grasslands preservation; ordinary people in big cities complain that the state is invading their privacy by specifying their laundry techniques and investigating their garbage disposal practices. Building on this line of inquiry, we wish to evaluate more systematically the many intended and unintended consequences of coercive environmental measures adopted by the state. A truly effective model of governance in the Anthropocene cannot afford to ignore the non-environmental implications of environmental pursuits. Therefore, we examine the promise of China's state-led approach along both environmental and non-environmental lines.

Our study reveals that there are admirable elements in the decisiveness of Communist Party policy makers on environmental issues, but there is also much to fear. Notable achievements have been made in sectors from renewable energy to the restoration of ecosystem services. At the same time, the crackdowns, targets, and technological surveillance tools used to implement environmental protection are also being used to assert and consolidate the hand of the state over the individual and over citizens' groups. We find that there is much to learn from China's determination to resolve its massive environmental problems, but we also caution strongly against the darker consequences of China's style of state-led environmentalism. Not only are individual and social freedoms sharply curtailed by China's approach but even the environmental successes are not always what they seem.

A preview of our main argument is in order. We set out to investigate the emergence of a new kind of environmentalism: a state-led, coercive, authoritarian style of environmental governance. What our investigation yields, however, is not a new environmental paradigm but an emerging political strategy to fold environmental concerns into the concatenation of the techno-political interests of the Chinese state. Building on prior studies that examine the broader, non-environmental implications of China's decisive moves in this arena, we try to provide a systematic portrait of "green" China's methodologies. As we follow the sprawling scope of Chinese environmental power from its industrial East to outer space, we discover a coordinated effort to align environmental interventions with the state's ambitious political agenda. This alignment has led to the wholesale subsuming of environmental goals and interests to the supreme leadership of the Chinese state. In the name of ecological wellbeing, the state exploits the environment as a new form of political capital, harnessing it in the pursuit of authoritarian resilience and durability. In this process, some environmental conditions such as urban air quality have seen marked improvement, but others such as desertification and deforestation have been made even worse.

These observations lead us to question the accuracy of the term "authoritarian environmentalism" for describing the empirical reality of contemporary China. The term suggests that authoritarianism is merely a vehicle in service of the honorable goal of sustainability. Thus, it implies an instrumental view of politics: the end justifies the means. Its use invites a leap of faith toward accepting authoritarian politics on environmental grounds. As readers will see, however, the cases in this book suggest an inverted picture, whereby authoritarianism is the end and environmentalism is the means. In some cases, there has been a measure of environmental success. In others, the environmental achievements are elusive, if not dubious. Common to all, however, is the intense consolidation of political and epistemic power in the hands of the Chinese state. In this light, a more accurate term than "authoritarian environmentalism" is "environmental authoritarianism." This formulation is more consistent with the empirical evidence presented in this book.

Towards Mutually Agreed-upon Coercion

Counterintuitively, the success of state-led environmentalism hinges not on a strong state, but on mechanisms that place state power in check. It is precisely the fragmented nature of Chinese state institutions, with their often conflicting lines of authority and tensions between the Party and the state, that has permitted *de facto* checks and balances. The Chinese state under the leadership of the Communist Party is no monolith. The state's fragmentation gives it an advantage in governing a vast and complex nation, making possible pluralistic deliberations even under authoritarianism (Mertha 2009; Spires 2011; Teets 2018). However, the state's efforts to consolidate and centralize power risk losing some of the elements that have contributed to China's environmental successes. China's progress in environmental governance would not have been possible were it not for the government's consultation and collaboration with scientists, citizens' groups, judicial authorities, entrepreneurs, and many other non-state actors that limit state power. The space for this is shrinking under an increasingly authoritarian regime. At the same time, some of China's environmental programs have gone awry because the state chose to ignore non-state voices. The promise of state-led environmentalism can be fully realized only if the exercise of environmental power rests on a broad base of knowledge, perspectives, expertise, participation, and, ultimately, support. By the same token, some of the darker consequences of coercive practices can be avoided if an autocracy remains sensitized to the wide range of environmental sentiments and practices in the society at large.

The effectiveness of state leadership in environmental affairs is thus premised on its incorporation of civil society inputs into the policy process. Some environmental initiatives we examine in this book, such as the mandatory recycling program in Shanghai, afforestation by monoculture in Inner Mongolia, and the sudden switch from coal to natural gas in Northern China, went awry because the state went too far, too fast. By contrast, the state has done much better when citizens feel empowered to participate in environmental governance, or deploy "supervision by the masses" (*qunzhong jiandu* 群众监督). In fact, in examining the practice of environmentalism under Chinese authoritarianism, we discover pockets of democratic strength. Democratic confidence remains strong when scientists and activists join together to fight against hydropower dams, citizens use their smartphones to record and report polluters, artists and filmmakers discover creative means to shed light on the darker side of Chinese modernization, and students organize campaigns to clean up the plastic-littered coasts. These democratic moments may be short-lived, and some may be one-off events, but they speak to the strength of citizen determination even in the face of authoritarian environmentalism. These pockets of democratic strength are pivotally important in keeping state environmental power in check and environmental undertakings on track.

Seen in this light, the authoritarian environmentalism hypothesis operates on a false coupling between coercive environmentalism and authoritarian politics. In other words, environmental coercion need not always be authoritarian in nature. As the empirical chapters in this book illustrate, the Chinese state has been able to achieve durable success in some cases such as the rehabilitation of the Loess Plateau, not because it acted in any way that was less coercive, but because the flexing of coercive muscle was based on extensive consultations with non-state actors ranging from international scientists to local peasants. Nevertheless, only with the backing of the state's coercive power did the complex and elaborate rehabilitation plan materialize. Coercion came after consultation. We note that consultation often entails the messy legwork of meeting, talking, understanding, and ultimately appreciating different positions and interests. Yet consultation is key to achieving the kind of mutually agreed-upon coercion that Garrett Hardin saw as the only way out of the tragedy of the commons. Just as international environmental treaties are agreed-upon coercive instruments between nation states, much of environmental governance in subnational contexts can be fashioned into coercive measures that emerge out of a consensus-building process involving diverse and broad representations.

We are not suggesting that agreed-upon coercion is an easy process, but it is essential if the abuses and missteps chronicled in this book are to be avoided. During the consultative process, the state must be at once forceful and humble, even-handed and responsive, decisive and prudent, focused and inclusive. But instead, much of what we document in this book is the abrupt wielding of coercive and capricious power by state officials against the interests and wills of the people. We show a pattern of coercion that all too often lacks long-term vision, thoughtful planning, or sensible implementation. Driven by short-term bureaucratic self-interest, many Chinese officials have misused coercive policy instruments under the noble disguise of planetary sustainability. The resulting policies have advanced the state's agenda for power consolidation but produced a mixed record in environmental and social terms. In the cases in which the state's worst instincts were moderated by international actors or civil society groups, the restrained exercise of power produced more durable policies for the betterment of human and ecological conditions.

In China, examples of *agreed-upon* coercion are woefully difficult to find. Understood from this perspective, China offers less a model for global action than a cautionary tale. In fact, herein lies the inherent contradiction of state-led, authoritarian environmentalism. The effectiveness of the model is heavily dependent on non-state inputs, broad-based consultations, "supervision by the masses," and similar processes that hold state power in check. Yet the authoritarian instinct is not to broaden and uphold such spaces of accountability and transparency, but to surveil, suppress, and subjugate them. As the state increasingly centralizes environmental power, it undermines the basis of its own efficacy. The state's aggressive moves to limit the space for civil society are thus a disservice to the state's grip on environmental power. To borrow a Chinese idiom frequently deployed by the spokesperson of the Chinese Foreign Ministry when responding to international criticism, China's brand of coercive environmentalism amounts to "lifting a stone only to drop it on its own feet," or *banqi shitou za zijide jiao* 搬起石头砸自己的脚. In the final analysis, mutually agreed-upon coercion is only attainable when the state remains open to criticism and dissent, responsive to the intended and unintended consequences of its policies, and able to adapt to the changing conditions of the earth – features that are not yet characteristic of the Chinese state.

We hope that readers will find the book useful in three main respects: as a historical explanation, as a contemporary portrait, and as a guide to the future. Historically speaking, China has adopted an unprecedentedly systematic approach to authoritarian environmentalism by centralizing environmental management in the hands of the state. This form of state-led environmentalism is a comprehensive political program that is, on the one hand, based on seven decades of Communist Party experience with state planning, and, on the other, compatible with a full range of non-environmental policies of the PRC such as community-level supervision, urban planning, and media control. In recent years, China has successfully gathered all this into a national and now global strategy. Unlike the World Bank and other Western-style actors, China makes little pretense to this approach being equitable or democratic. Chinese state actors are unapologetic about the centrality of the Party. Our study of China, therefore, helps explain how the Chinese state systematized the exercise of authoritarianism. We draw from and contribute to a range of debates in the social science literature and popular press concerning authoritarian adaptability, responsiveness, pluralism, and durability. Using environmental governance as a point of entry, we cast light on some of the most long-standing theoretical issues in the study of Chinese politics in particular and authoritarian politics in general. This first point is the historical value of the book.

In the present moment, China is seeking to legitimate various approaches of state-led environmentalism domestically as well as globally. It is actively marketing its systematized environmental governmentality through soft and hard power promotion of its "going out" policy and Belt and Road Initiative, not only to its own citizens but also to those beyond its borders. In the current political context of rising illiberalism on a global scale, China has an audience. We therefore need better to understand exactly what China is marketing, as well as the broad environmental implications of a global China. This second point is the contemporary value of the book.

Finally, we have eyes on the future. Unlike periods when other state-led projects transformed landscapes, as when communist "ecocide" brought irreversible consequences to vast areas of the USSR in the 1950s, or agricultural modernization transformed rural Brazil in the 1980s, we are in the midst of a planetary crisis. By positioning itself as a civilizational leader in the Anthropocene, China is already leaving significant marks on the planet and playing a decisive role in shaping the future of humanity. This is because of not only the sheer size of the Chinese territory and population, but also the scale of its appetite for resources, the intensity of its environmental interventions, and the increasing interdependence between China and the world. This third point is the forward-looking value of the book.

A few caveats are in order. Even though our empirical focus is the Chinese state, the current study has implications beyond China. The environmental measures we examine are by no means wielded only by the state; powerful non-state actors have used such tools throughout the world. For example, that the Chinese have sometimes removed local people to create bordered national parks with high entrance fees reflects their adoption of "best practice" from other parts of the world. Big international conservation groups, Western governments, and even individual philanthropists have constructed fortress-style protected areas and nature parks, often forcibly dispossessing or excluding local communities whose traditional livelihoods relied on access. One notorious example is the Patagonia outdoor goods company CEO who bought up huge parts of Chile only to become one of the least popular figures in the region. There are many examples of wildlife parks in Africa whose creation so angered local communities that they actively hunted the endangered species the parks were intended to protect. Yellowstone, Yosemite, and Shenandoah National Parks in the United States have similar histories of forcible relocation of native residents in the name of preserving nature.

Moreover, some of the authoritarian governmental tools we discuss in this book are not exclusive to authoritarian political contexts; they are often used in democracies as well. Quantitative goal-setting, for example, is standard fare in today's global environmental politics, challenging established systems of rule-making in global governance (Young 2017). From the two degrees Celsius global average temperature threshold to local fuel efficiency standards across the world, the enterprise of global environmental governance is built on the extensive use of quantitative tools familiar to bureaucrats tasked with mandates and deliverables. In the political and economic reality of democracies, such authoritarian pockets are many. Similarly, in the name of safeguarding "carbon sinks" and preventing defor-estation, Norway initiated the REDD-plus program to facilitate the transfer of funds from the developed world to developing countries, essentially transferring funds from wealthy countries to pay poor ones not to cut down their forests (the acronym stands for Reducing Emissions from Deforestation and forest Degradation). But the program can be highly unpopular with local people who have not been consulted and find themselves unable to use lands that have been in traditional usage for generations. Perhaps even more infamous are the "structural adjustment" packages that the World Bank and the IMF imposed on developing countries as loan conditionalities; critics have argued that they effectively remade recipient governance institutions so as to facilitate a vision of global trade and "sustainable" development that benefited Western corporate interests and forced livelihood changes in order to increase production of goods for export. These measures are top-down, heavy-handed, and problematic for those most immediately affected. In these and other examples of command-and-control environmental relationships outside of the China example, a diverse range of powerful actors sits at the command end, including big and powerful global non-governmental organizations (NGOs), multinational businesses, and international development agencies.

And now a few words about who we are and why we wrote this book. We have spent our careers reflecting on the politics of environmental protection in China. Yifei Li is a native of Shanghai who completed his PhD in environmental sociology at the University of Wisconsin-Madison and now teaches at NYU Shanghai. As someone who experiences China's authoritarian system on a daily basis while writing about environmental governance, he draws on his professional experience as an ethnographer of the Chinese state as well as his personal interactions with environmental activists, ecological migrants, journalists, and scientists. Judith Shapiro teaches international environmental politics at American University's School of International Service. Her intellectual focus has for many decades been the impacts of the Chinese state on ordinary Chinese people. She has written extensively about the Mao period, intellectual freedom in post-Mao China, and China's environmental challenges under Mao and in the present. Independently, we have been reflecting on China's implementation of a form of authoritarian environmentalism that is both attractive and worrisome. We are glad to be able to join forces to supplement each other's understandings and experiences. Because of the speed of China's rise, and the transformative depth and impact of this set of green authoritarian policies, a book addressing the implications of these phenomena seems urgently needed, even as the rate of change provides particular challenges. Emerging policies and techniques like the urban recycling mandate, the Belt and Road Initiative, big Earth data, and geoengineering technologies can be difficult to analyze because they change quickly.

In writing *China Goes Green*, our sources include personal experiences and conversations with a wide range of Chinese people, as well as our knowledge of the scholarly and policy literature about China, environmental governance, and the implications of China's rise. We also draw upon news reports from mainstream publications like the *New York Times* and *South China Morning Post* and insider news streams like *Sixth Tone*, as well as official data and reports from Chinese government agencies. Our case studies build on the scientific literature in forestry, conservation biology, environmental chemistry, data science, climate science, and related fields. We are by no means experts in these fields, but we draw from peer-reviewed publications and convey their findings. The book is intended to be both argumentative and empirically grounded. We aim to organize the challenges so as to clarify them conceptually and provide a basis for debate.

This book is organized along spatial and chronological lines. Chapter 1, "Asserting 'Green' Control: The State and its Subjects", examines the industrialized East, focusing on China's domestic environmental governance. In Chapter 2, "'Green' China Pacifies its Borders," we move to the less developed Western part of the country and border areas to focus on the forcible "ecological migration" of nomadic groups into settlements. Chapter 3, "The State on the 'Green' Belt and Road," studies the international implications of China's "ecological civilization," as the country rises to become a world superpower and seeks to export a development model that is both green and state-led. Chapter 4, "Global China Goes 'Green'," focuses on China's role in global trade, biodiversity, and climate, as the state finds its footing as a key contributor to the problems and a key actor in trying to find solutions. In these empirical chapters, we follow the protagonist of the Chinese state as it broadens and deepens its exercise of environmental power. We close with Chapter 5, "Environmental Authoritarianism on a Troubled Planet," in which we reflect on the implications of our work and point toward the future.

We hope that this book will appeal to both academic and general readerships. Scholars of environmental studies, political science, sociology, geography, East Asian studies, development, political theory, and international political economy may find the book of interest, as it speaks to the ongoing debates in the social sciences about authoritarianism, the East Asian developmental state, the decoupling of economic growth and ecological footprint, ecological modernization, globalization, and the challenges of the Anthropocene. We have also tried to write in such a way that the book will be of interest to students and activists who are seeking a way forward on a planet that is losing ground against humanity and that many of them will inherit.

The prevailing sentiment in the West about China and the environment often entails two faces – pessimism over climate change and insecurity about a rising China. We do not provide a falsely rosy picture to counter either of these sentiments. Instead, we stress the importance of a systematic, evidence-based understanding of China's exercise of environmental power. The empirical examples and cases in the chapters that follow have convinced us that the future of the planet hinges on the Chinese state's efforts to go genuinely green. To do so, the state must trust the Chinese people to participate in environmental governance through "supervision by the masses," rather than using a green cloak to obscure its current trajectory toward totalizing social control.

1

Asserting "Green" Control: The State and its Subjects

A chain of Chinese "oxygen bars" sells purified air for the modest price of 40 RMB for ten minutes of clean breathing, or 100 RMB for half an hour.[1] Water from the Himalayan springs of Tibet, which China supplied to world leaders during the G20 summit in 2016, sells for several times more than regular purified water. A "Beijing Pollution Fighters" WeChat group trades tips on the best home and car air purifiers, strategies to seal leaky windows, the efficacy of masks, and how to fit a facemask on a two-year-old. In China's highly developed East, lung disease and cancer rates are spiraling upward. Because such diseases may take years to emerge, current epidemiological patterns in China's developed areas can be traced to pollution exposure from the early reform-and-opening period of the 1980s after the death of Mao; in coming years, an even more dramatic public health crisis may be expected (Huang 2020).

---

1 We abbreviate US dollars as USD and the Chinese yuan, or *renminbi* 人民币 (meaning people's currency) as RMB. We use the conversion rate of 6.6886 RMB to 1 USD, the five-year average for 2014–18.

These Eastern regions are known both for great wealth and intense pollution of air, water, soil, and food. The manufacture of products for export and domestic consumption has turned vast rural coastal areas into urbanized workshops and factories, widening the wealth gap between the developed East and the less developed West. Glittering highrises, brand-name shopping malls, high-end hotels, gated communities with aspirational European themes, luxury automobiles, collector wines, high (and fast) fashion, and conspicuous consumption – these are the hallmarks of China's opulence.

The lifestyles of China's rising middle and upper classes put unprecedented strain on an over-capacitated ecosystem. Urban affluence contrasts with the poverty of the migrant workers who support the very rich and almost-rich as nannies, construction workers, motorbike delivery drivers, hair-stylists, masseuses, and manicurists. Yet no matter where a person sits on the wealth spectrum in industrialized China, it is almost impossible to avoid the pollution – a byproduct of the manufacturing that created so much wealth in such a short time – and the consumption that supports it. Sociologist Ulrich Beck (1992) calls this phenomenon the "boomerang effect" in the spread of environmental risks. The urban rich whose lifestyle choices produce outsized environmental harms ultimately cannot avoid being exposed to them.

Beginning soon after Mao's death in 1976, decentralization and economic freedom meant high growth rates, but also the fading of the Center's unchallenged grip on power. However, when President Xi Jinping became paramount leader in 2012, he reasserted control. Xi, who removed term limits on his position, is widely seen as the most authoritarian leader since Mao. In the age of "Uncle Xi," Beijing is re-exerting authority over localities not only to serve his power agenda but also to protect the legitimacy of the Communist Party in the eyes of a restive middle class upset about government corruption and pollution.

Meanwhile, in environmental matters, bureaucracies proliferate despite unclear areas of responsibility and lines of command, a hallmark of the bloated quasi-socialist state that exerts so much control over public life. Local leaders often benefit from pollution, and underfunded officials have even been known to rely on fines to enrich themselves or simply pay their own salaries (Jahiel 1997). Factory managers often take shortcuts and circumvent environmental regulations in order to maximize profits. The legal system for enforcement remains weak.

According to the economic theory of the Environmental Kuznets Curve, China is approaching a hypothesized point where profit from development will be put into pollution remediation, eventually leveling off pollution intensity before it decreases. A group of scientists has estimated that this tipping point will arrive between 2021 and 2025 (H. Wang et al. 2019). How will this transition play out in an authoritarian system? There are enormous benefits to decisiveness in these matters, but also considerable risks.

Crackdowns, targets, and behavior modification are key tools that the "green" Chinese Party-state is using to clean up the environment in its highly developed Eastern areas. Many urban Chinese blame the "system," or *tizhi* 体制, for some of the egregious problems of modern China. If the Communist Party of China does not address corruption, inequality, and environmental problems, its legitimacy will remain shaky. This is the context in which we must understand the Communist Party's intense drive to get a handle on pollution.

For the Party, this is not only a question of dealing with a problem that contributes to citizen dissatisfaction and hence the prospect of social instability. It is also an opportunity, or even a mandate for the state to consolidate control. Indeed, from the perspective of the Chinese state, the green agenda is closely linked to the authoritarian one because implementation failure could mean an increase in protests, or what the government euphemizes as "environmental mass incidents," or *huanjing quntixing shijian* 环境群体性事件.

The state's unease is evidenced, for example, by its repeated attempts in recent decades to head these off by providing centralized "complaint hotlines." These are intended to defuse frustration and gather data used to reward or punish local officials for their performance on a social stability metric. (This metric has contributed to abuses, as officials have brutalized potential petitioners when they attempt to leave home to petition higher authorities.) Despite such efforts, environmental protests continue to erupt, posing a serious challenge to the state's grip on power. Official sources suggest a steady annual growth rate of 29 percent in the number of "environmental mass incidents" since 1996 when record-keeping started (Yinan Wang 2014). Fear of *luan* 乱, or chaos, has been an entrenched anxiety since the anarchic phases of the Cultural Revolution turned China on its head and destroyed an entire generation. Environmental issues could, it is feared, be the wedge for public mobilization that they were in Eastern Europe. We would be remiss, therefore, to think that the state's enthusiasm for "ecological civilization" means China has become some sort of "eco-utopia" like Bhutan, which has been known for its pursuit of Gross National Happiness since the 1970s. Rather, in a bid to intensify its fragile hold on the Chinese populace, the Party has included environmental protection among a panoply of state goals that include poverty alleviation, corruption crackdowns, and building a "harmonious society."

To explain how the Chinese state came to rely so heavily on campaigns and crackdowns, and why so much of China's environmentalism comes from the top, or Center, we must see that the Party's choices and tools are limited to those of the authoritarian system it has created. Mistrust and even fear of public participation, civil society organizations, and democratic processes mean that the public space for environmental activism is carefully delimited, even if the boundaries can be murky and changeable across time and space. Risk-averse local officials, for whom stability outweighs transparency, await guidance from superiors before taking action (as seen in the catastrophic delay in announcing the coronavirus outbreak in 2020). The city of Kunming in southwestern Yunnan province can be freer than Beijing; months when there are no important meetings can be freer than those when major decisions are being made. Environmental non-governmental organizations (ENGOs) flourish, but always within the confines of collaboration with the state. Registration with the Ministry of Civil Affairs (for Chinese groups) and the Public Security Bureau (for foreign groups) is mandatory since the passage of new NGO laws in 2017. Teatime "chats" with security officials are necessary for the continued operation of well-respected environmental groups like Friends of Nature and the Institute of Public and Environmental Affairs (IPE), and for less prominent organizations like the conservation group Shanshui. Foreign-affiliated groups like Greenpeace, the Natural Resources Defense Council, and Jane Goodall's Roots and Shoots have an even more delicate row to hoe. Environmental civil society groups are fundamentally entwined with a state that has a felt need to keep close tabs on their every activity.

Some years ago, one of us, Judith, was approached by a Dutch foundation that wished to present a prestigious environmental award to Ma Jun, the founder of IPE. The decision-makers were hesitant about whether he was "sufficiently independent of the government." Ah, responded Judith, that is the wrong question.

Rather, the question is whether IPE has been able to function within the system and still achieve its aims of information transparency, citizen empowerment, public pressure, and strengthening institutions within the government (like the Ministry of Ecology and Environment) such that they can achieve shared goals of environmental protection and implementation of law. While environmental groups must tread carefully within the boundaries of the permissible, IPE has successfully worked to shift those boundaries and open up space for a longer list of acceptable strategies and activities. (Ma Jun got the award.) Similarly, Judith was approached by a Washington, DC-based ocean-protection ENGO seeking to open a Beijing office. They told her they planned to use the same strategies they use elsewhere in the world, including running grassroots mobilizations while maintaining complete independence from the government. Good luck, said Judith, but in China this approach just won't work. You must have allies or even sponsors within the state or little can be done. Even potential university partners are deeply entwined with the state.

In China, environmental governance challenges conventional Western ideas about the state–society binary relationship. A diverse range of non-state actors includes ENGOs and social enterprises, industrial associations and "public service units," or *shiye danwei* 事业单位. These actors work directly or indirectly under the shadow or sponsorship of the state. Some are affiliated with a state agency or even operate on the premises of their "supervising" governmental unit's secured compound. Business cards from people in "non-state" environmental groups often list government affiliations as credentials; reflecting the nation's socialist origins, state connections convey validity and the right to exist. In the local environmental programs in which we participate, official "letters of introduction" with red-ink chops from state agencies open doors and assure our contacts that it is safe to work with us. The state's penetration of civil society thus runs deep. However, just as ENGOs need state support to conduct effective environmental advocacy, so does the state depend on ENGOs to help reach the nation's vast and diverse populations. Environmental groups sometimes serve as its eyes and ears in monitoring pollution. They make up shortfalls in delivery of services including river and beach trash cleanups, and they clarify environmental messages in public awareness campaigns like those about shark fin and ivory (as we will see in chapter 4). This symbiotic relationship shapes environmental outcomes in a range of situations in China's industrialized East.

The Communist Party's uneasiness with civil society groups has created a particular, or even unique, style of environmental politics. As we now turn to the empirical parts of this book, we focus on a series of tools, techniques, and technologies that the Chinese state is using to achieve green goals. We begin with a focus on campaigns and crackdowns. Then we explore the state's use of targets and goal-setting. We end the chapter with a discussion of behavior modification, particularly as seen in the implementation of new urban recycling regulations.

Campaigns and Crackdowns

China's reliance on political campaigns (*yundong* 运动) dates to well before the 1949 revolution. During the Yan'an years (1937–45), when Mao's battered communists who had survived the Long March regrouped in a remote, cave-dwelling area of Shaanxi province, the Party used mass mobilization to engage ordinary people in support of the leadership and its policies.

Campaigns were intended to achieve a specific set of goals, often in a short time. They were an effective means of silencing critics, eliciting conformity and support, and engaging large numbers of people. China's political campaigns are infamous. They include the 1957 Anti-Rightist movement (intended to ferret out and label the enemies of the Party), the 1958–60 Great Leap Forward (intended to launch China from socialism to communism, to industrialize and overtake capitalist countries in iron and steel output, and to break all records in grain output), and the 1966–76 Cultural Revolution (intended to throw the country into a state of "continuous revolution," reassert Mao's vision and power, turn the entire country into a nation of soldiers engaged in a "war" against nature and against Mao's enemies from within and without, and wage "class struggle" against critics). There were also hygiene campaigns, like the one to rid China of "pests" like rats, flies, mosquitoes, cockroaches, and, unfortunately, sparrows, which were later proved to have eaten more destructive insects than grain (Shapiro 2001).

Even after the death of Mao in 1976 and the repudiation of most of these Mao-era campaigns as severe mistakes, not least because many of China's new leaders had themselves been victims, the Party continued to rely on campaign-style political movements (van Rooij 2006). For example, in 1983 a short-lived campaign against "spiritual pollution" was intended to crack down on "unhealthy" tendencies in literature and the arts. A 1986 campaign against "bourgeois liberalism" attempted to do the same. In both cases there was a lukewarm response from those charged with implementing them and from the masses, and the campaigns fizzled out. But the overarching political climate of the post-Mao decades has still been one of "cold winds, warm winds" (Shapiro and Liang 1986). The limits of the acceptable are constantly shifting and ordinary people remain off balance. Even today, everyone in Beijing knows that every March, at the time of the "two sessions" of high-level Party organizations, a politically conservative wind will blow and everyone must stay alert not to push boundaries or take risks. There are more residence checks and a greater presence of military and civilian security forces. Publications are postponed, book talks canceled, television programs suspended, internet censorship filters tightened, journalists furloughed, and petitioners and migrant workers rounded up and sent home.

There are also, of course, campaigns that are less overtly political, like those against walking on the grass or spitting in public. During a campaign in 2010, when Shanghai hosted a World Expo, the city government urged its citizens to give up the "backward habit" of wearing pajamas in neighborhood streets, even going so far as to recruit "community volunteers" to monitor and reprimand pajama-wearing locals. A more recent campaign against the "Beijing bikini," whereby men roll their undershirts to their armpits on hot summer days, has brought levity to such government efforts to mandate public behavior. Unfortunately, the time-honored game of mahjong is also under government attack as part of a stated effort to purify the social environment and improve the public image of citizens. For elderly retirees who rely on the game to pass time with their neighbors, this is a sad development. During the 2020 coronavirus outbreak, Anhui law enforcement officers were even seen smashing mahjong tables in people's homes as a way to stop residents from gathering in groups, while in Sichuan, camera-carrying drones hectored mahjong players to stop their games.

During such campaigns, the state manipulates public opinion through a coordinated set of activities. Officials mount red banners across the streets to display punchy slogans. Television and radio programs broadcast tuneful jingles about the campaign in order to spread it to the masses. Schools, hospitals, neighborhoods, and factories organize trivia competitions in line with campaign themes. Newspapers publish stories about exemplary citizens who achieve campaign goals for everyone to "learn from." Long lines of buses take teenagers and retirees to "must-see" educational films. Subways, buses, and taxis display themed ads. Celebrities are recruited as advocates. Schoolchildren are made to "volunteer" to distribute informational leaflets on the streets. All these campaigns share a top-down, directorial flavor whereby the state tells ordinary people what to do, whether or not they themselves aspire to be civilized subjects of the People's Republic. As we see in the next section, campaigns can also be punitive, with massive deployments of surprise inspections. These can have real consequences, not only for the economy and for pollution levels, but also for officials' careers.

Environmental Campaigns

The most well-known environment-related campaign is the one child family policy, launched in 1979 after the post-Mao government understood that China's exploding population meant serious challenges to its efforts to eradicate poverty. The draconian implementation of the policy is infamous, with family planning officials keeping tabs on fertile women's periods, and forcible abortions the norm. Women had to get permission from the state to get pregnant. Children born illegally lacked residence permits or the right to an education and health care, and they grew up with the stigma of being an "illegal second."

An influential 1990 book by former Environment Minister Qu Geping, who is often called the father of Chinese environmentalism, is called *Population and the Environment in China* (Qu and Li 1994, English translation). It argues that there is a direct link between population size and environmental degradation. In fact, many Western scholars of environmental politics believe this causal explanation is overly simplistic. While the famous I = PAT equation, or Impact = Population × Affluence × Technology, is widely seen as a decent starting place for understanding the root causes of environmental problems, the formula neglects the roles of culture, history, external economic forces, inequality, governance, and a host of other factors. The fact that Qu Geping believed that population size was the central problem underscores that China's earliest environmental efforts were profoundly linked to one of the state's egregious intrusions into the human rights of ordinary citizens. The one child family campaign further illustrates how an allegedly "scientific" policy proposed by technically minded engineers can have far-reaching consequences for multiple generations (Greenhalgh 2008). Nowadays, the one child family policy has been abandoned for multiple reasons, including gender imbalance and the worry that the demographic transition means China will soon lack sufficient able-bodied workers – a problem Chinese officials and economists call "diminishing demographic dividends" (Cai 2010). We now turn to more recent environmental campaigns, but first it is worth briefly introducing China's central environmental governance institutions.

Since the 1998 founding of the State Environmental Protection Administration (SEPA), the environment ministry has been given a steadily stronger hand. In 2008 it was elevated from an administrative body to the Ministry of Environmental Protection (MEP). When the MEP was seen as an ineffectual ministry as compared with others, it was gradually strengthened. In 2015, environmental civil society groups felt encouraged when they were permitted public comment during revisions of new environmental laws. They hoped the new laws would provide more punitive measures for violators such that factories did not simply write the cost of fines into their budgets, and that there would be cumulative punishments for those who did not correct infractions. They also hoped that the MEP would be given greater enforcement authority over provincial and local officials, who often had greater power than the central government administration because of a complex set of overlapping mandates and lines of responsibility. Finally, they wanted citizens' groups to be able to hold factories and even government agencies accountable in court. In many ways, they got what they hoped for, although some feared that the implementation gap would remain large (Ma 2015).

In 2018, the MEP was reorganized as the Ministry of Ecology and Environment (MEE), with an expanded staff and consolidated portfolio intended to reduce bureaucratic fragmentation, clarify roles, and eliminate redundancy. From the powerful National Development and Reform Commission (NDRC), the MEE assumed responsibility for emissions reduction and climate change; from other ministries it assumed watershed protection, underground water-pollution control, marine conservation, and agricultural pollution control. Revised environmental statutes allowed for more punitive fines and permitted officials to shutter non-complying factories. A network of environmental courts was established, with judges who had specialized training to hear pollution cases.

Recent years have seen ENGOs win some lawsuits against polluters now that a longer list of organizations is permitted to represent victims in court, although they still struggle to gain legal standing and to win judgments. The censuring of officials for environmental crimes has sometimes included loss of position, heavy fines, and even imprisonment. Since 2011, promotions and bonuses are officially supposed to be tied not only to economic growth and social stability but also to environmental protection, with some local governments withholding promotions for poor environmental performance. The perverse incentives that allowed officials to benefit from allowing polluters to operate are being gradually eliminated; local environmental officers are less likely to require a steady diet of fines to pay their own salaries. Citizen discontent with official corruption and pollution has been heard, and indeed it is consistent with the central government's efforts to reassert control over regions that went their own ways under Deng Xiaoping-era decentralization.

The state is crafting a strong response to pollution, and the campaigns seem to be making progress toward cleaning up China's dirty air and toxic waterways, although even the most optimistic admit there is a long way to go. Implementation has lagged behind rhetoric, with some areas reporting strong progress and others reporting mixed results. However, the dangerous small-particle air pollution (PM 2.5) has decreased significantly in some areas. During high-profile international and national conventions where the central regime sees its reputation at stake, host cities see marked improvements in air quality. Famous examples are the 2008 Olympics, the APEC (Asia-Pacific Economic Cooperation) summit of 2014, the national military parade of 2015, and the G20 summit of 2016. In 2019, the heavily polluted city of Tangshan saw production shut down so as to attempt to give blue skies to Beijing for the October 1 National Day military parade celebrating the seventieth anniversary of the establishment of the People's Republic of China. With characteristic irony, Chinese people refer to the sky during these events as APEC blue, parade blue, G20 blue and so on. With draconian top-down orders to close down factories, limit private vehicle use, suspend construction projects, and even seed clouds in and around the host city so as to use rain to cleanse the skies, these campaigns have delivered concrete results. The Chinese government considered the Olympic and APEC blue skies as key ingredients in promoting its international image. But the image crumbles after high-profile events. By design, these campaigns, which are not so much initiatives of the environment ministry as of other state organs, are not intended to produce more than a short-lived façade to show China at its best. Nor can local economies withstand such drastic coercive campaigns for long.

The Olympic and APEC skies had an unforeseen effect of reminding the Chinese that the sky need not be gray all the time, fostering discontent even as people enjoyed the respite from the pollution. In her highly influential 2015 documentary *Under the Dome* – now banned in China – journalist Chai Jing interviewed a six-year-old girl in coal-producing Shanxi Province, asking whether she had ever seen blue skies. The girl responded, "I have seen a little blue." Ms. Chai then inquired whether she had ever seen white clouds, to which the response was "no," and a confused look. Apparently, her village had never hosted an international summit.

Beyond the widely discussed "blue-sky" campaigns, the government's response to problems with air, water, soil, and food safety often comes in the equally dramatic style of unannounced inspections, sudden crackdowns, and blunt shows of force. In a throwback to the Mao-era language of violent struggle, the Party often employs militarized language. Responding to a mysterious virus that caused widespread "aporka-lypse" of blue-ear pig disease in the summer of 2007, for example, the State Council launched a "battle of rectification" for food safety, vowing to restore public confidence in China's food supply by holding local officials to account for the slightest lapse of vigilance

(Barboza 2007; State Council 2007). Pigs once again became the focus of a national "battle" in 2014, when the State Council mobilized local authorities to contain the environmental externalities of pig farming, targeting the problem of feces and waste discharge into waterways (State Council 2013b). The campaign escalated in 2016 into a full-fledged zoning code that banned small-scale pig farming from most rural areas (MEP 2016). By the end of 2016, hundreds of thousands of pig farms that had fewer than 500 hogs were forcibly demolished in the name of environmental protection. Devastated farming households were compensated at the meager rate of 60 RMB (9 USD) per square meter, and were "guided" into new livelihood options such as melon farming. Meanwhile, industrial pig farms were handsomely subsidized for their allegedly superior ability to comply with state environmental standards (Sun 2018). However, concentrated animal feeding operations turn out to be a far riskier way to supply meat. A 2019 outbreak of African swine fever wiped out an estimated 100 million pigs across China, driving up prices and threatening the pork supply. The State Council then announced a reversal in agricultural industrialization policy, pledging to subsidize the reopening of small-scale pig farms. Few farmers took up the offer (Q. Wang 2019). In the southwestern city of Nanning, according to the state-run *Global Times*, the local government had to issue pork ration books (Lei 2019). This was all too reminiscent of the not-so-distant Mao era of turbulence and scarcity.

Using similarly militarized language, ever since the 2013 "airpocalypse" that brought international notoriety to China's environmental crisis, the government has been waging a "war on pollution." Pollution control was dubbed one of the "three tough battles" to be won by 2020 along with reducing poverty and preventing financial risk, a pledge made by President Xi Jinping during his 2017 speech to the Communist Party's National Congress.

The anti-pollution battle is fought on many fronts. To fight the contamination of the nation's waterways, eight provinces in the heavily polluted industrial East launched campaigns in 2018 to clean up "bodies of black and smelly water" and pledged to restore water quality within the year. In Jiangsu alone, for example, provincial authorities targeted 129 surface waterways for immediate cleanup and footed the hefty bill of 223 million RMB, or 33 million USD (Jiangsu Provincial Government 2018). As part of a "2018–2020 Three-year Action Plan for Winning the Blue Sky War," the government launched waves of measures to clean up China's air. New coal-fired power plants have been prohibited in highly developed areas and some coal mines shut down; Beijing, Shanghai, and Guangzhou implemented restrictions on vehicle numbers (Greenstone 2018). In late 2017, manufacturing plants in entire swaths of the eastern part of the country were closed, revealing blue skies but also seriously disrupting supply chains. One businessman estimated that 40 percent of China's factories had at least temporarily been shut down, leading some international businesses to move supply chains to India and Bangladesh to try to meet Christmas orders (Schmitz 2017). As the *South China Morning Post*'s Jane Cai describes,

> An army of 5,600 inspectors, from not only China's environment ministry but also the Communist Party's anti-graft watchdog and personnel unit, were dispatched to the provinces to check whether local cadres were doing their jobs to protect the environment. This unprecedented action caused many local officials to overreact by shutting down all possible pollutant sources. ... Local governments were so aggressive in shutting down polluting facilities that the environment ministry had to step in, asking local authorities not to blindly shut down plants that could meet environmental standards. (Cai 2017)

In some cases, local officials who got wind of the crackdown preemptively closed factories to forestall inspections, while others falsified meeting records and other data. In the steel town of Anyang in Henan, factories were forced to implement production cuts despite the fact that they had already installed above-standard, low-emissions equipment (Stanway et al. 2019).

In summer 2019, another wave of surprise environmental inspections covering six provinces and two state-owned enterprises led to the censure of 130 officials, with 41 officials detained and fines imposed totaling more than 65 million RMB, or 10 million USD (Xinhua 2019a). Some foreign analysts believe that China is permanently shuttering low-value, high-polluting industries in an effort to shift the country toward higher-end "clean" manufacturing as befits its status as a newly developed country. Inspectors' destruction of boilers and other equipment used in non-complying factories seems to bear this out.

In August 2019, the city of Linyi in Shandong province, one of the cities with the worst air pollution performance, responded to the government crackdown with extreme measures. *Sixth Tone* reports that local governments shut down hundreds of businesses, including 400 plywood factories, 270 restaurants, and 24 delivery truck parking lots. Outrage ensued. In this case, the Ministry of Ecology and Environment criticized the Linyi government for the "dreadful consequences" of its compliance efforts (You Li 2019).

In the heat of a "war" on pollution, there is a tendency to employ urgent, blanket policies that allow for little nuance and may snare the innocent together with the guilty. For those on the receiving end, such campaigns can seem capricious. As we saw, some shuttered factories were actually in compliance with environmental standards but made to suffer the economic costs of lost production time. In the rush to judgment of a campaign-style crackdown, there is little opportunity for self-defense, and little effort to differentiate between major offenders and minor players. In one anti-air pollution campaign, for example, the state targeted those who were burning paper funeral money for the deceased to use in the afterlife, a centuries-old ritual important to the mourning of bereaved families. Such practices can have contributed hardly a fraction of the smog compared with that produced by large factories and automobiles, but good Marxism does not countenance an afterlife. A campaign to clean up Lake Erhai in Yunnan province led to a ban on almost all economic activities in the areas surrounding the lake, including garlic farming, leading entire families to lose their livelihoods. Those in the weakest positions to bear cultural and economic losses are being asked to do so.

There is a famous saying in Chinese, "killing the chicken to scare the monkey" – *shaji jinghou* 杀鸡儆猴 – which captures the idea that a small player may be sacrificed to send a warning to a more important one. Indeed, journalists who have interviewed people directly affected by the crackdowns report that small workshops and individual businesses have been hard hit. Instead of providing small and medium-sized enterprises the opportunity to upgrade their production facilities to comply with environmental standards, central inspectors have opted to use an iron fist, crushing the hopes of many grassroots entrepreneurs. In the name of eliminating environmentally harmful business operations, these campaigns have had an outsized impact on such smaller factories. Meanwhile, blatant violations by large state-owned enterprises (SOEs) have often been overlooked or excused (Eaton and Kostka 2017).

Justifications and Risks

Such campaigns may sometimes enhance enforcement and help factories make incremental shifts toward better performance, especially when local interests impede the legal system (van Rooij 2006; Kostka and Zhang 2018). Yet there is something worrisome about the way this is playing out. Why, one wonders, is there a need for campaigns and crackdowns in the first place? Why is there a pattern of flagrant violations of environmental laws and regulations? Why do factories shut when inspectors arrive, only to reopen as soon as they leave? Why are emissions reports routinely falsified? Why are effluent pipes concealed in riverbanks so that no one will see them? For a dramatic depiction of these and other evasive practices, see, for example, the 2010 film *Warriors of Qiugang*, which details the travails of Anhui farmers who try to shut the pesticide factory that has turned their community into a "cancer village" (Yang and Lennon 2010). At every turn the villagers tried to get justice according to the law, and at every turn they were stymied by thuggish local corruption on the part of factory owners and government officials.

If government officials, citizens, and factories had more confidence that policy and law would be consistently applied, such crackdowns and campaigns would not seem necessary. Instead, rule of law would be strong, the judiciary independent and capable of checking violations, and ordinary people empowered to bring lawsuits and gain access to lawyers. The political elite would be constrained by checks and balances on its power. This would create greater certainty for business and production as well as a cleaner environment.

However, the development of China's environmental legal system is not smooth. As an emerging field of legal practice in China, both the court system and environmental groups are still exploring ways to uphold environmental law. In the limited number of cases in which ENGOs such as Friends of Nature brought polluters to court under the 2015 environmental protection laws, there have been some successes but also many setbacks. Plaintiffs have advocated for better harm-assessment procedures, compensation mechanisms, and pollution remediation packages. However, there is a wide gap between environmental mandates and laws on the books and real-world enforcement outcomes on the ground. Sometimes the gap arises from the misaligned interests of central and local officials (Ran 2013; Mao and Zhang 2018). Other times, local conditions prove incompatible with the generic and even arbitrary provisions in the national requirements coming from the top (Jiang 2005). Yet other times, blatant environmental violations are left unregulated because these polluting practices have been the "normal" state of affairs for so long (Lora-Wainwright 2017). Given this implementation gap, environmental advocates cannot rely on the laws as they are written, and plaintiffs (as elsewhere in the world) often find it difficult to prove definite connections between pollution and public health. Moreover, in August 2019, a court in the city of Nanchang in Jiangxi province refused to hear a Friends of Nature case against a local water polluter on the grounds that the plaintiff was not eligible to sue, even though the group had filed similar cases elsewhere. The rule of environmental law thus remains in limbo.

From the state's perspective, the strength of the campaign approach is that it provides a high level of discretion. The length, reach, intensity, and scope of campaigns and crackdowns are dictated by the state. This tool of environmental governmentality is a prototypical form of authoritarian environmentalism, where the state retains totalized control over the process of environmental governance. Crackdowns and campaigns are face-saving ways for the central state to reclaim political legitimacy, especially when inspectors can place the blame for pollution on local officials. Operating under the direct authority of the Center, environmental inspection teams are effectively above the law, and certainly above the local government. This technique of environmental governance projects the Center as an impartial, uncorrupt environmental arbitrator in the service of the Chinese people. Meanwhile, faced with tremendous political pressure from top-down inspections, local officials sometimes take it upon themselves to over-enforce environmental regulations by closing all factories in an entire sector. In the end, environmental enforcement becomes contingent on the arbitrary dictates of the central inspection team and the fears and ambitions of grassroots cadres, as opposed to transparent, accountable environmental laws and standards. As Hebei province steel industry representatives complained, these inspections can be capricious and irresponsible, resulting in abrupt shutdowns, impracticable instructions, production and supply chain disruptions, fines unrelated to environmental matters, and unintentional contract violations (Hebei Province Metallurgical Industry Association 2019). Yet through these campaigns, the Chinese state recoups both consolidated control over its local counterparts and political legitimacy in the eyes of the people.

As we have shown, environmental campaigns offer short-term rather than lasting gains and all too often snare law-abiding citizens in their nets. Campaigns create the appearance of the state's strong environmental will, but they gloss over problems such as non-compliance, inequality, negative externalities, and arbitrary enforcement. In the end, campaigns produce an ad hoc patchwork, dashing hopes for extended sustainability. We now turn to a related, highly favored technique that shapes public behavior while allowing the state to assert control: target-setting, another method of social mobilization with roots in the Mao years and an invigorated home among China's technocratically minded policymaking elite.

Target-setting

During the wheat harvest in June 2019, farmers in the poverty-stricken agricultural county of Shangcai in Henan province were given an unusual order: machine harvesting was prohibited this season. Use your hands, the local government told the farmers. When journalists arrived, they saw entire wheat fields left to rot; some had been colonized by sooty mold because of recent rains. Farmers were devastated by their losses and infuriated with the government.

As it turned out, the culprit was the county's new automated air quality monitoring station. Like many other newly installed stations across China, it sent real-time readings of air pollutants to the now-powerful Ministry of Ecology and Environment. The county had been given specific clean-air targets. Local officials grew leery of machine harvesting because an influx of chaff can result in a spike in pollution readings. When confronted by journalists, an unnamed local official proclaimed that "in this tough battle of environmental protection, the interests of a very small group of people shall be compromised for the benefit of the vast majority of the people" (Lei and Liu 2019).[2] A day after the story broke on local TV news, provincial authorities issued a bulletin denouncing Shangcai officials for their "failure to fully comprehend the Xi Jinping thought on ecological civilization" (Zhao and

---

2 All translations are the authors' unless otherwise noted.

Zhong 2019). Too late, harvest machinery was allowed back in the fields.

Despite public derision in instances like this, target-setting remains a hallmark Chinese governmental technique. Targets are an ideal tool for governing a vast and complex nation through a centralized system. In the early decades of the socialist economy after 1949, economic outputs from steel production to grain harvest were subject to state planning. For each item, a national five-year, annual, or monthly target was set. These targets were then disaggregated into province-level goals, which were further broken down into local production targets. One infamous example of target-setting gone awry occurred during the 1958–60 Great Leap Forward, when peasants competed to reach ever more unrealistic standards in grain production, falsifying output in the name of patriotism and setting the stage for the great famine (Shapiro 2001). Target-setting is a parsimonious way of organizing national production, as it renders the complex conditions of the national economy into a two-dimensional spread-sheet. These methods remained prominent when Deng Xiaoping liberalized the Chinese economy in the early 1980s. In each iteration of subsequent five-year plans, target-setting continued to figure centrally in how the Chinese state exercises power.

When environmental protection emerged on China's core policy agenda in the 1990s, it was quickly harnessed to the familiar tool of target-setting. At that time, "sustainable development" had recently appeared in the global policy lexicon, but its meaning was contested, as it is today. Rendering the then-nascent term of sustainable development into concrete figures and charts was appealing because numbers seemed to give it specificity and apparent validity. In more recent years, fashionable terms like livability, resilience, and circular economy have also appeared in

Chinese policy documents in the form of dedicated target matrices. In the view of Chinese policy makers, unlike areas of public policy which are oriented toward supposedly subjective human beings, environmental policies are concerned with the supposedly objective natural environment. This in their view lends itself to straightforward measurement and reporting. Thanks to their training in technical fields such as microbiology, chemistry, and toxicology, Chinese environmental officials demonstrate remarkable faithfulness to the enterprise of quantitative target-making. Indeed, in our rich experience of presenting public lectures on environmental issues to Chinese academics, officials, and professionals, we have found that the idea that environmental challenges are inherently political, with winners and losers, comes to most Chinese audiences as a completely fresh analytical approach. Environmental problems are believed to belong within the purview of engineers and scientists.

Targets play a pivotal role in the organization of the Chinese state bureaucracy, especially in the process of cadre evaluation. Officials are promoted on the basis of how they perform on a bundle of targets assigned to them from above. This governance model results in a specific kind of accountability mechanism whereby government officials answer to superiors who evaluate them on a host of metrics. Such upward, bureaucracy-oriented accountability is in stark contrast with the kind of downward, public-oriented accountability typical in liberal democratic governments. The practice of target-setting dates to the Mao era of planned economy under socialism, when, thanks to Soviet tutelage, fulfilling production targets for "strategic materials" such as steel, aluminum, coal, oil, rubber, and rice could mean life or death for local officials.

Until recently, GDP growth targets had an outsized impact on cadre promotion decisions (Q. Wang 2013).

However, after more than a decade of experiments with calculating a green GDP (Pan 2004; Li and Lang 2010; Sun et al. 2014), the State Council announced in December 2016 that environmental targets would outweigh economic growth measures starting from 2017. Since then, there has been a rise in local environmental interventions as officials seek to claim green achievements. The change in bureaucratic incentive structures in favor of the environment is admirable, especially noting the significant efforts to clean up air, water, and land in response to the change. However, we also note risks in adhering dogmatically to quantitative environmental targets like these:

- Percentage of days in a year when air quality is at least good: at least 80 percent.
- Percentage of surface water that exceeds grade III: at least 70 percent.
- Percentage of surface water that fails to meet grade V: no more than 5 percent.
- Percentage of underground water rated extremely poor: approximately 5 percent.
- Percentage of contaminated farmland under safe utilization: approximately 90 percent.
- Forest cover rate: 23.04 percent.
- Grassland vegetation cover rate: 56 percent.
- Reduction in sulfur dioxide emissions: 15 percent.
- Percentage of national key protected wild animals under protection: at least 95 percent. ...

These and many other targets to be met or exceeded by the end of 2020 make up the bulk of the 194-page Thirteenth Five-Year Plan (FYP) for Protecting the Ecological Environment (State Council 2016). This main FYP is complemented by other ministerial-level FYPs for "special topics" such as environmental standards and environmental health. After the main FYP was finalized, offices within the MEE issued Five-Year Plans in their respective functional areas, including water, air, environmental monitoring, emissions control, energy efficiency, and industrial pollution mitigation. These sub-ministerial-level FYPs outlined more detailed targets that contribute to those in the main FYP. Then, at the subnational levels – in the provinces, municipalities, cities, counties, and villages – national targets became "responsibility packages" at each level of the state administration, manifested in a myriad of subnational FYPs. This system-wide quantitative exercise across the entire state bureaucratic organization, undertaken once every five years, is not meant to obscure the reality that a lot more target-setting takes place between the "big years" of FYP-making.

Targets Gone Awry

In this sea of plans and targets, the will of the state finds palpable expression. In September 2013, as part of the national plan to combat air pollution, the State Council pledged, among other things, to bring the share of coal in China's energy mix down to 65 percent by 2017 from the 2012 level of 68.5 percent (State Council 2013a). To achieve this target, the chief administrative authority followed up in June 2014 with a detailed energy reform plan, vowing to complete the switch from coal to liquefied natural gas (LNG) in the heavily polluted Beijing-Tianjin-Hebei metropolitan area by 2017, which amounted to a total ban on coal in the area (State Council 2014). These targets became enshrined into law after the amendment of China's Air Pollution Control Law in August 2015. In February 2017, under pressure, the Beijing-Tianjin-Hebei region, home to more than 110 million people in two municipalities and 26 cities spanning four provinces (referred to in many policy documents as "2+26"), outlined a package of localized targets. Beijing, Tianjin, Langfang, and Baoding would completely ban coal use by October. In each of the other 24 cities, a target was determined for the specific number of local households whose residential energy infrastructure had to be retrofitted to enable the switch (MEP et al. 2017). Four months later, in a move to ensure the successful transition, 13 of China's most powerful ministerial-level agencies jointly issued a sternly worded mandate reiterating the targets and demanding that cadres at all levels be evaluated on their performance in this regard (NDRC et al. 2017).

Under mounting pressure to meet targets by October 2017 lest they lose promotion opportunities or even their jobs, local cadres in the "2+26" area undertook drastic measures. The state-owned Beijing Gas Company invested a total of 8.5 billion RMB, or 1.3 billion USD, five times its average annual expenditure, to retrofit residential energy infrastructure. Shanxi province swiftly retrofitted 1.0142 million households, far exceeding its 0.39 million target. In Hebei province, 2.339 million households were retrofitted, exceeding the target of 1.8 million by 30 percent. Ultimately, the total coal reduction target was met far sooner than planned; the percentage of coal in the national energy mix dropped to 60.4 percent because of over-enforcement at subnational levels. In people's homes, as in factories, old coal-burning equipment was destroyed in the enthusiasm to make the switch. In the face of tremendous pressure from multiple central-level ministerial authorities, local officials were frightened into becoming overachieving environmental warriors.

All seemed fully prepared for LNG to kick in until Northern China's cold winter arrived. In mid-November 2017, gas companies across the region warned of tight supply. On November 28, Hebei had to suspend gas supply to commercial users while barely keeping up with residential demand. Natural gas prices skyrocketed. By early December, it was clear that the supply gap was too wide to be covered by emergency measures. Thousands of ordinary people were left in the cold, and the gas shortage crisis spread nationally to provinces as far from the frigid North as Yunnan in the Southwest. Even the *Global Times*, the Communist Party's propaganda organ, published an opinion piece on December 4 accusing local officials of "solving one problem at the cost of creating another even thornier problem" (Shan 2017). In the midst of this debacle, the Ministry of Environmental Protection had to roll back the LNG switch, issuing all governments in the "2+26" area a sparsely worded "extra urgent" communiqué which lifted the ban on coal. In short order, what remained of the region's coal-fired energy infrastructure came back online. To maintain stability, the Ministry sent 839 teams of inspectors to communities across the "2+26" area to give away electric heaters – a costly remedy billed to the central government's funds earmarked for air pollution mitigation (MEP 2017).

The switch from coal to gas failed not because target-setting did not work, but because it worked too well. Centrally mandated environmental targets effectively and powerfully percolated down the chain of command, resulting in systemic over-compliance on the part of local authorities. As a result, the central government found itself sandwiched between the insufficient supply of LNG and the demands of local governments that did more than their part. The loser was not the central government but ordinary citizens who went without heat when temperatures froze.

If the difficult transition to LNG seems like a temporary glitch, the problem of urban wastewater treatment (or lack thereof) has been a persistent issue in China's domestic environmental governance – an issue entwined with the target-setting governance regime.

Nearly a quarter-century ago, in 1996, in the Ninth Five-Year Plan, China set a target of installing ten million metric tons of daily wastewater treatment capacity by the end of the period. In response, many cities across China invested in new wastewater treatment plants. By 2000, more than half of water pollution-related fiscal spending went to building wastewater treatment facilities, which delivered more capacity than originally planned (Ge et al. 2003). However, it quickly became an open secret that most of these new plants were never used. Local officials were incentivized to meet targets by building new plants rather than by operating them. The Ministry of Construction (now Ministry of Housing and Urban-Rural Development, or MoHURD) decided to add a new target to fix the problem. In August of 2004, it was mandated that all wastewater treatment plants must be running at 60 percent of full capacity or higher during the first year, and 75 percent in the two following years (MoHURD 2004). Two years later, faced with widespread non-compliance or outright falsification in local data reporting, the Ministry organized a nationwide monitoring and verification campaign, threatening to punish violators (MoHURD 2006). However, when journalists investigated, some found that plants were turned on when the central inspection team visited and shut down as soon as they left (Yang 2014). Others saw brand-new water pumps bearing no sign of wear and tear (Yue 2015). Building the plants was a one-off cost, but operating them would require tapping regularly into the cities' coffers.

In recent years, the Ministry has made increasing amounts of earmarked fiscal transfers to local governments to support the everyday operation of wastewater treatment plants. However, new issues have emerged. On the one hand, because most plants were built in the late 1990s and early 2000s when China's standards for wastewater treatment were low, these plants are not equipped with technologies to comply with new requirements. On the other hand, because many plants were built in a rush to meet the Ninth Five-Year Plan's capacity target, they were not designed to connect to municipal underground pipeline networks, nor were municipal pipelines sophisticated enough to accommodate a separate system for wastewater. Cities now need to invest in extensive new pipelines if the wastewater treatment plants are to function. Consequently, many plants operate below standard, churning out muddy water not much better than what went into them. Many discharge directly into surface waterways. As a ministry official who wishes to remain anonymous told Yifei, the more they invest in the wastewater industry, the more the problems manifest themselves, which then call for even more investments. In the end, more than two decades since wastewater treatment emerged on the policy agenda, it has become a fiscal black hole, sinking public investments but returning little hope of cleaner water. The odd reality is that, in 2018, of the 436 polluters that the environment ministry fined for major pollution violations, 243 were wastewater treatment plants (Greenpeace 2019b). These plants, originally set up to mitigate pollution, now make up the single largest category of polluters.

The fiasco of the wastewater business should be a wake-up call for anyone who still has unconditional faith in target-setting. After repeated failures to improve the country's treatment of wastewater through centrally mandated targets, state officials sought help from Ma Jun, the founder of the Institute for Public and Environmental Affairs, the ENGO known for its work putting government air and water pollution data into the hands of ordinary citizens. In collaboration with Ma Jun, the government launched a "Black and Smelly Water" app for ordinary citizens to send geo-referenced reports of visibly polluted water through their smartphones. Analysis of data from the app shows verifiable improvements in the waterways that citizens flagged, suggesting some level of government responsiveness to this sort of citizen participation and "supervision by the masses" (Hsu et al. 2020).

A final lesson of this discussion of target-setting may be this: characteristic as it is of authoritarianism, target-setting is by no means unique to China, nor to authoritarian regimes in general. In global environmental governance, target-setting is more commonplace than ever (Young 2017). The quantified UN Sustainable Development Goals, for example, have not only defined national policies for many countries but also percolated into school curricula and ENGO mission statements. This may be linked to the drive for greater fiscal accountability and the need to show measurable results to donors. But it must not replace other forms of policymaking or we will lose the chance to craft long-term solutions that address problems at their roots. Moreover, a mechanistic focus on statistics and percentages tends to invite cooking the books and, as we have seen, leads to a perceived need for crackdowns and punishments. Thus, as a governmental technique, target-setting can go awry when quantitative goals are valued to the point of becoming sacred. Yet targets need not be sacred, for they are but a practical means toward effective environmental policymaking. They need to be revised or removed when they become counterproductive. The state would do well to take target-setting off the throne of authoritarian governmentality and instead mix it with other incentivizing strategies that can help loosen the central state's costly grip on power.

Behavior Modification

In June 2018, the newly formed Ministry of Ecology and Environment issued a public announcement titled

"Citizen Ecological Environmental Behavioral Code of Conduct," *gongmin shengtai huanjing xingwei guifan* 公民生态环境行为规范 (MEE et al. 2018). The announcement was co-sponsored by four other central agencies – the Central Commission for Guiding Cultural and Ethical Progress, the Ministry of Education, the Central Committee of the Communist Youth League, and the All-China Women's Federation – a move intended to show broad support within the sprawling state apparatus as the environment ministry took the lead to articulate, publicize, and attempt to enforce a new code of conduct. The document enumerated a long wish-list of environmental behaviors for the citizens of China, from "setting the air conditioner at no lower than 26 degrees Celsius in the summer" to "refusing to consume endangered wild animals." In a tone characteristic of socialist sloganeering, the document calls on Chinese citizens to "improve environmental self-consciousness and ecological civil competence." The public announcement culminated in an ambitious mandate: "be advocate, agent, and exemplar in environmental protection without being asked." As though these requirements were not enough, the National Development and Reform Commission released in October 2019 its "Overall Action Plan for Launching Green Living," *lüse shenghuo chuangjian xingdong zongti fangan* 绿色生活创建行动总体方案 (NDRC 2019). In it, the agency charts a mandatory program to "green" government operations, households, schools, residential neighborhoods, transportation, shopping malls, and public buildings for the entire nation. According to the Plan, all of society must embrace green living by the end of 2022. Taken together, these two documents epitomize another frequently deployed technology of environmental governmentality in China: mandatory behavior modification.

In the name of combating air pollution across China's industrial East, various behavioral bans have been introduced in the last decade. For example, there is a fireworks ban which abolishes a centuries-old tradition during Chinese New Year. From the state's perspective, the ban may have the additional benefit of combating feudal "superstitions" about driving off evil monsters, as such folk beliefs can be seen as threatening to the primacy of the one-party system. Many cities also ban open-pit barbecue stalls, wiping out a time-honored element of the Chinese night market streetscape. In rural areas, farmers have been banned from stubble-burning, ending an age-old method of farm waste disposal which has the side benefit of deweeding and pest control. These behavior modifications are part and parcel of the Chinese government's war on pollution. It is imperative to give up personal freedom on these matters for the sake of the greater good, the government proclaims on red banners that fly high. Mandated behavior modifications are often supplemented with exhortative persuasion in the form of public admonitions, warnings, and graphic signs. Such notices, often translated into unusual English, have been the delight of foreign visitors for decades: "Slip and fall down carefully," "After first under on, do riding with civility," "poisonous and evil rubbish," "the small grass is feeling ashamed to smile, please don't bother it," and so on. During the 2020 Chinese New Year, a time of family reunion that coincided with the coronavirus outbreak, red banners with colorful language were a common sight: "Visit relatives today, be visited by pneumonia tomorrow," "Gatherings can be homicidal," and "Undeclared patients with fever are enemies of the people."

The "green" revolution not only forbids entire categories of behavior, but also seeks to compel citizens to adopt specific patterns of environmental friendliness, whether by adding a mandatory fee to the distribution of plastic bags, giving buyers of electric cars free license plates (which, through competitive bidding, can in Shanghai normally cost close to 90,000 RMB or 13,500 USD), or offering subsidies to homeowners to retrofit their homes for energy efficiency. A 2013 move against food waste at government-funded banquets, the clean-plate or *guangpan* 光盘 campaign, associated with a general anti-corruption campaign, may not have been popular with officials but it did eliminate some egregious aspects of officials' behavior. Some of these measures may seem like standard regulatory adjustments to the free market's failure to account for the environmental cost of production, but they can also intervene intrusively into the fabric of citizens' lives.

Shanghai's new municipal waste mandate, which came into effect on July 1, 2019, is a case in point. Under the new regulations, all residents must separate trash into four unintuitively labeled categories: dry garbage (known elsewhere as landfill), wet garbage (compostable kitchen and garden waste), recyclables, and hazardous waste. However, people are only allowed to dispose of waste within a set four hours of 7–9 in the morning and 6–8 at night, when community "trash inspectors" are on duty. In each neighborhood, trash collection bins have been moved to a centralized location in order to monitor resident behavior and punish violators. The environmental rationale behind the policy notwith-standing, Shanghai's waste management strategy seems onerous to the vast majority of residents. Even the local government openly and unapologetically declared this policy to be the glorious start of "the era of coercion," or *qiangzhi shidai* 强制时代 in China's waste management. Many people cope with the new system by using "weapons of the weak," dumping trash on the side of the street under the cover of darkness or taking bags of garbage to work to be disposed of there so as to avoid the prying eyes of the trash inspectors. The new policy feels unfriendly to the overworked middle class in a city of 24 million.

Shanghai's new garbage policy is designed from the narrow vantage point of the state. The labels of dry and wet garbage make little sense, if wet wipes are supposed to go to the dry garbage bin and dry food into the wet bin. Yet these two categories are perfectly sensible from a state administrative viewpoint: The city now operates two daily fleets of garbage collection trucks, one (with 1,088 trucks) that goes to the wet composting facility and the other (with 3,197 trucks) to the dry incinerating facility (Deng 2019). From the perspective of the state, the contents of tens of thousands of color-coded bins are nothing more than raw material that feeds state-managed streams of garbage. Labeling them wet and dry could not have seemed more "legible" to the state, to borrow from James Scott (1998). Thus, the unintuitive labeling of garbage categories is reflective of the state's self-centeredness. Likewise, limiting the time periods and locations for waste disposal ends up inconveniencing everyone except the state. Seen in this light, the new waste policy of Shanghai seeks not only to modify citizen behavior to go green, but also compels citizens to adhere to a state-centric frame of mind.

Before the new policy was introduced, the city had a robust recycling industry, but it existed in a gray area that the state refused to recognize or support. Under the previous system, an informal economy of urban waste recycling was comprised of rural migrant workers who lacked legal residence permits and thus had no access to basic services like health care and education. Working as trash pickers in neighborhoods, within office complexes, or on main streets, they collected cardboard, bottles, cans, books, and even furniture. Daily, they hauled their sorted recyclables on overloaded tricycles to collection centers, which then sold the recyclables in bulk to factories (Morris and Schonberg 2017). It has been estimated that the informal recycling economy has employed between 3.3 and 5.6 million people in urban China (Linzner and Salhofer 2014). Most importantly, the informal system was highly effective in that trash pickers depended on recycling for their livelihoods; they were incentivized to extract as many recyclable materials as possible from the piles of trash. The city's new recycling program lacks such an incentivizing mechanism. But from the state's perspective, the eradication of the informal recycling sector has the multiple benefits of asserting state control over a robust and lucrative business, dissuading the supposedly "low-end population" of migrant workers from moving to the most glamorous metropolis in China, and returning rural migrants to their places of household registration (*hukou*) for ease of administrative management.

The Shanghai city government has resorted to a string of coercive means to elicit compliance from citizens. Community trash inspectors not only look through everything in the trash bag but also are empowered to issue tickets to anyone who violates protocol or refuses to comply. The punitive measures go along with the surveillance state China is building. Many of the trash inspectors Yifei interviewed spoke of an impending "orderly future" when trash bins would be equipped with high-resolution facial recognition cameras that would catch violators in the act. It will be very convenient, Yifei was told, because then everyone can dump their trash any time of the day. No more hourly restrictions! Indeed, such an "orderly future" does not seem far-fetched at all. Many gated neighborhoods have already installed turnstile facial recognition systems at their entrances, and facial recognition technology is now required for every new personal cellphone on the grounds that identity verification of online behavior will promote social stability.

Elsewhere, in the village of Yangde, 200 miles to the southwest of Shanghai, an experimental social credit system known as a "morality bank" awards villagers credit points for recycling and a host of other "virtuous deeds" (Ge 2018). It deducts points for "extravagant" funerals and birthday parties or other "acts of immorality" (Z. Wang 2019). The morality bank is a prototype of China's ambitious social credit system, designed to rate and monitor citizen reliability and creditworthiness based on a wide range of misbehaviors, from jaywalking to tax fraud. At a police big data center, surveillance material feeds into a computer program that analyzes real-time information to "predict" criminal behavior by flagging individuals the system deems suspicious. A team of police officers then manually screens the individuals, unbeknown to the suspects, for further background checks (Yan 2019).

The Chinese state has taken advantage of the 2020 coronavirus crisis to perform a test run of the social credit system. Under the aegis of the State Council, the Alipay app, which has more than 1.2 billion users worldwide, rolled out a green, yellow, and red color-coded "health pass" function, which rates citizens based on the government's repository of big data such as travel history, cellphone location reports, and health records. Holders of the green "health pass" are considered to have a low risk of contracting the coronavirus and are afforded personal mobility. If a yellow one pops up, however, the user is subject to two weeks of mandatory quarantine. The red color is reserved for citizens under medical isolation and treatment. In the name of virus containment, ordinary citizens are asked to produce their "health passes" to strangers such as subway security guards and even coffee shop baristas.

In a hint of what may lie in the future for more Chinese cities, an experimental all-seeing "smart city" known as the Xiongan New Area is unfolding 80 miles to the south of Beijing in what was a quiet rural backwater. Equipped with a mind-blowing assemblage of big data surveillance technologies, including, but by no means limited to, facial recognition, remote sensing, drone monitoring, phone location-based data mining, cloud computing, the internet of things, vehicle tracking, blockchain solutions, and see-through infrared cameras, Xiongan is positioned to be the "smartest" city ever built (Li et al. 2017). The Chinese president lauds it "the project of the millennium," and considers it the prototype of his grand Chinese dream (Xinhua 2019c). (We revisit big data technology in chapter 4.)

From constant badgering to omnipresent slogan-eering, from mandatory fees to outright bans, the Chinese state has utilized a slew of instruments in its efforts to modify citizen behavior. It continues to develop ever-more advanced technologies toward an all-seeing big-brother state. As China enters an era of coercion in the name of ecological sustainability, social costs are mounting. Migrant workers who previously picked trash are being expelled from major cities across China. Overworked middle-class urban residents have to adopt a compressed daily schedule to make it home for the two-hour window when trash-collection bins are open. Schools organize trivia games involving petty details: leftover bubble tea is wet trash, the paper cup is dry trash, but the lid is recyclable. Residents grow tired of being told what to do. Arguments between trash inspectors and residents erode community fabric. Many people become hostile to the environmental cause in general. Some of these social costs could have been avoided had the state opted to collaborate with the informal recycling sector rather than wiping it out.

Despite growing discontent, the city government tells an upbeat story of "citizens participating [in recycling] with heightened enthusiasm," which is backed up with, not surprisingly, numbers. For example, Deng Jianping, a bureau chief in the Shanghai Municipal Government, reports, "Since July 1, the city has processed a daily average of 4,400 metric tons of recyclables, or twenty times the figure from 2017, 8,200 tons of wet trash, a 130 percent increase from 2017, and 170,000 tons of dry trash, a 16 percent decline from 2017" (Deng 2019). The 20-fold increase in recyclables reflects a simple fact: much of what previously was recycled by mom-and-pop migrant trash collectors on flatbed tricycles has been diverted to the state-controlled stream of municipal recyclables. Deng's claim to environmental fame is actually premised on a statistical sleight of hand.

Environmentalism at a Price

Softer ways of shifting public behavior that feel less coercive to citizens might stand a chance of becoming integrated into public life for the long term. For example, ENGOs have championed the idea that people should carry their own chopsticks, both to cut down on deforestation from the tremendous waste of disposable chopsticks and to promote public health. Grassroots organizations have also undertaken advocacy efforts to publicize the devastation that Chinese consumption is wreaking on shark, elephant, and pangolin populations, which we explore in a later chapter. When backed with rule of law and government enforcement efforts, such grassroots campaigns can help the government to win popular support. By contrast, state-driven campaigns that stand on their own often alienate the very people and organizations they aim to engage.

Without doubt, some of these methods of state-led environmentalism have made significant strides toward sustainability. Punishing polluting industries and rewarding green behavior, China's government has gained success where it chooses to intervene. Often, the state acts swiftly and decisively, and is praised and admired for this. By standards of rapidity and rigor, China maintains an impressive track record of success in environmental protection. But as we have seen in this chapter, swift and decisive state action also comes with risks.

Many of these methods of state-led environmental management are oriented toward the rising middle class in Chinese cities. While some are inconvenienced by measures such as odd/even alternate-day license plate driving, they are mostly beneficiaries of state interventions into the environment. Meanwhile, the workers whose factories are forcibly shut down, the residents of politically disempowered areas where locally undesirable land uses (LULUs) are relocated, and the farmers in rural areas that become "cancer villages" are left out of the picture. The upshot is that state control in the environment works well for specific groups of people in specific areas, usually those who are environmentally, politically, and spatially privileged. It does not work so well for everybody else. The system perpetuates inequality by distributing environmental harms and social burdens to the already disadvantaged and environmental goods and social benefits to the already privileged. In parallel, in the business world, small and middle-sized enterprises take a disproportionate hit when the winds of environmental campaigns and targets blow.

Despite this, technocratic elites within the Chinese state often espouse faith in the heavy-handed state-centric approach to environmental governance. They freely and matter-of-factly deploy coercive techniques, citing the ecological environment as their justification. Through ramped-up coercive enforcement in renewable energy use, pollution mitigation, recycling, and many other policy areas, the Chinese state has been remarkably successful in expanding and deepening its control over society. Whether it is a household trash can or a factory boiler, everything is within the reach of the state. So is every person. As part of Shanghai's response to the coronavirus outbreak in 2020, for example, city officials installed wifi-enabled magnetic sensors on the doors of residents under quarantine. Every time the door opens, an alert text message is automatically sent to the head of the neighborhood, prompting a house visit. Under pervasive and invasive surveillance technologies, the citizens of China are more closely watched than ever.

The coercive environmental tools, techniques, and technologies we document in this book are often used in combination. In the case of the three focal tools described in this chapter, this is especially true. Campaigns, targets, and forced behavior modifications reinforce each other in the practice of authoritarian environmentalism on the ground. An example is the drive to "eliminate backward capacity," or *taotai luohou channeng* 淘汰落后产能, a policy that seeks to eliminate the most energy-intensive, emission-heavy, and resource-hungry factories in every sector. There are a number of problems: small businesses take a disproportionate hit; the definition of "backward" is elusive and subject to manipulation; implementation can cause unemployment in an entire segment of the economy; and total output has gone up in some sectors because "advanced capacity" enterprises received state subsidies. The state's wielding of these and other combinations of technologies, however, is by no means limited to the country's industrialized East. In the next chapter, we follow the Chinese state as it seeks to transform borderlands in the vast Western parts of the country, where it has been seeking control for much of its history.

2

"Green" China
Pacifies its Borders

"The sky is high and the emperor is far away," *tian gao huangdi yuan* 天高皇帝远. Beijing's uneasy relationship with border areas has a long history, with the reach of the "Center" stymied by malaria, Himalayas, deserts, and the resilience of ethnic groups with their own languages, cultural traditions, and sociopolitical organizations. Over the millennia, in contrast to the official narrative, the borders of the Chinese empire have shifted and remained porous. The task of state-building remains a preoccupation of contemporary leaders.

In this chapter, we turn beyond China's highly developed industrialized Eastern region to the less developed rural areas and Western regions. Chinese policy makers have become exquisitely aware of growing wealth disparities and of the dissatisfaction of those left behind in the economic boom. At the same time, they are persuaded that they must do more in the borderlands to alleviate the environmental crisis. Measures to stem biodiversity loss, wetlands conservation, and grasslands restoration are part of a panoply of initiatives that target less-developed regions, along with a poverty-alleviation program called "Opening up the West," or *xibu da kaifa* 西部大开发. Well-known examples of such environmentally focused policies include the Green Great Wall, also known as the Three-North Shelterbelt, or *sanbei fanghulin* 三北防护林, intended to fight sandstorms; the Conversion of Croplands to Forests project, or *tuigeng huanlin* 退耕还林, which retires farmland susceptible to erosion; eco-compensation programs; and protected areas and nature reserves. Some of these overlap geographically with the Belt and Road infrastructure developments that are the focus of the next chapter.

These seemingly well-intentioned policies for social and ecological goods are often implemented in a heavy-handed fashion. They may serve state goals of consolidation and control above and beyond what they nominally purport to address. In many cases they have an even deeper impact on people's lives than the state's interventions in the developed parts of China since they more thoroughly transform landscapes and cultures. Moreover, as we discover on closer examination below, even the claimed environmental successes are often mixed.

We begin this chapter with a discussion of afforestation as an example of what we will call "cookie-cutter policymaking," a uniform, one-size-fits-all approach to implementation known in China as *yidaoqie* 一刀切, or cutting everything with the same knife. Ambitious tree-planting goals have resulted in rapid increases in China's tree coverage in a short span of time. However, these afforestation projects have often caused serious disruptions to social cohesion in rural communities and resulted in long-term ecological decline due to their dogmatic implementation and insensitivity to local ecological conditions. We then address "green grabbing" through the example of dam building, whereby renewable energy goals are used to seize resources. Little attention is paid to what is being lost in terms of riverine ecosystems, local culture, and social justice. Finally, we focus on forcible reloca-tions, or what the state calls ecological migration – or sometimes biodiversity conservation. In the name of the environment, the state is intensifying control of border areas where ethnic minority nationalities have long had an uneasy relationship with Beijing. Using grasslands and wetlands conservation and the need for new nature reserves as official explanations, the state is profoundly transforming traditional livelihoods, cultures, and ways of life. The state adds these method-ologies – cookie-cutter policymaking, green grabbing, and forcible resettlement – to a quiver of techniques that also include the campaigns, target-setting, and behavior modification that we visited in the last chapter.

One-size-fits-all Policymaking

Like many others in her generation, "Kaye," one of Yifei's students in Shanghai, is passionate about the environmental cause. On her smartphone, she uses the Alipay app not only for routine payments but also to monitor her personal carbon account. The app gives carbon points to reward her daily behavior. Making an electronic payment earns points equivalent to the grams of carbon saved by not using paper money or a plastic credit card. Riding the subway earns points equivalent to the carbon saved compared with taking a cab. When Kaye's points reach a certain threshold, she can use her them to adopt a tree – a real tree planted in her name to combat desertification by the Ant Forest, an Alibaba subsidiary which the United Nations has named a "Champion of the Earth." A certificate pops up on the app showing the tree's profile, replete with information about species, registration number, general location, and the name of the organization that cares for the tree. The app assures Kaye of the tree's health with an animation of a happy green tree set against a background of green mountains, clear water, blue sky, and a few wind turbines. Today's tree is a shrub called the *caragana korshinskii* located in the Inner Mongolian Banner of Bayannur, which in the Mongolian language means Rich Lake.

Planting trees is a uniquely popular form of environmental action in China, not least because reform-era leader Deng Xiaoping was a staunch advocate for the activity. He declared in 1981 that March 12 would be China's Arbor Day, a public holiday for planting trees. The State Council issued a national resolution in 1982, passed by the National People's Congress as law in 1984, which stipulated that every male aged 11 to 60 and every female aged 11 to 55 had a legal obligation to plant three to five trees per year. Much of this has been accomplished through annual bursts of tree-planting activities in mid-March at schools, residential neighborhoods, state-owned enterprises, and governments at all levels.

What may seem like voluntary environmental action thus turns out to be Kaye's obligatory duty, even if relatively few Chinese citizens are aware of this rarely enforced legal requirement. Indeed, if Kaye earns three or more tree-planting certificates through the Alipay app in a calendar year, she can apply for a Tree-Planting Obligation Fulfillment Certificate from the National Afforestation Commission to display as she likes. Tree-planting has been so widely promoted as a public service that one of China's first ENGOs, Friends of Nature (formed in 1994), organized its earliest members to plant trees. As Liang Congjie, the founder, told Judith at the time, this was one of the least politically risky activities available and thus it was least likely to result in the organization being shut down. Even nowadays, tree-planting remains the safest form of activism under authoritarianism. Furthermore, it is a favored environmental action among the urban middle class. Just as the imagined wilderness of the American West occupies a unique place for Americans, the imagined pastoralism of the Chinese Northwest does the same for urban Chinese of the industrial East. The promise of restoring that imagined pastoralism by planting trees is especially alluring.

According to government statistics, Kaye is not alone. Between 1981 and 2018, an estimated annual average of 400 million people, roughly a third of the nation's population, participated in tree-planting, yielding a total of 70.5 billion trees planted over the course of nearly four decades (Y. Wang 2019). This figure is astounding, because the whole planet is estimated to be home to three trillion trees. In other words, if government statistics are read at face value, tree-planting efforts by ordinary citizens like Kaye have brought back nearly 3.5 percent of the entire planet's tree cover within less than four decades. Recent NASA satellite data confirm China's disproportionate contribution to global afforestation: The country is shown to account for a quarter of the planet's net increase in leaf area from 2000 to 2017, and 42 percent of China's contribution comes from its state-mandated afforestation efforts (Chen et al. 2019). By planting trees on a massive scale, China seems to have made the planet much, much greener.

However, a closer look complicates the apparent success narrative. China's soil erosion has worsened, and so have desertification and the intensity of dust storms. China's desert is estimated to be steadily growing at the annual rate of 10,000 square kilometers (Wan et al. 2005). Dust storms have seen a fourfold growth in frequency since the 1970s (Normile 2007). Chinese authorities have repeatedly overstated the success of afforestation projects in combating dust storms (X. Wang et al. 2010). Moreover, increasing numbers of studies reveal precipitously low survival rates for trees

planted through afforestation campaigns, ranging from
a mere 5 percent in the arid climate of Gansu to 34
percent in the national capital of Beijing (Cao et al.
2007; Lu et al. 2018). Seen in this light, the Chinese
government's self-reported figure of 70.5 billion trees
needs to be taken with a grain of salt.

How could afforestation produce opposing outcomes
of both increasing tree canopy and aggravated ecological
decline? The conflicting pictures of afforestation provide
an important empirical case to help us understand the
promise and peril of coercive environmental measures.
Examining China's astounding tree-planting efforts
brings into view the interplay of government mandates,
individual behaviors, forestry science, local knowledge,
and long-term ecological processes. As discussed in
chapter 1, however, such campaigns are unlikely to
have a lasting impact. In fact, the evidence below
demonstrates the risks of using a monolithic approach
to implementation. This analysis enjoys the benefit of
hindsight, as there are now decades of studies of the
effects of large-scale state-mandated afforestation in
China. The long-term negative ecological implications
of massive afforestation have become clearer after
sustained scientific observations of artificially afforested
areas.

Afforestation by Monoculture

Tree planting is central to some of China's most
ambitious environmental initiatives, from Conversion
of Croplands to Forests to the shelterbelt for sandstorm
prevention. It also appears in a host of mundane
policies: urban areas must meet mandatory green
coverage targets, just as rural areas have to demonstrate
forest canopy percentages. Infrastructure projects such
as highways and railroads are subject to mandatory

hedgerow coverage. While obligatory tree-planting figures prominently in the portfolio of Chinese afforestation policies, it is complemented by a growing suite of other policy instruments: state ownership of expanding networks of tree nurseries, urban renewal plans that incorporate trees, ecological "redlines" demarcating zones of forest conservation, regulatory interventions into the forestry industry, and restrictions on open-range herding, among others. All are geared toward securing the success of afforestation in China.

Trees and forests perform important ecosystem services. They help retain water, fix carbon, and restore soil fertility. However, as the two examples below will illustrate, the ecosystem services performed by trees and forests need to be understood in the complex ecological contexts in which afforestation occurs, including the species of trees being planted, their native environments, and their relationship to other elements in the local ecosystem – both natural ones such as relative humidity and local fauna and plant life, and human-created ones such as small sediment-holding dams and traditional farming practices.

Afforestation is integrated into the overall apparatus of Chinese state planning. At different levels of the government, afforestation is pursued in conjunction with land use planning and policies. From national Five-Year Plans to detailed local ones, afforestation is signaled on maps as a specific shade of green. These green patches can be farmlands, rural settlements, or deserts, but are deemed necessary to be reforested or afforested within a given timeframe in order to accomplish state-mandated targets. The rendering of afforestation in the form of green plots on planning maps typifies what James Scott (1998) calls "state simplifications." The government pursues a cookie-cutter approach to complex local issues in order to exercise sweeping state authority with uniformity and efficiency. This dogmatic "cutting everything with the same knife" approach has been used in Chinese environmental governance since the Mao era, and has retained popularity at multiple levels of the state apparatus (Shapiro 2001; van der Kamp 2017).

Simplification does not only manifest on the two-dimensional map, of course. In the three-dimensional real world, much of China's afforestation has taken the form of monocultural tree-planting. Afforestation by monoculture has obvious advantages from the viewpoint of the state, although single-species plantings are infamous among forest and agricultural professionals for increased vulnerability to disease, as the 1845–9 Irish potato famine reminds us. Uniformity also makes for a poor wildlife habitat; natural forests contain trees at various stages of life, allowing a range of shelter and forage.

But monoculture enables local officials quickly and effectively to implement targets from above, and also makes it straightforward for higher-level officials to account for, monitor, and evaluate local achievements. From the state's perspective, afforestation by monoculture presents a streamlined mechanism for administering and managing the environment of a vast nation. Commonly chosen tree species such as poplar, red pine, and locust are selected for their ability to grow quickly, so that forests can be seen within about two years (Cao et al. 2007; Jia et al. 2017). This enables state officials to present tangible evidence of afforestation success within their terms of office; the length of each bureaucratic assignment averages four years. From a fiscal perspective, the monoculture approach is a low-cost option because of economies of scale in nursing and transporting seedlings, training workers, and producing and applying chemicals to newly constructed forests.

As an expression of state-led coercive environmentalism, afforestation by monoculture is common. As

China has continued to set more ambitious afforestation goals, a state-owned business supply chain has emerged in support. From tree nurseries to aerial seeding operations, a specialized economic sector has grown up around afforestation by monoculture, making it unlikely that other models will supplant it. Moreover, with the recent availability of remote sensing, the State Forestry Administration can monitor nation-wide tree-planting efforts with data feeds from a full complement of government satellites. This will likely increase the central authority's emphasis on single-species plantations. Thus, China has set in motion a self-perpetuating cycle. State-owned business interests will continue to expand in accordance with China's afforestation targets, making the coercive monocultural approach the new normal.

The Loess Plateau as an Unscalable Success

The highly publicized environmental rehabilitation of the Loess Plateau (known in Chinese as Yellow Earth Plateau or *huangtu gaoyuan* 黄土高原) was China's first experience with large-scale afforestation and is widely heralded as a major success. Beginning in the mid-1990s, a team of Chinese and international experts worked with hundreds of villages to restore and conserve one of the world's most highly eroded landscapes, which spans five Chinese provinces. With funding from the World Bank, the project successfully revegetated 35,000 square kilometers, or roughly five percent of the Plateau. Both the World Bank and the Chinese government cite this as an exemplary case for ecological rehabilitation in China and even the world.

The experience of the Loess Plateau warrants closer analysis. Planting trees was central to the rehabilitation effort, but it was by no means the project's sole activity. In fact, afforestation was embedded in a larger framework of rural development that emerged through a long process of consultation with local communities. In the mid-1990s when the project started, a team of experts undertook two years of extensive outreach with farmers and villagers. They sought to understand the processes that led to soil erosion and some of the local practices that could help restore ecosystem functions. The consultation led development experts to focus on changing unsustainable farming and herding behavior as well as on understanding the Loess's complex topographical characteristics. The team then introduced an integrative rehabilitation program of tree planting, terraced farming, small sediment-holding dams, and, most importantly, a revamped land ownership structure which contracted parcels of land to individual households. These provisions turned out to be successful socially, because they provided sustained incentives for local households to care for the contracted land as long as they set aside plots for trees. They were also successful economically, because the terraced fields and orchards provided local livelihoods while the ecosystem was gradually restored. Furthermore, they were successful ecologically, because the selection of trees was based on the diverse soil structure and climate conditions across the Plateau. Newly afforested areas became self-sustaining, as they continued to be nourished by an intricate system of check dams and layered canopies, turning the region from a net carbon source to a net carbon sink. Significantly, as compared with the monocultures associated with so many tree-planting campaigns, shrubs and trees such as desert willow were planted on the steep slopes to stabilize the land, while walnuts and dates were planted on flatter patches to generate income (Zhao et al. 2013; X. Feng et al. 2016).

The Loess Plateau provides a point of contrast for evaluating the effectiveness of present-day state-led environmental programs. The state was decisive in its pursuit of ecological rehabilitation, but project leadership was devolved to local authorities, the community, and international experts dispatched by the World Bank. Even though the state played a dominant role in shaping the overall goals of rehabilitation, it empowered the team of experts to study and pursue strategies that made sense under local circumstances. From ecologists to sociologists, professionals from various fields contributed their knowledge at different stages of the project.

Furthermore, under a distributed leadership structure, the project sought to complement expert knowledge with extensive consultations with the local community. Building on local inputs about seasonal weather patterns, farming practices, and household economics, as well as on political mobilization and local engagement, the team of experts was able to arrive at a comprehensive understanding of the interlocking set of challenges on the Plateau. Detailed local knowledge was further complemented by land surveys and satellite remote sensing. After the team drafted an initial plan for rehabilitation based on these inputs, they worked closely with local communities to make sure the plan was sensitive to households who would have to make significant livelihood changes. Community buy-in was thus key to the rehabilitation of the Plateau.

The remarkable successes of the late 1990s and early 2000s notwithstanding, subsequent efforts to scale up and replicate initial reforestation achievements produced far less favorable outcomes. Local officials sought high-density planting of some of the fastest growing trees like poplars and locusts, and soil moisture levels across the Loess have seen a marked decline in recent years (Jia et al. 2017). In fact, aggressive efforts to scale up the afforestation of the Loess Plateau have pushed the limits of local water resources, straining an essentially arid ecosystem (X. Feng et al. 2016). Because of the government's failure to appreciate the underlying eco-hydrological mechanisms at play, tree-planting has exceeded the region's ecological capacity to sustain vegetation (Fu et al. 2017). In its haste to scale up, the state thus resorted to the *yidaoqie* technique of cookie-cutter policymaking, turning a blind eye to the "lessons" of the distributive governance model that gave rise to the Loess success in the first place.

The Industrialized Forest of Uxin Banner

The botched afforestation of the Inner Mongolian town of Uxin Banner (in Chinese, Wushen 乌审) is another case in point. Tucked into the desert between the tourist hotspot of Ordos and the "Kuwait of China" coal town of Yulin, Uxin is an inconspicuous settlement. It boasts an unusual title, however: It is China's first "Human Habitat Model Town." Uxin's claim to fame is the wholesale transformation of a desert into an urban settlement with more than 30 percent of the surrounding land under forest cover. Officials laud Uxin as a pioneer and model for green growth, as its development was driven by one of China's "dragon-head enterprises" – flagship projects in industrial agriculture, forestry, and renewables. The dramatic changes in the Uxin landscape typify a certain kind of environmental experience in the Chinese borderlands.

In the last two decades, encouraged by the widely publicized success in rehabilitating the Loess, many places in China's arid and semi-arid West began to plant trees. In Uxin Banner, folk and official accounts trace the beginning of local afforestation efforts to the work of a fearless local forester, Yin Yuzhen (Xiao 2016; Chen 2017). As the official *China Daily* story goes, Yin moved into her new husband's family's mud cave in

Uxin in 1985. Shocked by the lack of vegetation and poor living conditions, Yin took it on herself to plant trees. Her initial ambition was to experiment in her own backyard to combat the loss of soil cover so she could produce food for her own family. Her successful experiment drew attention from neighbors near and far, who began to contract their own family plots to Yin for ecological rehabilitation through afforestation. Twenty years later, in 2005, her efforts were recognized when the local party secretary discovered her trees in the desert and labeled her a model worker, or *laomo* 劳模.

The small tree-planting operation soon drew political and financial support. Roads were paved to allow trucks to deliver seedlings. The national power grid was expanded into Uxin to help modernize Yin's enterprise, which began to specialize in fulfilling government orders to meet afforestation targets. The business boomed, less because of her entrepreneurial ambitions than because of the local state's push for a large-scale afforestation success story.

Officials at the sub-provincial forestry administration sent her larger and larger batches of poplar seedlings and allocated new areas of desert for her to plant. Within a short time, Yin's backyard project grew into the Banner's most profitable activity, reportedly foresting 60,000 *mu* (roughly 15 square miles) of desert by the end of 2005, and far exceeding Uxin's afforestation target. Yin's success drew so much attention that China nominated her for a Nobel Peace Prize, perhaps with Kenya's Green Belt Movement founder Wangari Maathai in mind as a precedent. Propaganda materials continue to retell her story as a model in combating desertification, rapidly scaling a backyard ecological experiment into the transformation of arid landscapes in the entire region.

According to published interviews, however, Yin Yuzhen herself is unsure. She is pleased with the economic

gains from her industrial afforestation business thanks
to handsome subsidies from the local state, but she is
worried about the future. Before her rise to national
prominence, her mom-and-pop tree farm was small
but teeming with a diversity of plant life. Shrubs like
budsage held the dirt together. Sweetvetch was a food
source for cattle. Desert willow branches could be used
to make fences. Birch provided much-needed shade as
well as income from lumber. Through trial and error,
Yin had achieved a delicate ecological balance in her
backyard. Today, the farm's growth has come at the cost
of diversity. Yin laments that her plantations are devoid
of topsoil and remain dependent on watering (Xiao
2016). She has experienced firsthand what scientists also
know: Monocultural poplar or aspen "forests" deplete
underground water because of their deep root systems,
intensifying desertification and causing permanent
damage to the ecosystem. Her early experience showed
that for an ecosystem to be viable, it needs many
plant, animal, and fungal species to interact in mutual
dependency. A monocultural forest cannot thrive in the
long term, although trees planted and cut for regular
sale can make for a profitable business (Jiang 2006a).
Unfortunately, according to data from the official 2010
forestry census, 57.9 percent of the trees in Uxin Banner
are fast-growing poplars (Uxin Banner 2019).

In fact, in Uxin, afforestation by monoculture has
produced what scientists call a massive "natural" pump
that depletes underground water (L. Wang et al. 2010).
The pursuit of tree cover percentages may have intuitive
appeal, but when afforestation is achieved through
industrialized monoculture, it manufactures an oddly
homogenized kind of landscape that has little regen-
erative capacity (Jiang 2004; Burtynsky 2007). Swept
along by the state's target-based emphasis on afforet-
tation, individual entrepreneurs like Yin Yuzhen have
been co-opted into hyperbolic discourses and claims

about conquering the forces of nature (Shapiro 2001; Jiang 2005).

The analysis of monocultural afforestation in China demonstrates the salience of state power in shaping the social and ecological impacts of afforestation. Tree-planting can bring durable benefits when it is supported by an open, consultative state, but can also wreak havoc when dominated by a target-driven, hasty one. The initial success of the Loess Plateau rehabilitation project offers a beacon of hope for how thoughtful interventions can bring about significant ecological restoration. However, the project's lack of scalability and replicability presents a cautionary tale of how hasty environmental ambitions can misfire. Cookie-cutter policymaking explains the reliance on monoculture in afforestation and is related to China's fixation on models intended for nationwide copying. Even the Chinese government has become aware of the dangers of *yidaoqie*, denouncing it as a manifestation of bureaucratic formalism. Indeed, the environment ministry recently devised a campaign to "unequivocally crack down on environmental *yidaoqie*" (坚决杜绝环保一刀切), as it "harms the image of the Party and the Government" (MEE 2018). Yet the authoritarian instinct to pursue *yidaoqie* prevails. At the start of the coronavirus outbreak in 2020, local authorities in the epicenter of Wuhan issued an emergency order that required all citizens to wear a face mask in public or risk being tried under the Infectious Disease Prevention Law. The irony is that, just three months before, Hong Kong authorities had enacted an anti-mask law (Prohibition on Face Covering Regulation), banning all protesters from wearing face masks.

As a policy mechanism, afforestation by monoculture is by no means deployed only by the Chinese state or state-endorsed initiatives such as the Ant Forest. In July 2019, Ethiopia's prime minister Abiy Ahmed announced that his country had planted an astonishing total of 353 million trees on a single day, far exceeding the previous Guinness World Record of 50 million set by the Indian state of Uttar Pradesh in 2016. In February 2020, at Davos, even anti-environmentalist US president Donald Trump embraced the Trillion Trees Initiative, a global expansion of Africa's Green Belt Movement. The obvious benefits of trees notwithstanding, these high-profile planting sprees often produce more political benefits than ecological services. The grave situations of desertification and drought call not for one-size-fits-all quick fixes; rather, they point to the urgent need for lasting, coordinated, thoughtful commitments to locally sustainable innovations (Yifei Li 2019). However, as we have seen, local efforts at sustainability face tremendous challenges when the state insists on centralized measures.

Green Grabbing: Hydropower as Ecological Civilization and Modernization

Hydropower dams are among China's most contested major infrastructure projects. The state sees them as integral to its goals of reducing carbon emissions and increasing the percentage of renewables in the total energy mix, both of which are integral to the overarching platform of constructing ecological civilization. Indeed, hydropower is a far more significant area of growth than the country's impressive investments in solar and wind energy.

China's national energy target is 35 percent of electricity from renewables in the overall mix by 2030, up from 20 percent just a few years ago (Bloomberg 2018). This is praiseworthy in the eyes of anyone concerned with carbon emissions and global climate change, especially given that China until recently argued that it was entitled to burn fossil fuels just like developed countries that have benefited most from such practices. Those days seem long gone. China has acknowledged its responsibilities as the world's top carbon emitter and seems poised to assume a greater leadership role on this issue. As mentioned in the Introduction, in November 2014, the "APEC blue" summit meeting broke the stalemate between the world's two leading carbon emitters. President Barack Obama unilaterally committed the United States to stop building new coal-fired power plants, which allowed President Xi Jinping to avoid the appearance of yielding to a US bully. Xi committed China to reach "peak" carbon emissions by 2030 and to see a reduction after that.

In China, the effort to shift away from coal, oil, and their less-problematic cousin natural gas has meant prioritization not only of solar and wind energy but also of hydropower. But hydropower is deeply problematic for its enormous regional impacts. Ecosystem disruption, livelihood loss, and large-scale human resettlement have made dams highly controversial (Khagram 2004; Leslie 2005). Farmers' land is flooded. The currents that define watershed ecosystems can become stagnant. Fishermen are affected by changes in current and sediment flow. Fish are blocked from spawning grounds. Moreover, dam construction requires roads, which fragment landscapes and introduce even more human activity. Dams bring a host of industrial impacts due to the vast quantities of cement and other building materials required. Worldwide, dams have become among the most controversial of all energy projects (perhaps second to nuclear reactors), so much so that major funders like the World Bank have turned away from mega-dams. In 2001, the World Commission on Dams issued guiding principles on social and environmental impacts as a way to encourage governments to avoid some of the most destructive dams and mitigate the worst conflicts, but although China requires environmental impact assessments, it is not generally bound by these considerations.

Many of China's new hydropower dams are being built in mountainous Western areas where river currents are strong but seismic activity is frequent. The weight of the water in some catchment areas is thought to trigger earthquakes. In the region of the Three Gorges Dam, which opened in 2003, earthquake frequency increased from the pre-2003 average of 25 per year to the post-2003 figure of more than 600 (Liao et al. 2009). As water above dams filters into the ground as a result of massive weight, the earth's crust deforms and tectonic plates can shift (Sun et al. 2015). In fact, both Chinese and Western scientists hypothesize that a new dam at Zipingpu in Sichuan province produced increased seismic activity before the devastating 2008 earthquake in Wenchuan, which killed almost 70,000 (LaFraniere 2009).

China already has one quarter of the world's installed hydropower capacity, with 352 GW. Ironically, hydropower is at over-capacity in parts of China, and energy curtailment is common – installed capacity is not the same as actual use of renewables. To increase demand, in November 2019 the central government released a renewable energy policy which sets requirements for province-wide minimum consumption of renewable electricity. The International Hydropower Association (2019) is pleased: "The new standard will require designated electricity users to purchase an obligated amount of renewable energy certificates from renewable energy generators, which will further help to increase hydropower consumption and reduce curtailment."

Environmental activists from outside affected areas have worked with communities to try to stop dams that do not comply with environmental impact assessment laws and do not have adequate resettlement and compensation plans in place. But the state has a formidable weapon at its disposal: green grabbing, which we can define as using an environmental framework to justify the repurposing of resources and the dispossession of customary users.

Green Grabbing as a Tool of Government Control

One of the mechanisms by which the Chinese state imposes large dams on riparian communities is through a framing discourse that positions hydropower as a clean energy alternative required for the security of the state (Rousseau 2020). Hydropower is constructed as necessary for sustainable development and modernization. As John Flower (2009) puts it, state planners see "hydropower development as achieving socialist modernization through ecological engineering." Journalist Liu Jianqiang (2003) writes, "Ironically, it is under a Green banner that China has unleashed the hydropower sector, as part of 'energy conservation and emissions reduction.' A favorite slogan of Chinese hydropower companies now is that they are 'addressing climate change.' Particularly when they can combine 'addressing climate change' with the conversion of river resources into big money."

Notification of communities to be flooded and resettled is often piecemeal and compensation notoriously poor. But the government's environmental discourse complicates community resistance. By positioning hydropower as essential to meeting the nation's renewable energy targets and abiding by international commitments, the state has made it exceedingly difficult for affected communities to articulate and organize resistance, especially since they are often in remote areas where education levels are low, political power is limited, and information restricted. The wellbeing of these communities is neglected even as the Chinese government receives international acclaim for its achievements in green development.

We may understand green grabbing as a form of land grabbing, which has been given significant scholarly attention in recent years. Land grabbing, or the privatization of formerly public lands, involves the capture of land resources that were once public or untenured communal land, often by corporations or governments who then exclude traditional users and uses. A related seminal concept is that of "accumulation by dispossession" (Harvey 2003), which reflects the capitalist logic whereby local communities lose traditional access to land (or water) resources through privatization and the resources are then capitalized and/or resold.

Ironically, Harvey's Marxist critique of a capitalist strategy of claiming public lands for private ownership can easily be applied to "socialist" China. The rights of communities to riparian farmland and to the use of rivers for fishing and irrigation are often customary but unsupported by legal documents or land title. In China, despite post-Mao economic reforms, land still officially belongs to the state and is merely leased to households; it can be reclaimed at any time. The barriers to such state reclamations are low as compared with procedures to assert eminent domain in Western countries, leaving rural communities in the precarious situation of "dispossession without development" (Levien 2018).

"Green grabbing" frames this dynamic. Green grabbing occurs when traditional landholders are dispossessed and excluded from access to natural resources, often in the name of environmental goals. Green grabs can also be understood as neo-liberal privatizations of nature that are officially justified by the need to "save" it, whether for ecotourism, protection from deforestation (as in the case of the REDD-plus initiative to reduce emissions from deforestation and degradation) or, in the case of rivers, to harness their energy to mitigate climate change (Borras et al. 2011; Fairhead et al. 2012; Rousseau 2020). Cloaking the need for hydropower in the discourse of ecological civilization and modernization, Chinese officials hide the fact that the beneficiaries of big dam projects are often local government officials or state-owned hydro-power companies like the Three Gorges Corporation, China Resources, China Datang, Huaneng Power, or Huadian Power. Indeed, the energy may or may not reach energy-hungry big cities where it is needed and, as noted above, capacity often exceeds use.

The environmental discourse provides the state with an airtight rebuttal to resistance to land grabbing and helps it maintain social stability through suppression of public participation. The logic of green grabbing is that national environmental goals are so urgent that individual land rights must be violated. In this sense, the discourse is the mandate, while the grabbing is the coercive action of exclusion and dislocation. The discourse permits the activity to continue under a powerful configuration. By the same token, green grabbing does not always stop at "grabbing" but can mutate into green monitoring, green dissident purging, and so on. Green grabbing thus typifies a class of problems under authoritarian environmentalism, just as the "green bans" and coercive behavioral changes under the environmental mandate discussed in the preceding chapter typify classes of problems. Resettlement (addressed later in this chapter) may also be seen as one of the state's coercive techniques enveloped in a green justification.

Citizen Resistance: The Nu River and Tiger Leaping Gorge

Guojia xuyao 国家需要, "the country needs it," is often the helpless response of an ordinary Chinese citizen affected by a big infrastructure project. But there are notable exceptions. Some have argued that at the local level, dam-building can involve considerable non-state participation in the policymaking process (Mertha 2008; Tilt 2014). Local cadres are often caught between navigating top-down mandates and trying to maintain social stability, and thus authority is more messy and pluralistic than commonly believed, a sort of "fragmented mediation under hierarchy" (Habich 2016). In the case of several dams planned for the Nu and Jinsha rivers in China's Southwest, local officials and hydropower corporations, using national renewable energy targets as justification, saw financial opportunities in dam-building despite the fact that dams constructed in these locations were inconsistent with alternative official goals such as preserving world heritage sites and ecotourism destinations and safeguarding ethnic minority cultures. Local activists, NGOs, and journalists were eventually able to make a compelling argument to both higher-level authorities and the court of international opinion and get the dams scaled back, delayed, or canceled so that problems with environmental impact assessment and resettlement and compensation plans could be reconsidered. These outcomes were preferable to what has happened to ecosystems and communities when the state has built dams without the involvement and pressure of journalists, civil society groups, and community activists.

International interest in China's big dams is high, not least because the state sometimes constructs big dams through the mechanism of the Clean Development Mechanism (CDM) under the aegis of the United Nations climate treaties. The CDM allows developed countries to get credit for investing in less developed countries to reduce those countries' carbon emissions, since substantially larger reductions can be achieved by reaching for low-hanging fruit. China has the world's greatest number of CDM projects, many of them in hydropower: Japan gets considerable credit for dams toward its commitments under the UN Framework Convention on Climate Change for dams constructed in China. Unneeded dams are sometimes even built to capture CDM funding. When a dam is presented as an internationally recognized and supported project, communities are hard put to present their needs as significant.

Here we provide a closer look at two well-documented examples of citizen resistance to green grabbing for the purpose of dam-building. Both took place in the Three Parallel Rivers UNESCO World Heritage region of Southwest China. Here the Nu (Salween), Lancang (Mekong) and Yangzi (in its form as the Jinsha tributary) flow from the Tibetan Plateau into Southeast Asia and toward Shanghai. Here a diverse constellation of minority groups has depended on rivers for hundreds of years.

The first case involves the intervention of a group of environmental activists in a series of 13 dams planned for the Nu River valley, which runs along the Myanmar border. As told in the Canadian film *Waking the Green Tiger* (Marcuse 2011), the beauty and remoteness of the river, and the imminent threats to it, drew the attention of Green Watershed activists Yu Xiaogang and Wang Yongcheng as well as filmmaker Shi Lihong. *Waking the Green Tiger* excerpts Shi Lihong's film. It shows how activists bussed villagers from the Nu River dam site that the activists organized to visit the Manwan Dam on a parallel river, the Upper Mekong (Lancang in China). Many of the Nu River villagers had never left home and they departed in high spirits. But their encounter with displaced, impoverished Manwan women picking through a pile of trash shocked them deeply and mobilized them to demand a better outcome for their own communities. In Shi Lihong's film, a Manwan woman weeps as she tells visitors that the government promised that her poverty would be temporary but it has lasted decades. She is ashamed to invite them to her home.

Shi Lihong's recording was shared with multiple villages slated to be affected up and down the Nu and Jinsha rivers, causing them to resist the dams or, if resistance failed, to demand fairer compensation and clearer relocation plans. Some of the original 13 dams have now been removed from government consideration. The film's attention to the plight of those displaced by the Manwan Dam eventually resulted in better cash compensation for them as well, although the fundamental problem of lack of good arable land near flooded communities remains.

Our second example of foiled green grabbing is the cancellation of a dam that local hydropower officials planned for a world-famous canyon on the Jinsha River called Tiger Leaping Gorge. Situated near the World Heritage town of Lijiang, it is one of China's most famous scenic sites, named for a tiger fabled to have leapt the raging river at its narrowest point as it descends from the Himalayas. The government planned to build a dam there as part of an eight-dam cascade, allegedly foreseeing huge revenues from taxes on electricity generation. When journalist Liu Jianqiang published his 2004 exposé "Emergency at Tiger Leaping Gorge" in the influential Guangzhou newsweekly *Nanfang Zhoumo (Southern Weekend)* he revealed that preliminary dam construction had actually preceded government approval and that the environmental impact assessment was deeply flawed. Liu's article further described how prior dam resettlements had been marked by embezzlement of resettlement funds and the impoverishment of those who lost their homes.

Liu's story drew the attention of international media and sparked the intercession of higher-level officials. The dam was stopped in 2007 on grounds that it had never properly received central government approval. Liu wrote in a subsequent essay that the opposition to the dam at Tiger Leaping Gorge represented a confluence of new social forces. These included local activists from the affected community who garnered grassroots support, well-organized external environmental groups, and the power of the internet. Although Liu eventually lost his job because of his environmental exposés, one of the most famous free-flowing rivers of China continued to draw tourists and infuse money into the community (Liu 2013; Hilton 2017). Unfortunately, in the National Energy Administration's Thirteenth Five-Year Plan for years 2016 to 2020, the dam at Tiger Leaping Gorge reappears under a new name: the Longpan Hydropower Station. Official sources openly acknowledge that the name was changed in order to avoid public controversy. The dam was approved on an expedited track, and construction started in May 2016.

The stories of the Nu River and Tiger Leaping Gorge underline the importance of pluralism and public participation in helping the state make better choices about whether and how to build hydropower to help reach the admirable goal of reducing fossil fuels to mitigate both ground-level air pollution and carbon emissions. These cases are the exception rather than the norm, however, which explains why they have garnered so much national and international attention. Most alarmingly, as the Tiger Leaping Gorge story shows, pluralistic success may turn out to be short-lived, as the state continues to wield its power through a combination of tacit coercive techniques.

Unfortunately, it is debatable whether even such limited pluralism remains possible in the assertively authoritarian climate of the Xi Jinping years. Even during the comparatively more open years of greater organizing space for environmental groups, activists like Yu Xiaogang of Green Watershed were subjected to government disinformation campaigns. As Yu told *Grist* magazine after he was awarded the 2006 Goldman environmental prize in San Francisco, "There were many challenges – there are still many rumors about me, about my organization, about the management of the project. There are some rumors that the organization is illegal, and that any people who participate in it should be careful. Many people think I have a secret agenda" (Nijhuis 2006).

The Chinese government expects to double hydropower capacity by 2020. Justified publicly by their alleged carbon-saving and economic development potential, hundreds of dams are being built on rivers descending from the Tibetan Plateau, including the Mekong (Lancang), Nu (Salween), Jinsha, and Brahmaputra (Magee 2014; Eyler 2019). The Chinese government's top-down, mandate-driven dam-building spree extends not only to Western China but across borders into Southeast Asia, where communities are resisting China-funded dams in Myanmar and Cambodia, and where Vietnamese farmers and fishermen fear the loss of their livelihoods with the transformation of the Mekong Delta. Dam-building is also a major component of the Belt and Road Initiative, where China-funded infrastructure projects are being built in Southeast Asia, Africa, and beyond (see chapter 3). In countries where civil society groups are robust, the Chinese government is ill-prepared for the depth of local resistance, which is often led by local monks and nuns with the support of international environmental groups like the International Rivers Network. But the green grabbing phenomenon is facilitating the power of the state to co-opt and control rivers and exclude local people from traditional uses, livelihoods, and homelands in many parts of the world. Better outcomes are possible where civil society groups are active and the media can publicize dam-builders' plans. But such groups and journalists are at risk of political pressure, job loss, and even prison or exile.

As we saw, the dangers are formidable. Investigative journalist Liu Jianqiang was fired from his position at *Southern Weekend* after uncovering irregularities in the planned dam for Tiger Leaping Gorge. Filmmaker Shi Lihong was threatened by the police when she documented the livelihoods and landscapes slated to be inundated by dams on the Nu River. When activist Yu Xiaogang of Green Watershed mobilized communities to resist dams, his organization was subjected to government disinformation and warnings. Despite the state's efforts to disempower and suppress them, these courageous individuals actually helped the state to avoid serious mistakes. They empowered local communities to preserve their cultural heritage and receive better compensation when dams were built, thereby protecting natural landscapes and producing more sustainable social outcomes.

Ecological Migration: Sedentarizing Nomads and Building Parks

A final prime technique of green coercion examined in this chapter is forcible resettlement. Although such resettlements are also typically associated with dam-building, they are less well known as tools used in pursuit of other aspects of the state's green agenda: the sedentarization of nomads and the construction of national parks and protected areas.

The state has a deceptively appealing formulation for resettlement in the name of ecological protection: "ecological migration" or *shengtai yimin* 生态移民. Green resettlement is linked to the afforestation and green grabbing tools we outlined in the preceding pages, and also plays an infamous role in the construction of hydropower dams. Here, however, we will focus on how green goals are used to justify moving nomadic people into towns in the name of grasslands preservation, or *tuimu huancao* 退牧还草, literally "giving up livestock, restoring grasslands." Sometimes, but not always, this is done in coincidence with the creation of national parks, and more recently, with the construction of China's new network of national parks, which was announced by the State Council in September 2017. These nature reserves and parks also provide the state with a mandate to relocate people.

James Scott famously explained that the state does not like nomads (1998). Whether they are Roma gypsies, Sioux, Marsh Arabs, Kazakhs, or Mongols, nomadic people circumvent a state's felt need to make inhabitants "legible." Nomads avoid the organizing hand of the state. In China, the central government has struggled for centuries to bring the nomadic cultures of its border regions under its sway, not least because competing systems of governance and authority structures threaten the state's ability to extract resources, secure borders, and consolidate power.

One way the state has asserted control is by encouraging Han (the Chinese ethnic majority) to migrate to border areas to bring their "civilizing" influences to bear (Harrell 1995; 2002; Gladney 2004). Han culture overpowers minority cultures, practices, and beliefs as the state sponsors in-migration to borderlands to assimilate minorities into Han ways of life. Ironically, the increase in population has often meant that formerly sustainable human–landscape relationships have been disrupted and traditional practices that evolved in concert with local ecosystems have been forbidden. This is particularly obvious in Inner Mongolia, which we touched on in the discussion of afforestation in Uxin. Here, however, we also note that the increase in human population, primarily from Han Chinese relocated to border areas during the Mao years, brought with it an increase in livestock (Sneath 2000). In a classic example of the tragedy of the commons, overgrazing then caused grassland degradation and in some cases desertification (Y. Wang et al. 1979). This has only worsened with the intensification of animal husbandry for the cashmere industry. Indeed, the "desert" is now only a few hours' drive from Beijing, which experiences severe dust storms every year. The state has blamed indigenous Mongols and their sharp-hooved goats and sheep for the environmental damage, and embarked on a series of fencings, land privatizations, and prohibitions against pastured goats and sheep, to be replaced with animals that can be corralled within pens (Jiang 2006b). Nomads will be nomads no more.

Mongols reject the effort to corral livestock, as they see the nomadic lifestyle as an integral part of their cultural identity and heritage. Moreover, during implementation, the central government has failed to incorporate indigenous knowledge, including the well-founded idea that sheep that can smell fresh grass will not eat hay and thus starve at the very moment their strength is needed for lambing, and the need for livestock paths through restoration zones so as to access water and forage areas. The government's blame of nomads for ecological degradation ignores the fact that damaging farming methods such as land reclamation from lakes were introduced by Han migrants during the Great Leap Forward and the Cultural Revolution, against the conventional wisdom of local pastoralists. Moreover, the government has failed to consider that grazing requires flexibility to adjust to climatic shifts in rainfall, or that combining herds is highly efficient since only a small number of shepherds is required to monitor a group of animals. Impoverished and disenfranchised nomads and villagers have ended up employing "weapons of the weak" to dodge enforcement, grazing their animals at night to avoid detection, hiding animal numbers by cooperating with one another to exceed per-household quotas, and paying off local officials (X. Wang 2007). Yet the state, perhaps in an effort to make Inner Mongolia more "legible" (as Scott would have it) insists that it knows what is best for local people even as they protest that their very identities are under assault.

In the Far West, in the "autonomous regions" of Xinjiang and Tibet, a complex mix of Tibetan Buddhists and Muslims (who include Uighurs, Kazakhs, Tajiks, Uzbeks, and Kirghiz) also pursue the nomadic lifestyles of herders. Here the state has embarked on a radical program of "ecological migration" whereby nomads are being forced to give up their herds and move into settlements. This project is framed in terms of the win-win goals of poverty alleviation and grasslands restoration. Despite deep local dissatisfaction with the program and serious criticism from both Chinese and Western scholars (Gegen and Uyun 2003; Yeh 2005; 2009; Baile and Han 2007; Zhou et al. 2010; F. Du 2012; Y. Du 2019), the state has persisted with forcible relocation and sedentarization programs, even lauding ecological migration as a centerpiece of China's often elusive pursuit of ecological civilization. An estimated total of 2.5 million people, roughly the entire population of Chicago, was resettled under the banner of ecological migration between 1980 and 2010, and the state expects to resettle another 10 million who are considered "in need of ecological migration" in the future (W. Feng et al. 2016).

We must clarify that the rationale for this program is different from that used to justify the construction and operation of a huge network of compulsory Muslim re-education camps, a huge and important topic largely beyond the scope of this book. The camps are framed as anti-terrorism projects and are officially intended to cleanse inmates of "unhealthy" ideas and retrain them in useful skills before releasing them to their communities. That said, the ecological migration and anti-terrorism programs have the shared, if unstated, national goal of pacifying China's borders and Sinicizing its ethnic minorities.

The problem with ecological migration is not only with the program's social injustice and cultural dislocation. Rather, there is mounting evidence that removing herders from grazing is actually damaging to the environment, just as there is mounting ecological evidence that dividing grasslands up to individual households results in ecologically worse outcomes than larger-scale grazing units comprised of multiple households. Grazing has an important role to play in mitigating the negative effects of climate change on the grasslands, which is not surprising given the co-evolution of the Tibetan Plateau with grazers over thousands of years (Miehe et al. 2009). There have been numerous problematic claims about the success of China's grassland programs, including ecological migration, based on results from satellite imagery, which is not a good proxy for the quality and type of vegetation. Thus, ecological migration is not just an issue of brutal social policy but also of ineffective ecological policy that masquerades as climate adaptation (Klein et al. 2011).

There are additional problems. Eco-migration destinations face challenges that come with the influx of migrants: unemployment, insufficient resources, and new construction plans that do not reflect local conditions. Predictably, culture loss has been accompanied by disease, alcoholism, and societal collapse. In effect, ethnic minorities are required to adopt the lifestyles and cultures of the dominant Han Chinese. But such former nomads find it difficult to participate in the labor market in their new locations because of skill mismatch and lack of social connections (W. Feng et al. 2016). As a result, even though most nomadic families were self-sufficient prior to migration, the vast majority of them become dependent on state welfare in the new settlement (Zhou et al. 2010). Many are even forced to join the hundreds of millions of migrant workers seeking employment in the industrialized East (Li and Wang 2013). These problems in the destinations are often ignored when state media are directed to focus on celebrating green "success" in the newly established parks and reserves.

Protected Areas and National Parks

China is one of the world's most biodiverse places, known for pandas, snow leopards, Tibetan antelopes, cranes, and a host of other charismatic and highly endangered species. It is no accident that the World Wildlife Fund adopted the giant panda as its logo in 1961. Yet China also struggles to curtail the loss of habitat to logging, human incursion into fragile ecosystems, and land use transformation for agriculture. Erosion, hunting, climate change, and above all habitat fragmentation have made it urgent to set aside lands dedicated to conservation and the protection of biodiversity. To this end, the Chinese government has created numerous parks, nature reserves, and protected areas under the authority of the National Forestry and Grassland Administration, which in 2018 superseded the State Forestry Administration as part of a central government overhaul intended to address problems with bureaucratic redundancy and conflicting mandates. These parks and protected areas have satisfied the rising demand for ecotourism from the newly prosperous but they have fallen short of fulfilling the ecological functions they were originally set up to perform, such as wildlife conservation and ecological restoration (G. Wang et al. 2007).

In global conservation, there are several approaches to such parks. The "fortress conservation" model essentially builds a wall around a park and sharply limits human activity within it; the "buffer zone" model, as recommended by the International Union for the Conservation of Nature, defines a core and a series of peripheral zones which are open to light human activity and even residence. China has often followed the fortress conservation model epitomized by Yosemite and Yellowstone, with hefty entrance fees, tour buses, and restrictions on non-sanctioned economic activity within the park. Famous parks like Zhangjiajie, Jiuzhaigou, Huangshan, Yulong Xueshan and so on are not only refuges for biodiversity and protected areas for spectacular landscapes, but also big money-makers for those who control them. Fortunately, under a plan for a gigantic projected area in Sanjiangyuan 三江源 in Qinghai province at the headwaters of the great rivers of the Tibetan Plateau, perhaps because of the size of the proposed parks and the huge numbers of people who live within their planned boundaries, China has begun to experiment with the buffer zone model as well. As we see below, however, many people are being resettled and are unsure about their futures.

China in 2017 announced the creation of a network of centrally administered national parks including a giant panda reserve intended to link the increasingly fragmented pockets of panda habitat. Sanjiangyuan is the largest among the ten parks in the 2017 plan. With 47,500 square miles, Sanjiangyuan is larger than the other nine parks combined – more than 13 times the size of Yellowstone. Mandatory ecological migration started in 2005, more than a decade ahead of the public announcement of the national park plan. The vast majority of those resettled – 90 percent – were ethnic Tibetans (Z. Wang et al. 2010). On the official record, the total population in Sanjiangyuan was 223,000 in 2007 (Baile and Han 2007), a figure that dropped to 64,600 in 2015. The national park development plan involves unspecified targets for further population reduction until it reaches the projected "steady state" in 2035 (NDRC 2018). Similarly, the panda reserve will relocate 170,000 people in the three provinces of Sichuan, Gansu, and Shaanxi (Solly 2019).

Fortunately, in one pilot project in Qinghai, a gentler buffer-zone approach is being tried. Under the "One Family, One Ranger," or *yihu yigang* 一户一岗 program, one person per family is hired to collect trash and monitor the park for poachers (Larson and Wang 2019). The sheer size of the park and the human population of the region may make total relocation impossible, but uncertainty about who will have to move, and when, dogs local inhabitants.

From the perspective of Tibetans and other minority groups who are forcibly relocated from ancestral lands, the experience of ecological migration is similar to what Samuel Huntington (1968) called "forced draft urbanization and modernization," whereby peasants are forced to give up self-sustaining traditional ways and move into the city to embark on modern lives based on wage labor and consumer goods. In places like Sanjiangyuan, the shock of this forced urbanization is underappreciated by officials who have limited experience with Tibetan nomadic pastoralism (Baile and Han 2007). With their urban frame of mind, provincial officials see themselves as benevolent patriarchs who generously provide new housing to an ungrateful bunch of Tibetans. They shrug off Tibetans' grievances as excuses to extort more compensation from the state. To their minds, urbanization is self-evidently good and universally desired. Ecological migration, thus conceived, provides "backward" Tibetans with a once-in-a-lifetime shortcut to being modern. By contrast, local officials at the township level often see that ecological migration is ill-advised but feel they have little political space to resist it, or they may see it as a chance to capture needed funding for their own projects.

As in so many instances where a local resource is profitable, there are human winners and losers. In some cases, people whose homes were within the boundaries of a park are forced to move. Investment capital, often from outside the region, builds hotels, shops, and restaurants, and the government monopolizes tourist revenue through high entrance fees and mandatory bus tours. The promise that a park will spur local economic opportunities often goes largely unfulfilled. For example, on separate visits to the 500-square-mile park at Pudacuo in "Shangri-la" County in northern Yunnan, announced in 2007 and locally promoted as a crown jewel for China's protected area system, we found a fortress conservation-style park. Huge parking lots fed high-paying tour groups through a visitors' center and onto a stream of tour buses. These stopped at prescribed scenic sites to allow tourists to photo-graph waterfalls and interesting rock formations (boat ride available for an additional fee). "Entrance" to local minority villages was included in the ticket price, but locals were permitted free access into the park only three days of the year (September 15–17), when the county celebrated the anniversary of its 1957 "liber-ation from Tibetan serfdom." Even on these days, locals were not guaranteed access, because "traffic control" in the name of conservation prioritized entrance-paying tourists over non-revenue-producing locals.

Local people of Tibetan heritage told Judith that they were largely unhappy about the park. Some had been forced to give up their homes. Few of the promised economic benefits had emerged. Tour guides for the buses needed good Mandarin, which the locals did not have, and the fancy hotels that had sprung up near the park entrance were financed and owned by outsiders. Locals had formerly been able to provide horse rides to tourists and earn a little money by providing homestays, but they had been excluded from these small enterprises on grounds that the activities were not well regulated. Instead, investors who were experienced with catering to mass tourists were getting most of the business. Ticket fees did not return to the community but went primarily to park administration. Homestays were still on offer but only illicitly, and horse rides could only be offered near a remote park entrance to the west that had not yet come under full state control.

The merger of ecotourism and ethnotourism, which has become so typical of the Chinese travel industry, smacks of stereotyping, if not racism, even as it fragments and confuses local cultural identities. Commodification of both nature and people underlies many of the Chinese state's efforts to preserve biodiversity if we look closely at what is happening on the ground. Jack Zinda, who has studied the evolution of Pudacuo Park and its impact on local livelihoods, finds "less a win–win than a runaway victory for the prefecture government and affiliated tourism interests" (Zinda 2012).

As we have seen in the above examples of resettlement in the name of ecological protection, whether for conservation of ecosystems like grasslands or for the purpose of constructing a pristine natural area free from human intervention, the state has used green goals to assert control over ethnic minorities in frontier regions. While such efforts may be successful from the point of view of the state, and even from the point of view of those concerned primarily with short-term biodiversity conservation, they have often been implemented in such a way as to give short shrift to human wellbeing and cultural integrity even as they damage ecosystems in the long run. All too often, new commercial interests replace local economies and do their own sort of damage, as infrastructure projects to cater to mass tourism bring their own sets of environmental impacts. New protected areas and scenic sites are being "opened up" quickly to appeal to the mass tourism that has only recently come within reach of ordinary Chinese. The transformative impacts on both landscapes and local communities are already dramatic, and likely to become only more so.

Pacifying Borderlands in the Name of the Environment

The transformation of China's borderlands provides ample fodder for thinking about the promise and peril of state-led environmentalism. China is championed as the global leader in renewable energy. Under the country's aggressive green economic incentive programs, its Western borderlands have transformed into strategic zones for harnessing hydropower, wind, and solar energy. These developments have, in a relatively short time span, brought substantial changes to the national energy structure. Moreover, China manufactures the lion's share of the world's solar panels and wind turbines, helping to facilitate a global transition toward a green economy.

Yet the state's effort to pacify, subdue, and transform its borderlands comes with ecological and social risks. When afforestation campaigns are launched by state officials whose eyes are fixed on short-term results, they struggle to appreciate the complexity of forestry conditions in the borderlands – which are some of the most ecologically diverse places on earth. In the long run, these campaigns wreak ecological havoc, compounding the environmental problems they purport to solve. Likewise, when entire borderland communities are resettled for environmental engineering, grasslands protection, and national park projects, the supposed gains in ecological sustainability run into direct conflict with people's everyday needs, cultural identities, and traditions. When communities and livelihoods are traded for ecological gains, China's large-scale environmental projects look less rosy. These observations call for extra caution in managing borderland landscapes and communities, with a view toward recognizing their complexity and inherent value.

This chapter has explored three additional tools that the Chinese state uses to coerce environmental goals: cookie-cutter policymaking (as shown in the example of afforestation), green grabbing (as shown in the example of dam-building) and forcible resettlements (as shown in the examples of grasslands preservation and the construction of protected areas). We must note that tools such as target-setting, campaigns, and behavior modification are also widely used in China's less-developed West and scenic areas. But the methods introduced here are especially common in parts of the country where wealth disparities with coastal areas are striking and ethnic minorities predominate. Problems of environmental justice – whereby vulnerable populations do not benefit from resource extraction and are disproportionately harmed by environmental degradation – are typical of these regions. When China's push to go "green" through afforestation, renewable energy production, and biodiversity and landscape protection is coupled with the state's invigorated authoritarian agenda, the results are not always as benign, or as sustainable, as they initially seem. While green goals like expanding forest cover, increasing the availability of renewable energy, and setting aside protected areas are laudable, implementation often has its darker sides in the Chinese context. However, none of the darker sides are inevitable.

Many Chinese officials freely and matter-of-factly characterize the risks we document in this chapter with a twisted metaphor – "the labor pains of birthing green reform" *lüse gaigede zhentong* 绿色改革的阵痛. Compared with the weight of national interests, the responsibility of China's international commitments, and the promise of planetary ecological civilization, individuals and communities may seem negligible in the here and now. State officials deploy the "labor pain" metaphor to assure their citizens that sacrifices are temporary and corresponding gains are many. The promise of green development serves as the main justification for the supposedly short-term suffering of citizens. These "pains," however, are turning out to be chronic. Time and time again, the state unapologetically asks its citizens to bear the brunt of the many externalities of green development. These risks are systemic, not incidental, to the toolkit China wields in the name of sustainability.

The environmental gains of these approaches also remain unclear. Afforestation by monoculture increases tree canopy coverage but also brings ecological degradation to already vulnerable areas. Dams generate power but also disrupt the eco-hydrological balance of watershed ecosystems. National parks set aside large fragile landscapes for conservation and research but also invite the undue burden of mass tourism and may even have negative ecological impacts when grazing is excluded. In the end, the green justification for coercive environmentalism rests on thin grounds, even as the state has advanced a suite of non-environmental goals. Our case studies point toward the possibility of socially equitable and politically sustainable approaches of state-led environmentalism, but these cannot materialize without greater state receptivity to pluralistic consultations and partnerships.

3

The State on the "Green" Belt and Road

China's Belt and Road Initiative (BRI), previously known in English as One Belt One Road (OBOR) or *yidaiyilu* 一带一路, is one of the most ambitious infrastructure and energy development programs ever undertaken. It subsumes earlier foreign investments and aid projects dating to China's "going out" agenda of the late 1990s and now rivals the most powerful intensifications of the globalization of trade and investment of recent centuries. With nearly 150 countries and organizations already in active cooperation under the ever-expanding Belt and Road umbrella and multiple major projects underway, the BRI is already having dramatic consequences for China, for China's partners along the Belt and Road routes, and even for the international political and economic system.

To read the Chinese narrative of the program's potential, the initiative will bring prosperity, harmony, and economic development to the immediate partners and indeed to the whole world. It envisages an infrastructure network that will facilitate trade and connect countries to China through soft power and development.

Critics, however, see the risks as significant, including ecological and social impacts that may be irreversible; this is despite the official packaging of the project as one that promotes sustainability and human wellbeing. There are also economic risks of failed loans and inadequate financing, and geopolitical risks, as an authoritarian China seeks to counterbalance a Western-centric world order. Social and environmental impacts are receiving comparatively little attention from observers, except at the local level from the communities most at risk. This is unfortunate given this historical moment. The planet's ecological health is uniquely vulnerable and stands at multiple tipping points, while traditional cultures and social structures are buffeted and beleaguered by the forces of intensified globalization and resource use. In this chapter, we examine some of the tools, techniques, and technologies that undergird China's promotion of the Belt and Road.

The Belt and Road Initiative, first mentioned by President Xi Jinping at a university speech in Kazakhstan in 2013, is a colossal trade, development, and political initiative that initially focused on reviving the old Silk Road economic corridor on land across Central Asia to Europe (the "belt") and establishing a new maritime route around the coasts of South Asia to Africa and the Middle East (the "road"). Since then it has expanded dramatically, both geographically and conceptually, with signatories encompassing about one-fourth of the global economy. Although construction of roads, railroads, energy projects, and deep-water ports is at the center of the program, the BRI goes beyond infrastructure. Some of the human development and soft power aspects include anti-poverty programs, food and health aid, and education, including scholarships for students from BRI countries to study in China and the stepped-up installation overseas of Confucius Institutes, which promote Chinese language and culture so as to create a friendly constituency of foreigners interested in China.

So important does the BRI appear to be to the Xi Jinping administration and the Communist Party leadership that in October 2017 the program was enshrined through resolution into the Party Constitution, with the words, "following the principle of achieving shared growth through discussion and collaboration, and pursuing the Belt and Road Initiative" (Xinhua 2017a, official translation). Since then, the BRI has expanded to include member countries in Africa, Latin America, and Western Europe, the Arctic (called the "Polar Silk Road"), and even outer space (called the "Space Silk Road"). Despite the rapid expansion and enormous investment and attention, not enough time has elapsed for definitive conclusions about the BRI to be drawn. We know little about how or even whether the BRI vision will materialize, especially when we take note that the much-hyped Europe-bound freight trains – a signature BRI achievement – have been running with empty containers (Sun 2019). We do not know how China will respond to concerns about inadequate social and environmental safeguards for many projects and criticism of its sponsorship of coal-fired power plants in recipient countries, or whether China will be able to reconcile its public commitment to building "socialist ecological civilization" domestically with its support for environmentally destructive projects and activities beyond its borders. Yet the pace of the initiative's introduction, the breadth of its acceptance by major powers and institutions, and the sheer ambition of its blueprints require global attention, not least because discussion in these early phases may shape outcomes for many years to come.

The Belt and Road Initiative rests primarily on bilateral agreements between China and participant countries, bolstered by multilateral meetings. In this chapter, we explore China's use of authoritarian tools as they intersect with "green" aspects of the BRI at the national and sub-national levels, reserving discussion of China on the global, planetary stage for the next chapter. The key relevant methods of state-led environmentalism include the win-win framing of green developmentalism, the projection of ecologically friendly soft power, and the use of big data in governance on a transnational scale. Before we delve into these governmental techniques, an overview of the BRI's relationship to the environment is in order.

The Belt and Road Initiative and the Environment

There is a fundamental contradiction between China's BRI-related efforts to create global economic integration through investments in infrastructure and energy and its public commitments to decarbonize and model a vision of an ecological civilization suitable for the world. As we have noted, both ecological civilization and the Belt and Road Initiative have been written into the CCP's constitution and are core directional principles for the country. But as we see below, in practice China has been displacing some of its most environmentally destructive activities onto Belt and Road countries, including building coal-fired power plants and hydro-power dams and opening new mines for copper, iron ore and other minerals. Some of this may be in response to over-capacity at home and to the need to create new markets and source raw materials internationally.

The BRI is presented officially as "green," with China's Ministry of Ecology and Environment convening an April 2019 Thematic Forum on the Green Silk Road, and major government-run Chinese investment banks agreeing to adhere to "Green Investment Principles." Yet Chinese policy makers seem patently insensitive to the environmental and ecological impacts of infrastructure development and commerce. Highways, railroads, pipelines and deep-water ports fragment and transform habitats. Increased trade promotes transportation involving fossil fuel emissions. Using an unfortunate metaphor, President Xi Jinping said in a 2017 speech to the 19th Party Congress that China is "in the driver's seat" with respect to preserving the planet for future generations. But there is a huge gap between the Chinese promise of shared prosperity and green development and the realities on the ground. Even if construed as being as well intentioned as possible, the Belt and Road Initiative could mean the death knell for significant portions of the planet's biodiversity and for its climate infrastructure, as transportation and energy projects transform fragile ecosystems and increase global carbon emissions.

The most contentious and immediately damaging aspect of the BRI is the export of coal-fired power plants. In fact, infrastructure and development projects along the Belt and Road will be predominantly powered by coal, despite China's commitment to UN Sustainable Development Goals and the Paris Climate Accord. Such plants do not seem to comport with China's vision of a "green, healthy, intelligent and peaceful" Silk Road (WWF 2018). But China is already the world's largest exporter of coal-fired plants, and the Belt and Road Initiative will entrench this status. Indeed, a 2019 study by Greenpeace East Asia indicates that since 2014 China has put much more into coal-fired power along the BRI than into wind and solar, with 67.9 GW of coal to only 12.6 GW of wind and solar (Greenpeace 2019a). In Indonesia, China plans to supplement Indonesia's electricity shortage through coal investments by SOEs, many of which are seeking new opportunities as China's own coal consumption is starting to abate. In 2016, for example, the Power Construction Corporation of China entered into a joint venture with Indonesia's PT Intraco Penta to build the 360 million USD Tenaga Listrik Bengkulu power plant. The Beijing-based ENGO Global Environment Initiative found that China's support for such high-carbon projects increased when funders like the World Bank, the European Investment Bank, and the US would no longer support them (Ren et al. 2017). China's commercial banks face few restrictions on funding coal-fired plants, which allows China to export outdated excess production capacity. They contribute significantly to China's overall carbon footprint if its overseas investments are included in the calculation (Gallagher and Qi 2018).

The dynamic is clear: China's "shadow ecology" or hidden environmental footprint (Dauvergne 1997) means that, even as China pivots toward more sustainable development domestically, its overall impact on the global environment remains enormous and is not trending toward sustainability. China is shifting its carbon output to less developed countries through the BRI initiative, indicating that China's domestic efforts to go green have not translated into investments abroad (Tracy et al. 2017; Hafeez et al. 2018). This is a classic example of what many environmentalists call "displacement of environmental harm" or "dirty migration," an environmental justice problem and moral hazard whereby, when politically well-connected groups and institutions resist such activities, they are moved to the more vulnerable. Beyond coal, other forms of carbon-based fossil fuels such as natural gas and oil are also problematic. One of China's principal goals for the BRI is to ensure energy security, and its partnership with Central Asian countries rich in oil and gas will mean that it can transport energy more safely without being vulnerable to controversies in the South China Sea and US interference in sea lines of communication (SLOCs). China-funded (and in some cases -operated) pipelines in Central Asia have already had effects on the local environment. The North Caspian Operating Company, for example, had to replace pipelines in 2014 due to leaks (WWF 2018).

Even renewable energy resources such as hydro-electric, solar, and wind power have environmental consequences as the Belt and Road Initiative seeks aggressively to tap into them. As we saw in the previous chapter, dam-building significantly disrupts ecosystems by impeding the movement of migratory fish and the distribution of sediments and nutrients. Dams change river flows and lead to human relocations and loss of livelihoods and culture. The Belt and Road Initiative is creating significant impacts all along the Mekong river (called the Lancang in China). In the Mekong Delta in Vietnam, upriver Chinese dams are putting 64 species in danger and are limiting water flows on which millions depend (WWF 2018). In Cambodia, the latest big Mekong River dam, the Lower Sesan 2, was rejected for funding by the Asian Development Bank but is going forward with support from a subsidiary of China's Huaneng Power. The dam will significantly disrupt Cambodia's Tonle Sap, one of the world's largest fresh-water lakes. The lake is the primary resource for the nation's fishing families, many of whom live on the lake. Hundreds more dams are in the planning stages; Brian Eyler has written that they will be the final blow to a once-mighty river now in its last days (Eyler 2019).

Apart from localized environmental degradation from BRI energy projects, there are systemic environmental risks. International shipping in oceans, rivers and lakes, as well as the construction of road and rail infrastructure result in numerous general impacts. Among them are: the proliferation of exogenous species, hypoxia from fuel waste, disconnection of rivers from floodplains, and new barriers to migratory mammals. Habitats are fragmented into islands, promoting accelerated extinction rates. Increased transport contributes to global emissions of greenhouse gases.

Deep-water ports are the crown jewels of the Belt and Road Initiative. Nervous Western defense analysts have labeled the Chinese developments a "string of pearls" around South Asia and into the Middle East, leading Chinese officials to reject the idea that there is any deliberate underlying strategic intent in how they are selected (Brewster 2017). The ports have profound impacts on coastal ecosystems, the livelihoods of small-scale fishers, and coral reef systems. The most controversial include the Gwadar port in Pakistan (which predated the BRI but has been subsumed under it), the Hambantota port in Sri Lanka, and the Kyaukpyu port in Myanmar. All are connected to China via important overland economic Belt and Road infrastructure – the China–Pakistan Economic Corridor and the China–Indochina Peninsula Economic Corridor – and connect China westward to markets in Europe and in the Middle East.

From a global conservation perspective, the Belt and Road Initiative threatens irreversible changes to vulnerable ecosystems that stand in the path of its development plans. In an analysis of the overlap between proposed Belt and Road corridors and ecologically sensitive areas, the World Wildlife Fund shows coincidence with the habitat of 265 threatened species, 39 of which are critically endangered and 81 of which are endangered (WWF 2017). In addition, the corridors intersect 1,739 Important Bird Areas or Key Biodiversity Areas and 46 biodiversity hotspots. The study finds that land-use changes, deforestation, emissions from construction including heavy use of concrete, and emissions from transportation will cause enormous habitat loss. The highways that cut across tropical and subtropical forests will have huge negative impacts on valuable carbon sinks, even as they bring a vast increase in secondary human impacts because of improved access.

Notwithstanding the concerns enumerated above, however, there are environmental opportunities associated with the BRI, as we will see in the next section as we explore the support that key multilateral agencies are offering to the program. If implemented with a rigorous focus on mitigating negative environmental side-effects and enhancing positive environmental services, the initiative could strengthen sustainable development and environmental protection around the globe. Indeed, some Chinese investors are going above and beyond what the Chinese government recommends in terms of social and environmental screenings in an effort to improve the investment experience for all concerned. A new paradigm could yet be forth-coming. Much depends, however, on whether Chinese policy makers can develop a nuanced understanding of social and environmental impacts of China's footprint. Recognizing the BRI's tremendous risks and potential, it is essential to examine the tools, techniques, and technologies of state-led environmentalism beyond China's borders: the win-win framing of green devel-opmentalism, the marketing of "socialist ecological civilization" and the quest for soft power, and the promotion of global green technocracy.

Win-win Green Development

In China's framing, the Belt and Road Initiative is a big win for all parties involved. President Xi Jinping's much-reproduced speech, "Work together to Build the Silk Road Economic Belt and the 21st Century Maritime Silk Road," delivered on May 14, 2017 at the opening ceremony of the Belt and Road Forum for International Cooperation, concludes with a series of statements on what the Initiative is a road *for* – peace, prosperity, opening, innovation, connecting different civilizations. A supporting five-minute video with portentous background music depicts a sincere President Xi explaining how he conceived of the Belt and Road. He is shown as a courageous but ever-so-human visionary, troubled by the world's pain and willing to step up to the task of finding a new path. He is shown as remembering his boyhood home in Shaanxi at the mouth of the old Silk Road, when he used to dream of camels and increased prosperity through international trade. He is presented as daring to have a vision to help a world plagued by war, famine, and global uncertainty, a world searching for direction and leadership. Images of wind turbines and airplanes shift us toward hope. President Xi states that he was inspired by the ancient Silk Road to realize shared dreams "shining with the wisdom of the East." Core principles are to be "extensive consultation, joint contribution, and shared benefits." As a win for a troubled planet as well as a win for the ancient wisdom of the Middle Kingdom, the Belt and Road Initiative conveys President Xi's win-win green developmental promise to the world.

The Belt and Road Initiative is framed as open and inclusive. It is to represent a veritable chorus of countries. The video depicts projects through a whirlwind world tour, many of them in emerging economies, often with awe-struck local children filmed as the main beneficiaries. We see an Uzbekistan high-speed rail tunnel, a Belarus industrial park, unspecified Russian cooperation projects (unveiled by deconstructing nesting dolls), the Maldives "Friendship Bridge" with a Chinese kite flying above it, and Malaysian container ships. For a laurel-wreathed, toga-clad Greek fisherman, there is the Piraeus port. For a Sri Lankan child reaching toward a lightbulb, there is the Puttalam coal-fired power plant. For a bowler-hatted Briton, there is the happiness brought by China–Europe railway freight. Djibouti, Fiji, Addis Ababa, and Kazakhstan are represented too, with varying degrees of cultural stereotypes like dancing, grass-skirted Fijians. Toward the video's end, an airborne, gloriously painted Pakistani truck soars over the Karakoram Highway. These are to be win-win partnerships, as symbolized by a soccer ball, a child blowing bubbles, hot-air balloons, and a Van Gogh-like drawing floating in the sky in a marriage of Eastern and Western culture. "History is made by the brave," we are told (Xi 2017, official translation). Children of many ethnicities are running excitedly toward the future.

On the occasion of the fifth anniversary of the announcement of the BRI, the official *People's Daily* produced yet another music video, and featured a story about it on its front page. It is based on the 1971 Coca Cola jingle, "It's the Real Thing." Loose-knit, largely unrehearsed groups of mostly foreigners, apparently international students at Tsinghua University, dance and sing about world peace, perfect harmony, and turtle doves – rather than a cold bottle of soda. "It's the real thing" becomes "It's the Belt and Road" (Yang 2018). The irony of linking the BRI with the consumer brand most closely identified with Western capitalism may have been lost on the video's producers.

The framing of the Belt and Road Initiative as a project offering the world mutually beneficial development goes much further than presidential remarks and propaganda videos. An official declaration states that "the Belt and Road Initiative is not a zero-sum game with winners and losers, but creates win-win, multi-win, and all-win outcomes" for China and its BRI partners (Xinhua 2019e). In a commentary published in *Fortune* magazine entitled "Why the U.S. Shouldn't Sit Out the Belt and Road Initiative," China's ambassador to the US Cui Tiankai offers this evidence: Belt and Road investments have created more than 300,000 jobs in China's partner countries within just six years. In the logistics industry alone, in Duisburg, Germany

– home to the world's largest inland port – 6,000 jobs have been added, showing that infrastructure improvements bring tangible benefits. The ambassador concludes by enumerating the major US companies that have contracts through Belt and Road projects: Honeywell, General Electric, Caterpillar, and Citibank. "Embrace this opportunity," the ambassador reproves a recalcitrant United States (Cui 2019).

Indeed, the win-win framing has become a key tool to promote and defend the Belt and Road, especially in response to critics who accuse China of advancing security and military interests under the guise of a seemingly neutral Belt and Road. The spokesperson for the Chinese Ministry of Foreign Affairs, Hua Chunying, provides a colorful rebuttal to a US think tank report that questions China's win-win claims and casts doubt on the country's motives (Thorne and Spevack 2017). Hua fulminates, "I would like to remind the relevant people who cooked up this report that if they continue looking at others as well as the world with dark thoughts and through tinted glasses, they will see everything as darkness and traps. On the contrary, if they are open and broadminded enough, they will find a sunlit world that is bright and warm" (Hua 2018a, official translation).

To further press their case, official Chinese statements blame the existing Western world order for the inequitable distribution of developmental benefits. The Belt and Road Initiative is thus positioned as providing an alternative to the wave of protectionism sweeping the Global North and the hegemonic voices of the US and Western Europe in international economic and financial institutions (NDRC et al. 2015). Against this background, the BRI is central to China's proposal to spearhead a global "community with a shared human future" – *renlei mingyun gongtongti* 人类命运共同体 – an aspirational phrase that is enshrined in the Constitution of China in a 2018 amendment.

Notably, in response to mounting criticism of the environmental problems we reviewed earlier in the chapter, Chinese authorities have stretched the win-win frame to suggest that both human prosperity and ecological sustainability can flourish on the winning end of the bargain. The win-win has gone fully green. The Belt and Road Initiative now officially follows a set of "Green Guidelines" that "promote the win-win goals of economic development and environmental protection" (MEP et al. 2017). In a public speech, President Xi Jinping further suggests that the "green" BRI represents the globalization of China's quest for ecological civilization. Here, once again, Xi blames the West for contemporary environmental ills: "industrialization produced unprecedented material wealth, but also brought irreversible ecological damage" (Xi 2019). Perhaps, it is suggested, China can show us another way. In fact, Chinese official propaganda organs interpret Xi's speech to mean the beginning of a new era in which China expands the "community with a shared human future" formulation into a "community with a shared human and natural future" (Zhao 2019). Green wins, so it seems.

That said, by lending large sums to develop infrastructure in Belt and Road countries, China finds itself in a win-win situation quite different from the "win-win" solutions it touts as part of its public rhetoric. If the loans are repaid, China has lost nothing. But if countries are unable to return the loans, China can gain *de facto* ownership of key infrastructure projects which are often of high geopolitical value. For example, Sri Lanka handed over the key strategic port of Hambantota because it defaulted on its loan. The deep-water port in Gwadar, Pakistan is effectively under Chinese control, with China contracted to make 91 percent of all port income for the next 40 years (Manuel 2017). Either way, China gains secure access to trade routes, key geopolitical bases, and influence. Critics commonly call this aspect of the Belt and Road Initiative debt-trap diplomacy.

China's focus on the win-win frame has earned it an unlikely ally: the United Nations. For example, the United Nations Environment Programme (now known as the UN Environment) signed a 2016 Memorandum of Understanding with China "to cooperate to promote a sustainable Belt and Road." With support from the Chinese Ministry of Commerce's pool of "South-South cooperation" funding, UN Environment offered a green outlook:

> UN Environment's vision for its Belt and Road engagement is to incorporate environmental sustainability considerations across the different areas of focus of Belt and Road Initiative. The ultimate goal is to ensure that investments made under the Belt and Road Initiative contribute to the achievement of the 2030 Agenda for Sustainable Development at the global level. (UNEP 2018)

In the same spirit, the United Nations Development Programme (UNDP) was another early Belt and Road supporter, signing a Memorandum of Understanding with the government of China in the same year at the margins of the UN General Assembly, followed by an action plan in May 2017. One UNDP policy document, "Development along the Belt and Road," produced in collaboration with the China Development Bank and the Peking University School of Economics, argues that "with a shared vision, the Belt and Road can create a viable model for long-term, sustainable growth by giving the Sustainable Development Goals (SDGs) a central role in the initiative's quest for economic prosperity" (CDB et al. 2017). Since then, the 17 Sustainable Development Goals (adopted in 2015 by the UN General Assembly with a target to achieve them by 2030) have brought the UN and China closer than ever. Goals like poverty alleviation, gender equality, education, clean energy, sustainable cities, and climate action are attractive to all. United Nations Secretary-General António Guterres remarked in April 2019 that "The five pillars of the Belt and Road – policy coordination, facilities connectivity, unimpeded trade, financial integration, and people-to-people exchanges – are intrinsically linked to the seventeen Sustainable Development Goals. These are conceptual pillars that can be translated into real life progress for every people" (UN 2019). As Xinhua noted, a month later President Xi

> recalled that he put forward the Belt and Road Initiative in 2013 to realize win-win cooperation and common development among countries, adding that the initiative, highly compatible with the UN 2030 Agenda for Sustainable Development in terms of goals, principles and implementation approaches, has received positive response and support from the international community. (Xinhua 2019f, official translation)

The effort publicly to link China's Belt and Road Initiative and the UN's Sustainable Development Goals reflects the broader problem of political legitimation in international development and environmental governance. The alignment of BRI and SDGs lends China a powerful imprimatur of international legitimacy, transforming the supposedly non-political UN into China's *de facto* advocate for Belt and Road projects. Chinese state-funded scholars have tried painstakingly to "prove" through selective evidence that, like the SDGs, the BRI is guided by the purposes and principles of the Charter of the United Nations (Hong 2017; Jin 2018). Yet much of this effort remains discursive at best. Existing infrastructure projects on the Belt and Road are rebranded as SDG-compliant without substantive change. The UN backing of the BRI, despite the well-documented contradictions between the SDGs and the realities on the Belt and Road, shows the agency's deference to China's enormous international economic and political power. It also shows how much power China already wields within UN institutions. Admittedly, it can be better to try to shift an ocean liner's course from within. But through its wholesale adoption of Chinese official narratives, the UN appears to dismiss the environmental and social concerns of many of its members. The 2019 appointment of Qu Dongyu, who simultaneously holds the office of China's Vice Agricultural Minister, as the Director-General of the UN Food and Agriculture Organization is widely seen as China's successful maneuver to align the agency's scientific and aid missions with Chinese national priorities. With the help of the seemingly neutral SDGs, Belt and Road development is thus being framed as self-evidently positive and necessary.

The unprecedented scale of its developmental ambitions notwithstanding, China is by no means the first to deploy this type of depoliticized win-win framing to justify developmental projects. In his classic study of development in Lesotho, anthropologist James Ferguson (1990) describes how, under the guise of apolitical framings of development as purely technical undertakings, the "development apparatus" engaged in highly political acts of oppression, exclusion, dispossession, and ecological destruction. Ferguson's work highlights a central problem of depoliticization: it can lead to the discursive silencing of the inherently political qualities of development. China's win-win framing is but the contemporary reincarnation of what Ferguson calls the "anti-politics machine." With the collaboration of the UN, China has found in the

SDGs an unassailable expression of green win-win developmentalism, allowing it to command the world to "embrace this opportunity." As we see in the next section, the exercise of authoritarian environmental power on the Belt and Road also has a people-to-people aspect that emphasizes its projection of a soft face.

The Quest for Soft Power

On a recent May Day in the Beijing Capital Airport, as Judith waited to pass through immigration and customs, she was amazed to see an enormous number of young Africans in line. Striking up a conversation, she learned that this group of high school students from Ghana would be spending several months in the capital learning Chinese and taking courses in Chinese culture and civilization, with all their expenses paid by the Chinese government. Later, while in residence at Tsinghua University, she noted the huge increase in the number of visiting graduate students from Africa, Pakistan, Malaysia, and other countries, on the Belt and Road. Most were on scholarships and looking forward to launching better careers through expertise in Chinese language and culture. Similarly, Yifei constantly receives emails from students and scholars in countries that China considers BRI allies, from Argentina to Zimbabwe. The emails offer extended praise of Chinese higher education. The writers are seeking acceptance to NYU Shanghai, which they think can parlay into a full scholarship from the Chinese government to study and live in China. (Unlike local universities in China, NYU Shanghai is not eligible for this program.) These young people represent the human realization of a projection of soft power that has cushioned apprehensiveness about China's arrival in the Global South.

They will help implement China's vision of a South–South cooperation that bypasses the big players in the developed world.

In 2004, China established the first Confucius Institutes in Seoul, Korea and at the University of Maryland College Park in the US. Since then, some 500 Confucius Institutes have been scattered throughout the world, representing an early generation of China's soft power initiatives. Sponsored by the Ministry of Education, these institutions partner with universities to offer instruction in Chinese language, cooking, taiji, and calligraphy, K-12 and community outreach, and celebrations of national holidays, often with generous budgets and relatively little asked of the recipient institution (Albert 2018). In the developed world, they have been controversial for lack of intellectual freedom, with more than ten US institutions closing them down after objections about restrictions on debate from faculty and the American Association of University Professors. Members of the US Congress have threatened to withhold government funding to host public universities because of the Confucius Institutes' ties to the Chinese state, and many in the US have shut down, including the flagship campus at the University of Maryland, which was shuttered in 2020. That said, they are welcomed by universities in areas which cannot easily otherwise provide the international programming that the Confucius Institutes offer. In the developing world, the opportunities they offer seem particularly exciting, as they provide students a roadmap toward a future that seems increasingly to be intertwined with China.

The first generation of soft power efforts may have involved some naïveté and wishful thinking on the part of the Chinese state. But wrapped in concepts of a green Belt and Road, ecological civilization, and the China Dream, China's new wave of soft power exports has found a receptive audience in the developing world.

Indeed, China's offer of a "solution package" to developing countries seems to be of general appeal. As a Pakistani journalist writes,

> The China model offers a fast track to development ... An "ecological civilization" ... entails a series of ideas and measures meant to guide China and the world towards a greener future, covering everything from renewable energy to afforestation. ... China has been exploring a new path of high-quality development that prioritizes ecology and highlights green development. (Khan 2019)

Perhaps even more appealing is China's essentially value-free approach: it is singularly focused on the efficient delivery of tangible, pragmatic developmental outcomes from roads to ports, forgoing concerns about human rights and equity while paying lip service to the SDGs. The material wealth of China's glamorous cities is dangled as an incentive. In this context, China's new soft power maneuver is increasingly oriented toward marketing a vision of green development drawn from its domestic experience. With China's model, it appears that developing countries can have it all: glittering skylines and fast cars together with an ecologically friendly development model that will preserve the planet for future generations. This eminently confusing message is being packaged through increasingly sophisticated media tailored to a wide range of audiences.

Even in the developed world, China's efforts to present itself in a favorable light have grown more subtle. Media introduce "new China" through soap operas and paid ads in respected outlets such as the *Economist*. Billboard videos in New York's Times Square market China as a brand, featuring superstars like basketball player Yao Ming, tennis star Hu Na, and pianist Lang Lang. The government-run English-language newspapers *China Daily* and *Global Times* are widely distributed in major global cities, often for free. China Central Television's (CCTV) international division has renamed itself China Global Television Network and produces channels in multiple languages. China Radio International broadcasts to the world. All seem to heed President Xi Jinping's call to "tell China's story well" (Lim and Bergin 2018). There is nothing inherently nefarious about these efforts; public diplomacy is a standard activity of most internationally minded governments. However, since the Chinese state's version of reality is often patently manipulated and censored, the clumsiness of some of the messages can seem disturbing or amusing. During the government's all-too-important "two sessions" plenary meetings in March 2019, for example, the state propaganda apparatus released on its 12-language platform an unintentionally hilarious music video of a little-known performer identified as Su Han. Rapping about the "true essence of our country's development" against a backdrop of natural landscapes, he propounds in near-unintelligible English, "greening project's never forgone by / never gonna be the earth invader / ... gotta be the ready one player / when in front of dirty polluter / ... so we turn the entire space into oasis" (Xinhua 2019d). Ironically, because of rap's association with rebellious youths, hip hop culture had been the target of a national media crackdown on "immoral culture" in early 2018.

These efforts are not limited to grooming China-friendly future young professionals and presenting a kinder face to the world. China's soft power efforts also include environmental management programs organized by Chinese governmental agencies and universities for officials from the developing world, particularly from BRI countries. Chinese state units, from central and local government agencies to the prestigious Academies of Sciences, host training sessions, workshops, and capacity-building programs for officials and academics from partner countries to "learn from the sacred text," or *qujing* 取经 – a metaphor with Buddhist origin commonly deployed in this context. China is projected as the unassailable source of developmental wisdom.

These outward-facing educational programs have a pre-BRI origin in China's "going out" policy. In 1998, the Ministry of Commerce held the first such workshop, designed to teach African economic policy makers about the success of China's reform and opening up policies. During the first decade of its operation, the educational arm of the Ministry of Commerce maintained a low profile, offering an annual average of merely ten workshops (Jin 2010).

Since the early 2010s, however, China has aggressively stepped up its charm offensive through fully funded environmental education programs. Under the Hu Jintao administration which ended in 2013, China's green educational outreach grew exponentially. At the ASEAN-China Summit in Southeast Asia in 2010, for example, then-Premier Wen Jiabao announced the launch of the Green Envoys program, or *lüse shizhe jihua* 绿色使者计划. Over the next two years, the initiative brought more than 500 environmental officials and scholars to Beijing to be informed about "China's advanced experience in environmental legislation and law enforcement" (China-ASEAN Environmental Cooperation Center 2013).

Under the Xi presidency, in 2014 the Green Envoys program was upgraded to the Green Silk Road Envoys program in support of the then-nascent Belt and Road (Ding and Shi 2017). The expanded initiative seeks to disseminate China's environmental governance techniques to a target audience of "environmental officials at all levels, university students, researchers and technicians of China and countries along the Belt and Road" (MEE 2019b). Activities under the Green Envoys rubric range from highly technical trainings such as environmental surveying and mapping workshops to youth summits on issues such as low-carbon transportation, but they all help buttress China's image as a purveyor of environmental knowledge. These workshops, often held in Beijing, feature the "success" of Chinese environmental governance by offering field trips to places such as futuristic "model eco-cities" on the outskirts of the city in addition to presentations of the latest Chinese environmental technologies by state scientists at top universities and academies of sciences. In many official news releases about such workshops, organizers are keen on reporting the vast numbers of non-Chinese government officials traveling to the former imperial capital. This is perhaps reflective of a deep-seated frame of mind among Chinese officials that constructs China, especially Beijing, as the center of a heavenly mandated world order (French 2017).

The Green Envoys program now brands itself as the soft face of the green BRI. It cultivates "people-to-people bonds" toward the larger goal of building a "community with a shared human and natural future." In fact, Chinese environmental officials consider such soft power maneuvers an indispensable ingredient in transforming China into the leader of global environmental governance (Jiang et al. 2018). In a policy brief issued by the semi-governmental China Council for International Cooperation on Environment and Development, Chinese top policy makers call on the Green Envoys program to "share China's ideas and practices [in] realizing ecological civilization and green development," and "to guide environmental protection enterprises to 'go global' in an orderly manner" (CCICED 2019). Even though the specifics of such "guidance" remain unclear, the Chinese government clearly intends to remain "in the driver's seat" moving forward.

Much of this is framed in terms of South–South cooperation, providing an alternative to the US-centric global system. Some Western observers have even identified an emerging "Beijing Consensus" as contrasted to the World Bank-led Washington Consensus, although Beijing rejects this formulation. Rather, Chinese environmental policy makers use a counter-discourse that features the "China Dream" as contrasted with the American Dream. Few Chinese are able to articulate what the China Dream might mean in real terms. But few fail to understand the underlying messages: China is emerging as an alternative superpower; China is being restored to greatness by building ecological civilization; China is regaining face on the international stage by garnering praise from the United Nations and other multilateral institutions. This allows individual Chinese to feel proud of their country, even as it promotes the continued leadership of the Chinese Communist Party. In the words of Jorge Chediek, Director of the UN Office for South-South Cooperation,

> The vision of China, based on the development of infrastructure, cultural connectivity, and intellectual connectivity ... has promoted a new vision for the world, a new vision of prosperity, a new vision of sustainability, which is extremely compatible with the ideas and the best practices of the United Nations. (quoted in Lin 2019)

China's quest for soft power has come a long way, and will most likely continue to evolve into ever more sophisticated engineering of its national image for both its own citizens and the world at large.

We have thus far focused primarily on the discursive qualities of China's green claims in the context of the BRI, but we hasten to add that China is by no means content only with wielding persuasion and attraction. Besides ambitions for resources, trade, and market access, China seeks also to advance less tangible, but no less real, technologies of green governmentality through digital infrastructure. This brings us to another powerful tool in China's green arsenal: the export of green technocracy.

Green Technocracy

Data is China's answer to many of the environmental objections to the Belt and Road. The promise of a digital Silk Road seems almost self-evident to Chinese policy makers. China pledges to support its BRI allies to "leapfrog" into the digital age, thus skipping the dirty phase of fossil fuel dependence that has characterized the West's rise to global dominance. To Chinese officials, data-enabled "smart" development is part and parcel of ecological civilization's promise of a low-carbon, green, innovative future on the Belt and Road (Z. Wang et al. 2017). More importantly, according to the official narrative, the "digital gap" is the root cause of global inequality in the twenty-first century, where the digital have-nots find themselves cut off from economic opportunities and social services in an age of connectivity (Yong 2019). China therefore sees itself as doing the developing world a generous service by providing low-cost technological solutions to its BRI partners. With state-of-the-art technologies in artificial intelligence, quantum computing, big data, smart urban infrastructure, blockchain, and related fields, China promises to connect everyone, everywhere, at every moment of time.

Digital development is at the heart of what China sees as low-carbon, clean, green growth for the underdeveloped countries along the BRI. The use of digital technologies has the potential to reduce paper consumption, save carbon emissions from "unsmart" transportation, and promote energy efficiency with the help of smart building control systems. As we will explore further in chapter 4, however, the infrastructure for digital technologies is costly from an environmental point of view, as its manufacture depends on rare-earth minerals that are toxic to extract and because e-waste disposal perpetuates environmental harms in disadvantaged communities.

The complex relationship between digital technologies and sustainability notwithstanding, China continues its pursuit of technological dominance in the name of ecological civilization. From governmental service platforms to everyday personal devices, Chinese technological providers stand ready to go. Indeed, technologies from Chinese enterprises have already transformed the lives of many in the developing world. When Yifei was teaching at New York University's Abu Dhabi campus in 2017, a taxi driver from India struck up a conversation by passionately announcing his allegiance to China. "I love China," he exclaimed, "because of your people, my people all have smartphones now." He merrily waved his Huawei phone as he spoke, while following the GPS directions of a Xiaomi phone mounted to the dashboard.

The impact of Chinese technologies is by no means felt only by immigrant workers like the cab driver. As Chinese tech giants come to dominate the digital market in economies along the entire Belt and Road, the lines of demarcation between private and public investments from China are increasingly blurred. Companies like Huawei serve as exclusive technological providers for government-to-government service contracts. In Central Asia, the Kyrgyz Republic is trying to build smart cities with Huawei technologies and has accepted a five-year Belt and Road loan from China to foot the hefty bill. In Europe, when announcing Italy's intent to join the BRI in March 2019, prime minister Giuseppe Conte explicitly affirmed his support for Chinese firms Huawei and ZTE, against the tidal wave of US sanctions (Balmer 2019).

Under the Belt and Road Initiative, China and the United Arab Emirates have formed particularly close political and economic ties. As the Emirates seek to transition from a hydrocarbon economy to tech-centered post-oil development, China's digital Belt and Road offer seems like a perfect match. Abu Dhabi's pro-government paper *The National* lauds the country's "fertile ground for Chinese smartphone conglomerates to come knocking," citing its remarkable smartphone penetration rate of 73.8 percent (Stewart 2019). During President Xi Jinping's visit in 2018, Emirati Minister of Economy Sultan Bin Saeed Al Mansouri was quoted as praising the BRI as "China's gift to the world" (Xinhua 2018) – a compliment that would be reciprocated a year later by Chinese Foreign Minister Wang Yi, who called the Arab world's second-largest economy "a shining pearl along the Belt and Road" (WAM 2019). What official news agencies on both sides fail to mention, however, is the two authoritarian states' shared interest in internet censorship and citizen surveillance through increasingly advanced technological means.

As the Chinese state develops and deploys an increasing amount of digital technology under the pretext of nice-sounding values – safety, development, transparency, accountability, efficiency, and sustainability – the prospect of an all-seeing state worries many both within and outside of China. In chapter 1, we discussed China's effort to build a social credit system to monitor and profile individual citizens. A parallel social credit system for businesses has also grown steadily. This system seeks to gather and monitor a wide range of corporate behavior through a centralized big data platform that China calls "the Internet Plus." The rapid rollout of this system has prompted the European

Chamber of Commerce in China to warn its members to "prepare for dealing with approximately 30 different ratings and compliance records based on upward of 300 concrete rating requirements" (European Chamber 2019).

Internationally, China's move toward the digital Belt and Road is no longer just aspirational, but has translated into operational, on-the-ground digital infrastructure. China is finding a market hungry for its know-how in censorship and surveillance. In the Ecuadorian capital of Quito, for example, much of the city's policing is accomplished through thousands of Chinese-made high-capacity street cameras that feed images into a computerized control center developed by Beijing (Mozur et al. 2019). The popularity of Chinese technologies among Belt and Road governments has led the Center for a New American Security to warn that "privacy and freedom will pay a toll" (Kliman and Grace 2018). Despite widespread skepticism and wariness in the West, however, the demand for low-cost Chinese digital technologies remains robust in the developing world.

In fact, China has signed bilateral agreements with some of its closest allies on the Belt and Road for the transfer of Chinese data technology. Whether it be the Ministry of Science, Technology, Innovation and Communications of Brazil or the Ministry of Information and Communications Technology and Innovation of Rwanda, Chinese technology providers have found friendly homes away from home. Some of the early bilateral and trilateral digital connectivity programs, such as the China-Mongolia-Russia corridor and the China-Pakistan corridor, have been subsumed under the so-called Asia-Pacific Information Superhighway, a signature project of the UN Economic and Social Commission for Asia and the Pacific (ESCAP). The UN regional commission is unreservedly optimistic about its dependence on Chinese technologies, declaring that the "ESCAP-China cooperation strengthens synergies between AP-IS [Asia-Pacific Information Superhighway] and BRI initiatives respectively to attain mutual benefits, sustainable development, and strengthen economic relations among the ESCAP member countries" (UN ESCAP 2017).

Outside the BRI umbrella, China's internet tycoon Jack Ma promised to create one million jobs in the US by bringing his companies' digital technologies to the other side of the Pacific. Ma's plan was to reincarnate much of rural America into "taobao villages," a term that describes parts of rural China's rise to economic prosperity when digital technologies penetrate, thanks to Ma's now-omnipresent online shopping platform (Lin and Stevens 2017). Ma later recanted the promise during the height of the trade war.

Taken together, these smart data technologies for communication, surveillance, and monitoring are part and parcel of China's export of green technocracy, which is expected to work in tandem with the other two tools we have examined in this chapter, win-win development framing and soft power projection through people-to-people initiatives. Data from digital sources are China's way to try to demonstrate hard evidence of the BRI's win-win approach to development. The constant data feeds are to provide real-time readings of whether China's BRI partnerships are achieving SDGs, as well as how China itself is doing. Moreover, the rise of China's tech industry on the global scene is broadly discussed as having symbolic significance as China begins to exercise "scientific soft power" in the service of international development.

Indeed, the technological offers from China seem impossible to resist. What could be wrong when all China does is to supply objective scientific information for policy makers to pursue evidence-based approaches, so that all nations along the Belt and Road can benefit from better policies? Yet, a bit of historical perspective encourages us to rethink this; Chinese state-funded data scientists are not the first to propose a monopoly over environmental governance, or what we might call green technocracy. In his critique of the conservation movement in the United States in the 1980s, Indian environmental historian Ramachandra Guha rebuts American biologists who claimed to speak for the natural world. At the time, advances in American life sciences led researchers to believe that the planet would be better off if they ran it. Guha writes that the haste to replicate American scientific success on a planetary scale risked uprooting human communities while celebrating the ability of environmental science to "save" the planet (Guha 1989).

Since the publication of Ramachandra Guha's article, scholars and practitioners have grown wary of universalizing scientific claims and increasingly sensitive to the historically specific ways in which people in different places relate to their ecological environments. In this context, China's seemingly generous offer of green technologies warrants closer scrutiny. Drawing from a comprehensive range of data sources that include remote sensing, local surveys, and field measurements, China's drive for big, and even bigger, data coverage for the entire planet purports to lead the next generation of integrated science–policy interface. When Chinese state scientists, in a spirit not dissimilar to that of American biologists of the 1980s, write articles that stress the "progress of Earth observation in China" (Guo et al. 2018), they have been blinded by overconfidence in their own enterprise. In fact, China is fast approaching what media scholars Nick Couldry and Ulises Mejias (2019) dub "data colonialism": a frightening penetration of digital technologies into the fabric of everyday life that leads to the intense appropriation of people, land, and resources.

Perhaps in anticipation of such criticism, Chinese state researchers have made an unusual promise: "People will be able to use big data in their lives, and in the meantime force the government and various institutions to be responsible for their policies" (Guo et al. 2018). Placing the government on the receiving end of coercive force seems like an unlikely, if not completely unrealistic, proposal in the context of China and its rapid expansion along the Belt and Road.

That China's digital platforms may help foster governmental transparency is at least possible. In January 2019, the Chinese Academy of Sciences unveiled a five-million gigabyte database known as the "CASEarth Databank," which aims to provide Chinese government officials and "countries involved in the Belt and Road Initiative" with continuous information about topics as wide-ranging as microbes, wealth, topography, and natural disasters (Z. Zhang 2019). It remains unclear whether and how citizens will be able to use the Databank to hold the government accountable. In the end, transparency will only be attainable if big data is shared.

A Morass of Contradictions

There is an enormous discrepancy between the official Chinese rhetoric surrounding the BRI's "shared prosperity," "extensive consultation," and "green development" and what is happening in practice on the ground. Government-sponsored environmental management trainings are window-dressing if riverine ecosystems are destroyed by big dams, coastal fisheries are transformed by deep-water port construction and traffic, and fragile lands, from deserts and mountains to rainforests and dry forests, are transected by highways, railroads, and pipelines. Chinese investors' lack of experience of consulting indigenous groups and local communities is obvious, even as some governments begin to reconsider the hidden price tags attached to Chinese easy money. Communities and civil society groups across the Global South are mobilizing against the environmental and social impacts of many China-funded infrastructure projects.

There is still a critical window of opportunity to examine the enormous impact of so much wealth invested so quickly. Neither donors nor recipients are well versed in considering the ramifications of such rapid transformation. Chinese investors are all too often driven by geopolitical considerations, profit motivations, and a need to export expertise and infrastructure, while recipient governance systems all too often do not allow for transparency, accountability, and protection of the vulnerable. Only a small-minded person would fail to see that the BRI umbrella offers developing countries an opportunity to bring populations out of poverty. But sometimes too much, too fast, is a recipe for regret.

The top-down, government-to-government approach favored by China in its relations with BRI countries makes local civil society organizations and networks particularly important as counterweights to press for better outcomes. Local resistance to China-funded dams and mines stretches from Southeast Asia to Latin America and Africa. Increasingly, this resistance from vulnerable local people is finding support from activists within China, as ENGOs and activists come to learn about some of the negative impacts of their country's activities overseas. This is not only because of shared commitments to such key environmental causes as wildlife protection and mitigating climate change but also because they are concerned about China's international reputation. Forming partnerships with like-minded groups, some Chinese ENGOs are trying to help their government and international corporations to avoid some of their worst missteps, like failing to consult with communities or to conduct robust environmental and social impact assessments. Although Chinese journalists sometimes are required to leave critical thinking capabilities at home when they venture overseas to report on BRI projects, the South–South model is starting to apply not only to inter-government relations but also to a global civil society that includes Chinese actors. For example, *Chinadialogue*, a London- and Beijing-based online forum for environmental reportage, has run a series of stories on China's international impacts, including topics like the export of coal-fired power plants and the decimation of Kenya's donkey population due to Chinese demand. Their partnerships include Dialogochino, a Spanish-language project intended to inform Latin Americans about China's impacts, and the Third Pole, a project about environmental change in the Himalayas. Another example of such Chinese international engagement is the activism of the Chinese human rights and environmental lawyer Zhang Jingjing, whose China Accountability Project is dedicated to helping indigenous groups adversely affected by international Chinese investments. With projects from Peru to Guinea, she is working with local groups to create resistance through local courts. In Ecuador, for instance, she filed an amicus legal brief about a Chinese privately funded mining company's failure to consult with indigenous groups as required by Ecuador's Constitution and the UN Declaration on the Rights of Indigenous Peoples. Her intervention may have carried enough weight to make the difference in putting the Rio Blanco mine on hold.

As Chinese SOEs come to understand and, under pressure, adopt environmental safeguards in their overseas operations, their domestic environmental performance may see improvement as well. Relatedly, as the BRI continues to expand across the Eurasian continent and beyond, the call for multilateralism and transparency may become difficult for China to ignore. China's global ambition could turn out to be a golden opportunity for better environmental governance for a troubled planet. Everything seems to hinge on China.

In an effort to project its power onto the world, the Middle Kingdom has repackaged state-led environmentalism as China-led environmentalism for the world, which entails the export of technologies, infrastructure and, importantly, coercive governance tools. As we have seen in this chapter, through financing mechanisms such as the China Development Bank and educational investments such as China-based training programs for officials from the developing world, China projects itself as the source of best practices in global environmental affairs. Yet much of the new infrastructure has enormous implications for resource extraction, habitat loss, and increased carbon emissions. An increasingly confident and assertive China appears to be advancing a new global order of development, but there are numerous questions about the new order's compatibility with planetary sustainability. As the global Sino-sphere comes into focus, the planet must count on China's full commitment and action.

The Belt and Road experience to date raises concerns about social justice as well as biodiversity loss and climate change. We worry about the impacts even as we recognize that many projects are highly sought-after by developing country governments and communities. Understanding the dynamics of the BRI requires a multidisciplinary approach. Political ecology's focus on marginality, vulnerability, conflict, and extraction combined with international political economy's focus on the impacts of trade and financial flows clarifies the stakes at a moment when many projects are still in the planning stages. The Belt and Road may be introducing new forms of "slow violence" toward the most vulnerable – disruption and displacement that occurs gradually and often invisibly in an age of hyper-extraction and environmental degradation (Nixon 2011).

As we have seen, the Belt and Road Initiative has the potential to be an environmental and social disaster. Most concerning are Beijing's lack of mandatory controls on investors and the dearth of NGO input into Chinese investment processes. Further challenges include weak host country governance and corruption, as well as the Chinese reluctance fully to commit to high environmental and sustainability standards. Another factor is the sheer rapidity of change in China's place in the world and economic might. However, there is also a chance to make progress toward systemic sustainability and environmental protection. By leveraging "green finance," China might fund the BRI with conditions for sustainable development policies attached. Promoting sustainable infrastructure and energy development would be relatively easy for China because of its price-competitiveness in solar, wind, and other green technologies. Furthermore, the expansion to smaller, but largely untapped infrastructure and energy markets presents opportunities to export China's sustainable development technologies, goods, services, and excess capacity. China must be willing to uphold its own domestic green economic policies and commitments abroad. If this shift is to occur, however, it must occur quickly, and both China and recipient countries must be willing to tread carefully where the environmental and social risks are so high. Much is at stake for China, and for the planet.

4

Global China Goes "Green"

"A specter is haunting the world – the specter of 'global China.'" Playing on the opening line of *The Communist Manifesto*, labor scholar Ching Kwan Lee (2018) signals that China is already the global center of gravity. Above and beyond the extraordinary lineup of bilateral and regional projects on the Belt and Road, China's presence is being felt at a global scale. China's power and prowess are not merely haunting the world but actively reshaping it. The imprint reaches from the Sri Lankan port of Hambantota to a People's Liberation Army Base in Djibouti. It extends from a China-owned satellite station north of the Arctic Circle in Sweden to the Pacific island of Tulagi, where China owns exclusive development rights. Thanks to the interdependence of the world economy, the immense purchasing power of the Chinese state and middle class, the vast global network of the Chinese diaspora, and the rapid advances in Chinese science and technology, the People's Republic's omnipresence is at once economic, social, technological, and ideological. Welcome to the age of global China.

In the environmental realm in particular, the arrival of global China is both feared and desired. For some observers in the West, it is comforting to think of China as playing a decisive leadership role in global environmentalism. Under the Trump presidency, the retreat of the United States from global environmental affairs – especially the planned withdrawal from the landmark 2016 Paris Agreement on climate change – has opened unprecedented political space for China. Radical rollbacks of US domestic environmental policies, from wildlife conservation to water pollution control, present a jarring contrast to China's official discourse committing the country to constructing "ecological civilization" at home and overseas. Trump's allegation that climate change is a hoax perpetrated by the Chinese sends a chilling message to the global community. In Europe, Brexit threatens to undercut much of Britain's existing environmental legal framework (Carrington 2019). The hoped-for leadership of an awakened West willing to assume responsibility for the long-term damage and disproportionate benefits of its own industrial revolution has not materialized. Overall, the gloomy outlook of Western environmental politics, and the collective failure of the global community to arrest climate change, leave many looking for hope elsewhere. In its bid to become a responsible global power, China is eager to fill the vacuum. "In the face of uncertainty and unease around the globe," remarked UN Secretary-General António Guterres in a 2019 address to dozens of heads of state, "I want to recognize China for its central role as a pillar of international cooperation and multilateralism" (UN 2019). Sweet words for a country hungry for just this sort of recognition.

In Chinese philosophy, there is a strain of modernist technocratic thought that is captured in a famous set-phrase, "Man Must Conquer Nature" or *rending shengtian* 人定胜天. This slogan is associated particularly with the Mao years, when it was held that rivers could be made to run uphill through sheer force of human ingenuity and labor. Nature was seen as something distinct from humans, an enemy force meant to be overpowered in a quasi-military battle. Hillsides were clear-cut in order to fuel all-night backyard furnaces to smelt steel, sparrows were eradicated in mass mobilizations, tropical rainforests were supplanted by rubber plantations for war preparation, and lakes were bombarded with boulders in an attempt to create more arable land. These are just a few examples of Mao-era campaigns with disastrous ecological and human consequences (Shapiro 2001).

After so much human suffering and environmental degradation, many thoughtful Chinese felt encouraged by the national rhetoric about harmonious society and ecological civilization. They hoped that the nature-conquest mentality had dissipated. But it appears that the technocratic governance model has emerged stronger than ever. In the age of global China, and especially under the muscular authoritarianism of President Xi Jinping, the modernist orientation subsumes environmental goals and is framed as leading societies in continuous linear progress toward a bright future. Technocratic innovation under the wise leadership of the Chinese Communist Party, it is held, will bring great benefits to all humankind.

Technocratic authoritarianism is by no means limited to China. At the root of many of the tools and techniques we are exploring in this volume lies a philosophical orientation toward the natural world that James Scott, in his 1998 classic *Seeing like a State*, called a belief in high modernism. However, as indicated in Scott's revealing subtitle, *How Certain Schemes to Improve the Human Condition have Failed*, when "engineers, planners, technocrats, high-level administrators, architects, scientists, and visionaries" help an authoritarian state to implement grandiose plans, the results are often disastrous, especially when the state also seeks to assert control over citizens and territory and when civil society is weak.

It is no accident that many of China's top leaders, from former Premier Li Peng to former President Jiang Zemin, were trained as scientists and engineers, nor is it an accident that many of China's climate-related policies come out of top science and engineering schools like Tsinghua ("the MIT of China") and the University of Science and Technology, which is overseen by the key government think tank, the Chinese Academy of Sciences. The technocratic mindset is especially evident as we turn to a final set of techniques the Chinese state is using to assert authoritarian control in the name of the environment. These include: manipulating the global trade in waste, rare earths, and biodiversity; engineering the atmosphere for blue skies and rain; and carrying out outer space environmentalism to gather big data and to research geoengineering to combat climate change. These efforts are intimately linked to geopolitical and strategic agendas. In employing these tools, China's leadership avoids the messy business of dealing with environmental issues as problems of lack of sociopolitical will or of spatial and temporal injustice, and seeks instead to impose top-down solutions by fiat: Chinese technocracy to save the world.

Mastering the Trade Game

In its bid to advance technocratic leadership, China seeks to assert itself as a scientific superpower. However, China's path to global prominence in science and technology has been constrained by the country's economic status as the world's factory, a situation that China's leadership is urgently attempting to change.

Situated near the bottom of the global value chain, the Chinese economy has gravitated toward the low end of mass manufacturing rather than the high end of research, development, and innovation. Chinese officials, from the president to ordinary bureaucrats, routinely lament the economic structure as being characteristic of the "extensive model," or *cufang xing* 粗放型: it utilizes vast quantities of resources, energy, machinery, and labor in an inefficient fashion to achieve high-quantity economic growth. They long for the alternative "intensive model," or *jiyue xing* 集约型. This would intensively, but efficiently, utilize limited quantities of the same inputs in the service of high-quality development. From the controversial "Made in China 2025" strategy to make China the global leader in high technology to the lesser-known "National Brand Project" launched by China Central Television to raise the status of high-quality domestic products, Chinese planners have made concerted efforts to move the enormous economy up the global value chain, one commodity at a time. Global trade, or what they see as the country's woefully undervalued position in international markets, looms large in their calculations.

When China opened its doors with the reform-and-opening policies of the early 1980s under the Four Modernizations of Deng Xiaoping (in Agriculture, Industry, Defense, and Science and Technology), few imagined that the country would become an economic superpower. In the early days of opening to the outside world, China saw itself as a humble student of the rules of international trade and commerce. Decades of domestic turmoil and international isolation had left the state and the country's newly liberalized market eager to reenter the global economy. The key to a smooth reentry, top Chinese leaders reckoned, was to "internationalize" the country by adopting existing global rules, the most prominent of which were trade rules (Zweig

2002; Hsieh 2010; Gong 2011). During the first three decades of reform and opening, the axiom of development in China was to "connect with the international track," or *yu guoji jiegui* 与国际接轨 – a metaphor that captured the country's urge to rejoin and rebuild.

As China gradually assumed the role of manufacturing low-cost goods and became a major trading partner for the world, international concern mounted that the country might not be following the rules of global trade. Although subsidies and tariffs have long been wielded by both developing and developed countries hoping to nurture some industries and protect others, the fear was that China might be abusing these tools. When China was admitted to the World Trade Organization (WTO) at the end of 2001, that controversial decision was taken in part to provide trading partners with leverage to make China play more fairly. Important WTO cases involving China have included accusations that the country was dumping steel at low cost in order to undercut the steel industries of the US and Canada. The Chinese, for their part, have accused the US of targeting China's solar panel manufacturers by imposing unfair import tariffs; the US argues that China subsidizes the industry in an effort to corner the global market.

Even as China learns to stand up for itself at the WTO, it is attempting to reformulate multilateral organizations that were founded after World War II without its input. From the Bretton Woods institutions of the World Bank, the International Monetary Fund, and the International Finance Corporation to the WTO itself, China is now either offering alternatives (as with the China Development Bank and Asian Infrastructure Investment Bank) or inserting its personnel and values into existing institutions such as the United Nations, as we saw in the preceding chapter on the Belt and Road. In the case of global trade, China is positioning itself as a new rule-maker unbeholden to the institutions it had little part in establishing.

In the era of the Trump trade war and intensified economic globalization and resource extraction, China is no longer heeding Deng Xiaoping's 1980s dictum to "hide our strength and bide our time," or *taoguang yanghui* 韬光养晦. Rather, it is flexing its muscles and asserting its presence. Moreover, it is refusing to continue to be part of a "race to the bottom" whereby it served as a dumping ground for industries and pollution that were unwanted by stronger players. That worked as a vehicle for explosive growth, but that time has passed. In fact, Chinese leaders are quite open about the fact that the Deng era of humility is long gone. The Ministry of Foreign Affairs describes Deng's "hide our strength" dictum only as bygone history (Tang 2012). The official *People's Daily* flatly dismisses Deng's approach as outdated, boasting that the Chinese economy is "no longer the sampan it once was before the reform, but a cruise liner ready to travel afar" (Peng 2019).

Banning Global Waste Imports

On July 18, 2017, China notified the WTO of its plan to impose a ban on 24 categories of waste imports starting from January 2018. "To protect China's environmental interests and people's health," the notification reads, "we urgently adjust the imported solid wastes list and forbid the import of solid wastes that are highly polluted" (WTO 2017). The global solid waste industry panicked, not least because China had been the destination of 45 percent of global plastic waste since 1992 (Brooks et al. 2018). China's decisive move alarmed recyclers and governments, especially in North America and Western Europe. But it also galvanized support from environmental justice groups like the Basel Action

Network, which applauded the possible end of the Global North's ability to hide the consequences of its own overconsumption and to displace environmental harm to the developing world.

The 2018 waste import ban was of unprecedented scope and thoroughness, but it was by no means China's first attempt to intervene. We provide below a review of China's escalating efforts during the decade-long leadup to the ban. During the course of the Chinese state's sustained efforts to regulate the waste trade, it remained uncharacteristically sensitive to affected citizens in the domestic recycling industry and emerging circular economy, to local livelihoods and employment, as well as to the voices of Chinese and international environmental advocacy. Like the other coercive environmental measures we discuss in this book, the Chinese state's interventions were forceful. But unlike in the other cases, the impact of the waste import ban was buffered by the length of time it took to implement China's interventions. Ordinary people and industry professionals inside the country had time to prepare and adapt.

The global waste trade is subject to the Basel Convention on the Control of Transboundary Movements of Hazardous Wastes and Their Disposal. Signed by 53 nations including China, the Basel Convention came into force in May 1992. It entails a set of obligations for member states to minimize and ultimately ban the global trade in hazardous wastes. However, the treaty is widely criticized for its absence of enforcement provisions. Even though China became a signatory to the Convention in 1990, at the time it look little action to regulate the growing volume of hazardous waste entering its borders.

In April 1996, a papermill in the village of Xiyu near Beijing drew national attention. Its warehouse exuded foul odors and fluids, prompting villagers to complain to the Beijing Bureau of Environmental Protection.

Local officials investigated and found 29 shipping containers of mixed garbage – 639.4 metric tons – that was of apparent foreign origin. The papermill owner had expected high-quality post-consumer paper from the United States which he had intended to recycle, but instead he had been given contaminated materials. Local officials had no experience with waste imports, so they reported the problem upwards. The case went up the chain of command to then-Vice Premier Li Lanqing. Embarrassed by the apparent lack of regulatory oversight, the Vice Premier ordered a crackdown on foreign waste imports, which was carried out by an unprecedented multi-agency taskforce (Ge 2008). According to the official Environmental Yearbook for 1996, more than 200 container ships were turned away at Chinese customs as a result of the crackdown on illegal waste imports that year (MEP 1997).

However, as we saw in chapter 1, many of China's environmental campaigns and crackdowns are short-lived. This was no exception. Despite the high level of publicity about the Xiyu case, the country's waste imports saw steady growth throughout the 1990s and 2000s (Brooks et al. 2018). Had the story ended there, it would have been yet another case of blunt-force environmental crackdown without durable effects. But in 2002, the Basel Action Network, an international non-profit organization, brought global attention to the previously little-known town of Guiyu in Guangdong Province. Their documentary film, *Exporting Harm* (Puckett 2002), presents a riveting picture of environmental injustice. A major center of the global illegal electronic waste trade due to its proximity to the international shipping hub of Hong Kong, Guiyu was shown to be home to tens of thousands of unprotected recyclers who extracted valuable metals by baking circuit boards on coal stoves in their backyards.

Greenpeace, in collaboration with anthropologists at Sun Yat-Sen University in Guangzhou, popularized images of impoverished Guiyu children exposed to harmful piles of e-waste. A 2008 investigative report screened on the CBS television show *60 Minutes* further publicized the situation. A Chinese Academy of Sciences study then found that multiple toxins in the air, soil, and water of Guiyu, including heavy metals and organic contaminants, were hundreds of times higher than the regional average (Peng et al. 2009).

Between 2002 and 2012, Guiyu authorities repeatedly tried but failed to eradicate the e-waste industry; the vast majority of rural households in the area depended on baking circuit boards and separating cathode ray tubes as their only means of livelihood. Guiyu officials openly lamented the futility of campaign-style governance over the problem (Xinhua 2015). An official economic census conducted in May 2012 found that Guiyu was home to 5,169 small electronic waste recyclers employing a total of 17,282 individuals (MEE 2019a). The administrative cost of enforcing environmental regulations against more than 5,000 family businesses in rural China would have been prohibitive. Official CCTV even aired its own investigative documentary in 2013, reporting that nine out of ten Guiyu children suffered from heavy metal poisoning.

Even as the government struggled to control the e-waste sector at the family and village levels, authorities also began to respond to mounting domestic and international pressure to enforce Basel import restrictions at Eastern ports. Through "Operation Green Fence," in effect from February to November of 2013, Chinese customs pursued 1,090 violations with a combined cargo weight of 883,000 metric tons and a value of 3.83 billion USD. As a result, the amount of plastic waste imports declined 17 percent over the year before (Wei and Zhang 2014). The goal of Operation Green Fence was to establish a standard for importable waste such that the most blatant violations of the Basel Convention would be intercepted and punished with shipment repatriation. Yet in actuality, shipments rejected by China were diverted to Southeast Asia for reprocessing before they were China-bound once again.

In an additional effort to get a handle on the trade, between 2012 and 2015 the government shut down 2,469 small businesses in the Guiyu area – nearly half of the local e-waste economy – and offered affected households employment opportunities at a newly built industrial park where recycling facilities were in compliance with Chinese environmental regulations. Nearly 3,500 local residents took up the offer, thanks to an improved work environment and average monthly wage of approximately 4,000 RMB, about 600 USD, roughly the same as the median income in the province. The Ministry of Environmental Protection dubbed this strategy the "block-unblock linkage," or *shudu jiehe* 疏堵结合: blocking incoming streams of illegal hazardous waste while unblocking people's pursuit of alternative employment (MEP 2019a).

Operation Green Fence had far-reaching implications for the Chinese recycling industry. The majority of backyard coal stove operations shut down voluntarily because of the reduced supply of cheap, low-grade recyclables and the increased cost of environmental compliance. Some medium-sized recycling businesses moved to places like Vietnam and Malaysia, but many took government subsidies to upgrade their plants to comply with the new rules.

In January 2017, the waste problem once again appeared in Chinese headlines, when environmental filmmaker Wang Jiuliang released his documentary *Plastic China*, which follows two families whose miserable lives depend on sorting and recycling plastic waste of obvious foreign origin (J. Wang 2017). The film went viral, prompting Chinese authorities to purge it from the internet. One of us, Yifei, invited Wang to speak at a private screening of the film in Shanghai scheduled for later that year. Wang declined, explaining that he was under intense government surveillance.

A month later, on February 7, 2017, Chinese customs launched "Operation Sword," further tightening scrutiny of incoming cargo container ships. By year's end, Chinese customs had reportedly rejected 866,800 metric tons of "foreign garbage" (Du 2018). Operation Sword followed the same set of technical specifications as Operation Green Fence, but the scope of cargo inspection was now more complete, making it all but impossible to import non-compliant shipments of recyclables. Many observers, including Wang Jiuliang himself, viewed the escalated enforcement as the government's answer to *Plastic China*, despite the censorship of the film. Rumors circulated that a complete ban was under discussion (Lo and Yeung 2019).

When the notification to the WTO finally arrived in July 2017, then, industry insiders were not surprised. Even though China framed the new policy as a restriction, it amounted to a near-total ban. By the time it came into effect in January 2018, much of China's domestic recycling industry had gone through multiple years of restructuring, and international shipments had been subject to inspections for years.

China's decade-long interventions into the waste economy have far-reaching implications. Domestically, the recycling industry has been transformed from an unregulated informal sector with hundreds of thousands of family-owned shabby, toxic operations into a state-subsidized network of environmentally compliant industrial parks. Due to the much-reduced availability of foreign paper and plastic waste, the cost of paper and plastic products in China has gone up precipitously, incentivizing citizens and businesses to reduce and reuse. The dwindling volume of waste imports has encouraged Chinese cities to devise urban recycling programs so that locally generated waste can be processed and repurposed, as we saw in chapter 1. Seen in these lights, the domestic impacts have been largely positive. Since then, China has continued to tighten its control over waste imports, banning 16 more categories in December 2018, eight more in July 2019, and another 16 in December 2019 (Kou 2019). In January 2020, China's National Development and Reform Commission and Ministry of Ecology and Environment jointly issued an order to "completely prohibit the import of post-consumer plastics," in addition to a detailed phase-out schedule for plastic straws, take-out containers, and other single-use plastic products (NDRC and MEE 2020).

Internationally, the picture is muddled. Some Chinese medium-sized recyclers, with the help of investors, have relocated to new "pollution havens" in places as far from China as Tanzania (Xia 2019). Admittedly, the displacement of environmental harm to less developed countries reflects uneven global development rather than Chinese state intervention, and China can hardly be faulted for this outcome even as resistance is mounting against the new routes of the waste trade. Neighboring countries such as Vietnam and Thailand have introduced their own bans in the face of the flood of diverted shipments heading their way (Reed 2018). These efforts have given rise to a landmark Basel Convention amendment in May 2019, known as the Norwegian Proposal, which adds plastic waste to the Convention and is slated to go into effect in January 2021. (The United States declined to sign, as it has declined to sign most other environmental treaties, but it will largely be bound by the amendment in practice as other governments take action.)

The experience with environmental harm in villages such as Xiyu and Guiyu is symptomatic of a much larger problem of global environmental injustice (Pellow 2007). Thanks to international filmmakers and advocacy groups, China's e-waste problems became high-profile international stories that were hard to dismiss as Western bias. The stories embarrassed the Chinese government as it tried to claim credit for promoting planetary ecological civilization and led it to take action. As a result, the global waste economy may soon be history, after decades of egregious shifting of toxics from the wealthy to the vulnerable. This may finally uncover the real costs of production and force industries to rethink their use of materials. Indeed, when it becomes clear to consumers that there is ultimately nowhere to throw things "away," the entire pattern of cradle-to-grave global consumption may have to change.

However, even if we applaud China for refusing to be a dumping ground for rich countries' trash and toxics and support the global resistance to the trade in hazardous waste, we must also note that China has weaponized the ban in its trade war with the United States. On March 23, 2018, a United States representative to the WTO denounced the ban as having "caused a fundamental disruption in global supply chains for scrap materials, directing them away from productive reuse and toward disposal" (Miles 2018). Chinese Foreign Ministry spokesperson Hua Chunying dismissed the charges, saying that they are "unjustifiable, illegitimate and have no legal basis," before calling US officials "hypocritical" (Hua 2018b, official translation). This exchange took place amid rising concerns about a full-blown trade war.

As the war heated up, on May 2, the Chinese customs authority imposed an "extra urgent" measure requiring mandatory open-container inspection of all American shipments of recyclables. This brought the business to a near-complete halt. After the release of a conciliatory US–China joint statement on May 19, a truce seemed in sight and on May 22 customs authorities issued another "extra urgent" measure granting a rare inspection exemption for Canadian transshipments of US goods. The waste import ban thus became part of China's trade war arsenal of weapons, tightening and loosening according to the temperature of US trade relations. In fact, the war image is apt for both metaphorical and literal meanings: the state-run tabloid *Global Times* compared the waste ban to the 1839 Chinese crackdown on opium imports that ultimately led to the First Opium War between the Qing and British empires (Zhao 2018). Thus, the environmental merits of the waste import ban notwithstanding, the policy has strategic implications. Such geopolitical, non-environmental consequences are even more pronounced in the case of China's interventions into the global trade in rare earths.

Withholding Rare Earths

As the trade war between the two largest economies escalated, on May 20, 2019 President Xi Jinping paid an unusual visit to the city of Ganzhou in the mountainous southeastern province of Jiangxi. The first stop of his short trip was a company called JL Mag, the world's largest supplier of rare earths – natural elements that are used in manufacturing hi-tech products such as telescope lenses, aircraft engines, cellphones, and computer screens. Accompanied by China's top trade negotiator Vice-Premier Liu He, President Xi toured company headquarters and offered "important instructions" to enhance sustainability in the rare-earth industry. Xi and Liu's visit to JL Mag was widely interpreted as a signal that China planned to leverage its monopoly over the global supply of rare earths to gain an upper hand in the trade war (Areddy 2019). Indeed, a week after the visit, the official Chinese Communist Party *People's Daily* published an editorial that described rare earths as a "trump card," or *wangpai* 王牌, in China's trade conflicts with the United States. The editorial used no shortage of colorful language: "the US is intoxicated in its delirious complacency, but will slap itself in the face when it sobers up," it fulminated: "consider yourself warned!" (Wu 2019).

Near the bottom of the periodic table, rare earths include 17 metallic elements that are actually not especially rare, although the feasibly extractable supply is limited. Known deposits of rare earths are scattered throughout the earth's crust. Rare earth is thus a misnomer that has little to do with the geological qualities of the elements, but everything to do with the difficult chemical processes required to separate and refine them, and the high degree of politicization of global supply and demand (Klinger 2018). Rare earths tend to occur in nature together with hazardous elements such as uranium and heavy metals. As a result, the mining of rare earths is one of the most ecologically damaging undertakings on the planet. For example, cerium, a rare earth extensively used in professional lighting devices in the film and television industry, is extracted after crushed ore is dissolved in sulfuric and nitric acid, leaving behind massive amounts of poisonous waste as a byproduct. Near the Inner Mongolian city of Baotou, decades of the rare-earth mining boom have left behind what locals call a "rare-earth lake," a toxic dumping ground for untreated waste that spans approximately ten square kilometers, roughly three times the size of Manhattan's Central Park (Maughan 2015). In the vicinity, land has turned barren, livestock have died mysteriously, and residents have fled from ancestral homes (Li 2010).

In part because the environmental costs of rare-earth mining have led many countries to refrain from the industry, China enjoys a *de facto* monopoly over global supply and is presently responsible for 85 percent of global rare-earth production (Dutta et al. 2016). Interestingly, how this came to be is similar to the cases of afforestation, green grabbing, and ecological migration discussed in chapter 2. The development of rare-earth mining, particularly in Inner Mongolia during the Deng Xiaoping era, reflected the regime's efforts to pacify the borderlands and minority populations through rapid industrialization and modernization (Klinger 2018).

In recent years, China has shown increased willingness to use its monopolistic position for political ends. On September 7, 2010, the Japanese coastguard detained a Chinese fisherman for straying too close to the disputed Diaoyu/Senkaku Islands in the East China Sea. The incident escalated into a diplomatic crisis, giving rise to public protests in both Japan and China and the suspension of high-level exchanges between the two governments. A concert by the popular Japanese boy band SMAP, originally scheduled for October in Shanghai, was canceled because of political tensions. By the end of the month, Japanese hi-tech manufacturers were complaining of not receiving their shipments of rare earths, leading to speculation about a Chinese embargo (Bradsher and Tabuchi 2010). Chinese authorities publicly denied this. Yet the Ministry of Natural Resources did not hesitate to reprint an editorial claiming, "the West is terrified when China weaponizes rare earths," and "China should master the use of this weapon" (Xu 2013). Japan released the fisherman shortly after concerns emerged over the apparent embargo.

The *New York Times* economics commentator Paul Krugman sees the incident as evidence that China "showed no hesitation at all about using its trade muscle to get its way in a political dispute, in clear – if denied – violation of international trade law" (Krugman 2010). Scholars view the episode as part of China's increased mastery of "economic statecraft" – the use of economic arrangements such as embargoes and boycotts to serve foreign policy goals (Kalantzakos 2018). With its increasing economic clout, China is indeed frequently deploying these techniques. After Norway awarded the 2010 Nobel Peace Prize to imprisoned Chinese dissident Liu Xiaobo, who has since died, Norway's salmon exports to China plummeted by 70 percent and have not recovered (Huang and Steger 2017).

China's phantom embargo of rare earths did not go unchallenged. In March 2012, several countries led by the United States filed a case with the WTO's dispute settlement mechanism. The US accused China of violating international trade laws by assessing duties, imposing restrictions, and manipulating prices in the trade of rare earths (WTO 2012). China's response was that it had intervened in the sector on environmental grounds (State Council 2012).

To be fair, there are ample environmental justifications for curbing Chinese rare-earth mining, production, and export. The main reason China became the world's leading source of rare-earth products, after all, was the country's poor environmental safeguards. The low prices of Chinese rare earths were deceptive in that they failed to reflect the environmental costs of production. According to official sources, in Ganzhou, which President Xi visited at the height of the trade war, annual revenue from the rare-earth industry totaled 6.5 billion RMB in 2011, but the cost of rehabilitating the contaminated ecosystem would have been 38 billion, or nearly six times the industry's annual earnings (Xinhua 2012). Moreover, the production of rare earths in China has until recently been plagued with an immense black market of unregulated mines that is estimated to be 2.2 to 2.8 times the size of the legal one (Liu 2016). Black market mining makes no pretense at following environmental standards. In this context, China's response to US allegations has considerable validity. Indeed, some of the efforts to restructure the industry have sought to establish and enforce stricter environmental standards within China (Hayes-Labruto et al. 2013; Wübbeke 2013). That said, there is little evidence that the export restrictions resulted in any reduction of rare-earth production in China. This, among other factors, led the WTO panel to rule against China in August 2014. China complied with the decision by dropping restrictions in January 2015.

This legal resolution did not prevent China from brandishing its rare-earth "trump card" four years later. In fact, the Chinese government now enjoys unusually favorable conditions for managing the rare-earth supply chain as it wishes. Since 2011, the state has gradually consolidated rare-earth production into six state-owned conglomerates. The industry is now centered in a few key locations such as Baotou and Ganzhou (NDRC 2016). Such state-mandated restructuring of a "strategic" industry enables the Chinese government to exercise unprecedented control over rare-earth production and their global consumption. Perhaps Deng Xiaoping's 1992 epigram is more true than ever: "Rare earths to China are like oil to the Middle East" (State Council 1993).

Curbing the Endangered Species Trade

After investigating so many state-led, top-down exhortations, directives, targets, and campaigns that masked other agendas, it is refreshing to be able to record a significant success. This is the reduction in Chinese demand for one prominent species in the cascading global biodiversity collapse: sharks. Shark fins are used in East Asia in expensive soups and are believed to have a range of medicinal properties, although scientists tell us they are primarily cartilage with neither taste nor nutritional value. The endangerment of the ocean's apex predator has implications for much of the ocean's biodiversity, as sharks are central to well-functioning ocean ecosystems; like other apex predators, they regulate the balance of predator-prey organisms in the food chain. Moreover, finning is an exceptionally cruel way to harvest animal parts since the captured and mutilated shark is cast back into the ocean to drown. This message has gotten out to Chinese consumers, and the price of shark fins in Guangzhou, Hong Kong, and some of the world's other major seafood trading hubs has plummeted for lack of demand. This outcome represents a collaboration among governmental and non-governmental international institutions, the Chinese state, and civil society groups. It involves the Chinese state's willingness to implement and enforce the Convention on International Trade in Endangered Species (CITES), to which China has long been a signatory and which has banned the international trade in many species of shark. It involves government bans on shark fin soup on government banquet menus. It involves new domestic regulations that prohibit the import of shark fins that are not attached to the animal, thus making the trade far less lucrative.

Importantly, the government has permitted international civil society groups like the International Fund for Animal Welfare and WildAid, in partnership with Chinese celebrities like basketball star Yao Ming, to conduct major public information campaigns to change perception about shark fin consumption. With billboards in major cities and even electronic advertisements in subways, this campaign has been so successful that most luxury hotels and high-end restaurants have removed shark fin soup from their menus (although the word is that there is often a back room where fins can be had for a price). Domestic environmental groups have also played their part. The Alashan Society of Entrepreneurs and Ecology has been advocating for banning shark fin consumption since its inception in 2004. The organization's programming ranges from the national "shark-fin-free restaurant" campaign to lobbying efforts targeting high-profile representatives at the National People's Congress. The fragmentation of Chinese state bureaucracies allowed Alashan to influence the most progressive segments of the People's Congress, including 30 high-profile entrepreneurs who served as People's Congress representatives. The entrepreneurs' anti-shark fin bill overrode the resistance of medical and trade establishments, and in June 2012 the State Council, China's highest and most powerful administrative body, banned shark fin consumption at official meals. Ordinary people have gotten the message as well. It has now become increasingly unfashionable to serve shark fin soup at weddings. Domestic civil society groups continue to pursue advocacy for better environmental laws and regulations. Responding to the 2020 coronavirus outbreak, Friends of Nature enlisted the support of environmental lawyers, ecologists, journalists, and dozens of other ENGOs to urge the Chinese legislature to eradicate illegal wildlife trade and consumption, which are the root causes of the infectious zoonotic diseases that spread between animals and humans.

Public information and shaming techniques have inspired and supported governmental efforts and created a truly remarkable shift in citizen behavior within only a few years. A 2005 WildAid survey showed the public's indifference toward the problem of consumption of shark fins, but the same survey five years later suggested

that 56 percent of Chinese respondents were aware of
the WildAid campaigns, and 82 percent committed
to refusing or reducing consumption (Bai and Zhang
2012). The impact of these changes in China is felt
globally. There has been a steady decline in the global
shark fin trade since the mid-2000s, and the decline
in trade has resulted in a corresponding drop in the
quantity of shark fins "harvested" on a global scale
(Eriksson and Clarke 2015).

The same groups, in partnership with the Chinese
government, are making similar efforts to educate
Chinese consumers about elephants, which are being
decimated for their ivory and, it is feared, will soon
become extinct in the wild if trends continue. Ivory is
prized in China as a medium for carving and is now
within the reach of the newly wealthy, with access to
the source facilitated by China's increasing presence in
Africa and the complicity of organized international
criminal syndicates (Power et al. 2012). Other severely
endangered species are also finding advocates. One of
them is the pangolin, a small anteater-like animal whose
scales are used in traditional Chinese medicine and
which is poached from Southeast Asia literally by the
ton. Numerous species of turtle, and precious trees like
rosewood and mahogany, are similarly endangered, not
least by the huge increase in Chinese demand, but they
have received much less attention.

In a dramatic move, the Chinese government banned
the sale of ivory, including antique ivory, on December
31, 2017, and on several occasions publicly destroyed
stockpiles of ivory confiscated at borders. Yao Ming has
again lent himself to a civil society campaign ("Ivory
Belongs to Elephants") and posed for photos looking
exceedingly tall next to a cute baby elephant dressed
in a little plaid sweater. The Chinese government's
interventions have brought down the scale of illegal
poaching in Africa and caused the global price of ivory

to plummet (Zhou et al. 2018). However, the trade in illegal ivory remains brisk, in part because of other driving forces such as persistent poverty and corruption in countries where elephants are found (Hauenstein et al. 2019). Meanwhile, even though the ban has driven domestic sales to a black market, it has had the unintended consequence of driving up ivory purchases among Chinese tourists abroad. A 2019 World Wildlife Fund survey shows that 27 percent of Chinese international travelers admitted to purchasing ivory products, up from the previous year's figure of 18 percent (WWF 2019).

It may well be that the value of ivory for its beauty and status is more deeply entrenched in traditional Chinese cultural values than that of shark fin soup, and it will be that much more difficult to save one of the planet's most intelligent and charismatic species. The pangolin has another set of challenges: it is not well known, it is easy to catch (when threatened, it rolls into a ball that a poacher can pick up), and it lacks the elephant's charisma even as it is used for both medicine and food. The global trade in pangolin is highly lucrative, and it benefits local officials who are easily paid off. Civil society campaigns to raise awareness of the pangolin's plight are in their infancy. If the government focused on the illegal wildlife trade with as much enthusiasm as it has paid attention to the trade in recyclables and rare earths, then biodiversity-focused civil society groups would gain much-needed support.

One of the only positive impacts of the coronavirus outbreak is that the state has listened to petitions from a coalition of ENGOs to ban the consumption of wildlife permanently. The success of the new laws will depend upon implementation and enforcement, as well as citizen acceptance and compliance. This must be aided by the full participation of civil society groups who can monitor markets and educate an adventuresome citizenry drawn to consuming wild animals for their purported medicinal benefits and culinary rarity. There is a common saying that Chinese gourmands will eat "anything on four legs that isn't a table." For global biodiversity to survive Chinese middle-class consumption patterns, this will have to change.

Engineering China's Atmosphere

China's efforts to engineer the atmosphere for domestic purposes are just getting underway, yet they are already more ambitious than those of many other industrialized nations. The list of interventions is long: it includes: seeding clouds to create blue skies for special events; altering precipitation patterns over the Tibetan Plateau to compensate for glacier melt due to climate change; conducting research and pilot projects on carbon-mitigating techniques like carbon capture and sequestration; sending "resource" satellites into space to monitor ecological changes (and much else); and making plans to mine the moon, all in the name of protecting the environment. Below, we briefly introduce what China is doing in each of these areas. So much is changing in these highly technical sectors, and so quickly, that there is relatively little settled evidence. Taken together, however, they point toward a set of policies that are more reminiscent of the nature-conquest mentality of the Mao years than of earlier Chinese philosophies that advocate "harmony" between the heavens and the earth.

Blue Skies or Bust

China has long experimented with cloud-seeding in order to guarantee those blue-sky days about which we heard in discussions of target-setting and campaigns. Although there is little scientific consensus to confirm that cloud-seeding reliably works, China does it with some regularity, as before the 2008 Olympics, the 2014 "APEC blue" summit, the 2015 "parade blue" celebrating the 70th anniversary of the defeat of Japan, and the 2017 BRICS (Brazil, Russia, India, China, and South Africa) summit in Xiamen. Before the Shanghai 2010 World Expo, the city's "weather guarantee committee" was fully prepared to deploy cloud-seeding technologies, but the sky cleared on its own ahead of the opening ceremony. Before the Olympics, Beijing seeded clouds in neighboring regions to try to guarantee rain-free skies for the opening and closing ceremonies on which it had staked so much.

Cloud-seeding involves sending drones or small planes into cloudy or polluted skies to distribute silver iodide or other chemicals in an effort to form crystals that induce rain or snow and thus cleanse the air – water drops attract soot, sulfates, and organic particles. The chemicals can also be shot into the air by rockets. On the opening day of the Olympics on August 8, 2008 alone, for example, China launched a total of 1,104 cloud-seeding rockets (Cao and Li 2008). Many countries practice this form of weather modification, particularly at airports, and experiments in the US by the National Oceanic and Atmospheric Administration and other agencies have been ongoing since the 1960s. But China's program is considered the largest by far. During a 2009 drought, Beijing shot so many iodide sticks into the air that a three-day snowstorm closed Beijing's main roads, indicating that these measures do sometimes have an effect. The use of cloud-seeding rockets is becoming ever more commonplace; in response to a three-month period of drought, Anhui provincial authorities fired 327 such rockets in October 2019 alone (Tian 2019).

According to official data, between 2012 and 2017 the Chinese government spent 8.8 billion RMB, or 1.3 billion USD, on weather modification "for the sake of ecological civilization" (Xinhua 2017b). Cloud-seeding has led to regional tensions, with some areas accusing others of "stealing" rain and others complaining about adverse effects of introducing so many potentially toxic chemicals into the environment (silver iodide is toxic to fish but governments claim its effect on humans is negligible). Moreover, the government's focus on creating blue skies for big international events causes resentment, as ordinary people sometimes feel that foreigners are treated better than they are and the blue skies are just a sham to give the government face.

Constructing "Sky River": Weather Modification on the Tibetan Plateau

Glaciers are melting rapidly on the Tibetan Plateau, which is often called "the water tower of the world," or "the Third Pole." The major rivers of China, Southeast Asia, and South Asia all have their sources in the Himalayas and other mountains of China's Far West, including the Yangzi, Yellow, Indus, Brahmaputra, Ganges, and Mekong. Global warming is causing the glaciers that supply these critical water systems to melt. The initial bounty of extra river water will eventually vanish, imperiling major water-poor cities, including Beijing with its tens of millions of residents. While ordinary Chinese people, even the well educated, are often less immediately concerned about climate change than about ground-level ozone and the small air-pollution particles that lodge in their lungs to cause cancer, China's technocratically minded policy makers are well aware of the long-term threats posed by climate change. Falling water tables are parching North China, rising seas frequently inundate sections of densely populated Shanghai, Guangzhou, and Tianjin, and intensified cyclones and droughts are already levying tremendous human and economic costs throughout the country. Thus the Chinese government, in partnership with its top research institutions and universities, is paying great attention to mitigating climate change by reducing carbon emissions and, as we will see below, to the potential of technologies to deflect sunlight and recapture carbon. The state is also adapting to climate change by building flood control mechanisms like sea walls and encouraging the development of "sponge cities" that can absorb excess water. Shanghai even has a mechanical shoreline gate similar to that in Rotterdam. One of the most dramatic of these efforts to adapt to climate change involves a plan to change the weather at the roof of the world.

On the Tibetan Plateau, the government is building a cloud-seeding system of combustion chambers that send particles of silver iodide into the atmosphere to induce cloud-formation, with the goal of increasing precipitation with such volume and regularity that it would be equal to 7 percent of China's water consumption. As the *South China Morning Post*'s Stephen Chen explains in an investigative report, some 500 experimental chambers have already been deployed in Tibet, Qinghai, and Xinjiang, with a plan for tens of thousands more. These relatively inexpensive chambers (as compared with the drones, small aircraft, or rockets used for the short-term cloud-seeding described above) burn solid fuel that produces ice-like iodide. This is then carried upward by monsoon breezes from South Asia to interact with water vapor and form snow- and rain-releasing clouds. Thirty planned weather satellites will monitor winds over the Indian Ocean so as to guide the chambers with real-time data. The project is to be jointly implemented by the China Aerospace Science and Technology Corporation, Tsinghua University (which proposed the project in 2016 and named it Sky River or *Tianhe* 天河), and the government of Qinghai province. The aerospace corporation president told the *South China Morning Post* that the project "will make an important contribution not only to China's development and world prosperity, but also the wellbeing of the entire human race." It is difficult to imagine how fundamentally altering the weather on the Tibetan Plateau could contribute to human wellbeing. In an echo of the "rain-stealing" complaints around blue sky days in Eastern China, skeptics have noted that intercepting moisture in Tibet would likely reduce it in South Asia, with potentially devastating effects (Chen 2018).

Outer Space Environmentalism: The Digital Belt and Road

China is investing in a satellite-based global digital infrastructure platform known as the Digital Belt and Road (DBAR), the scale and data-processing capacity of which are expected to be unparalleled. According to the *Bulletin of the Chinese Academy of Sciences*, the DBAR platform grew out of a 2014 project that successfully established a comprehensive digital "panorama" of Central Asian countries based on remote sensing data from Chinese satellites. Integrating a wide range of data on urbanization, climate change, water, and agriculture, the 2014 study allegedly "received favorable comments from state leaders" and was therefore granted substantial government funding for rapid expansion. The resulting DBAR platform aims to encompass the Belt and Road Initiative corridors and ultimately the entire globe (Song 2016).

The Digital Belt and Road began to lay out its infrastructure in December 2016, when China unveiled its first fully domestically owned overseas satellite station in the northern Swedish iron-mining town of Kiruna, chosen for its strategic advantage in accessing polar-orbiting satellites (Chinese Academy of Sciences 2016b). Politically, Sweden is one of the few European countries that are not part of the North Atlantic Treaty Organization, or NATO, and is thus less beholden to US interests. Kiruna is no stranger to China. Due to land subsidence from decades of mining, the people of Kiruna even moved two miles east to New Kiruna in order to expand the mine for Chinese exports. Despite China's claim that the satellite station only performs scientific investigations, its launch has provoked concerns over its possible contribution to China's global surveillance and military missions (Elmer 2019). The Swedish state-owned company Swedish Space Corporation managed to press ahead with the project despite such reservations.

These concerns may have merit. In the "Beijing Declaration on Earth Observation for Belt and Road," Chinese state-funded scientists demand that the Digital Belt and Road "be given the fullest support by countries along the Belt and the Road" (Chinese Academy of Sciences 2016a). At the same time, China argues, "Many countries cannot afford to train experts in Earth-observing techniques or install ground stations to monitor soil nutrients or air quality" (Guo 2018, p. 26). Thus, the Chinese state is creating a monopoly on gathering, processing, and sanctioning scientific investigations within its international sphere of influence, with the help of big Earth data.

The Digital Belt and Road bills itself as the nerve center for a range of such data gathered through satellite remote-sensing, aerial photography, and ground-based monitoring. It aims to provide detailed information on such potentially sensitive areas as land use change, population density, traffic, and energy use, as well as event-based observations of natural disasters and food supply. On September 12, 2019, a Long March 4B rocket was launched from the city of Taiyuan carrying a Ziyuan 1-2D satellite developed by the China Academy of Space Technology. A perfect example of the green discourse that is used to explain these initiatives can be found in the Xinhua report of the launch, which states that the satellite is intended for:

> natural resources asset management, ecological monitoring, disaster prevention and control, environmental protection, urban construction, transportation, and contingency management. (Xinhua 2019b)

A microsatellite included in the launch is named Ice Pathfinder, or BNU-1 (run by Beijing Normal University). It will track polar sea ice changes and identify ships in polar waters. China's intentions in the Arctic and Antarctic have elicited intense geostrategic concern. This small satellite underlines the coincidence of China's "green" commitments with its strategic agenda. Indeed, China is pushing ahead with a plan to build space-based solar power stations, a concept originally developed by Caltech in the US but not implemented. While the renewable energy potential of this technology is obvious, Central Military Commission's Zhang Yulin, deputy chief of the armament development department has also commented, "The earth-moon space will be strategically important for the great rejuvenation of the Chinese nation" (Xinhua 2016).

Geoengineering the Earth's Climate

As noted, the Chinese government is acutely aware of the risks and costs of climate change. Given the technocratic orientation of the government, it is no surprise that the state is sponsoring one of the world's largest geoengineering research programs through the Ministry of Science and Technology.

Worldwide, two main categories of geoengineering responses are being explored. The most commonly known are carbon dioxide removal (CDR) or negative emissions technologies (NETs), which involve capturing carbon dioxide from the atmosphere and reinserting it deep into the earth. The second, solar radiation management, involves techniques to reduce the amount of incoming solar radiation that can be captured by greenhouse gases. Proposals include sending aerosols into the upper atmosphere to reflect sunlight to replicate the cooling effect seen following large-scale volcanic eruptions. Also under research and consideration are ideas to increase the reflectivity of other planetary features by making clouds more reflective or using "space reflectors" to block sunlight.

As with cloud-seeding, China is by no means the only country actively investigating these technologies; the US, UK, Germany, Japan, India, and other countries have research programs as well. China officially adopts a precautionary approach to intervention in basic geophysical processes and it is not at this point conducting outdoor experiments, unlike those planned for some preliminary US projects. Rather, China focuses on modeling, on seeing how techniques used in combination with each other might interact, on evaluating risks, and on trying to ensure that developing countries which are most impacted by climate change have a strong voice in any emerging geoengineering governance regime. The country wants to help write the rules, especially since there is a possibility of inadvertent or deliberate weaponization of geoengineering techniques, and of catastrophic repercussions if governments or private entities embark on real-world experiments without fully understanding potential impacts.

That said, China already has several carbon capture and storage projects in various stages of construction and operation, and is developing knowledge and technological capabilities that could be utilized for more elaborate carbon dioxide removal schemes. The Yanchang Integrated Carbon Capture and Storage Project in Shaanxi province captures carbon dioxide from nearby coal-burning plants and injects it into an oil field to improve oil recovery rates; the CO_2 is also used for carbonated beverages. Other projects, some in partnership with the European Union, are in various stages of funding and development. Chinese scientists are quick to point out, however, that neither carbon capture nor solar radiation management resolves the urgent problem of ground-level ozone. As noted in earlier chapters, dealing with air pollution is a non-negotiable task for the Chinese state because of public health impacts and citizen dissatisfaction.

Mining the Moon

China is also not the only country actively pursuing the idea of mining the moon. The Europeans, with tiny Luxembourg positioning itself to be the center of European space research, have plans for a moon-mining project to begin by 2050. China is the first country, however, to successfully land on the far side of the moon. In January 2019, to the admiration of space scientists worldwide, the Chang'e 4 made a historic landing on the deeply cratered surface, a feat guided by indirect communication through a satellite and then in the final phase conducted entirely by computers on the lander itself. The moon's far side is inaccessible to direct observation from earth and a presence there would allow observation into the reaches of parts of deep space that have so far been blocked. It is hoped that it will be a rich source of helium-3, a non-radioactive isotope that can be used for nuclear fusion and has the potential to meet global energy needs for centuries. It is also expected to be a rich source of rare-earth minerals. Chinese activities here are not necessarily nefarious. But security-oriented observers have commented that since the far side is not observable from earth, a hostile power could position a weapon capable of attacking and incapacitating satellites on which communications depend, and no one would be the wiser (Trevithick 2019).

Moon-mining seemingly has the mission to resolve environmental problems like finding energy sources that are alternatives to fossil fuels and securing access to new sources of the rare-earth metals on which so many high-tech products depend. China also has plans for a space-based solar power array that would be far more efficient than building solar power on earth, and along with other countries it is interested in gaining access to the minerals to be found in asteroids. But as with so many of China's "green" initiatives, there is a potential for a dark side that would further the state's techno-authoritarian goals.

The Sleeping Lion Awakes

Through a host of aggressive environmental entanglements, global China seeks to project itself as a "green" rule-maker and "green" technological superpower. But there are grave risks when technocracy and authoritarianism wrap themselves in a green flag. Lack of transparency, consultation, participation, or access to information can be particularly dangerous when an authoritarian power is insecure about whether it can maintain domestic support. China's leadership is preoccupied with the country's global reputation and it is alert to the potential for a repetition of the humiliations of recent history at the hands of foreign powers. The country is feeling its way at a moment of exceedingly rapid geopolitical and environmental change. While many of China's global interventions have been positive for the environment, the risk is that insecurity, inexperience, and arrogance can promote poor or even dangerous decisions. China's commitment to emissions reductions in the Paris Agreement in 2016 was heartening. However, it was characteristic of a defensive Chinese state that its top climate official in August 2019 blamed the US–China trade war when it was unable to meet its pledge (Xu and Stanway 2019). In fact, in September 2019 China opened a new railway system dedicated to shipping coal from Inner Mongolia's mines to Jiangxi province, called the North–South Coal Express, with an annual capacity for shipping 200 million metric tons of coal. It is clear that the Chinese economy is unlikely to shed its coal addiction anytime soon. Even as the world outside China collectively reduced coal power capacity by 8.1 GW from January 2018 to June 2019, China's coal fleet grew by a whopping 42.9 GW during the same period (Shearer et al. 2019). When domestic use is combined with the increased capacity of Chinese-funded coal-fired power plants on the Belt and Road, China's hoped-for leadership on the climate change issue comes to look like so much smoke and mirrors.

"China is a sleeping lion. Let her sleep, for when she wakes, she will shake the world." This well-known but often misattributed comment is believed to have been made by Napoleon Bonaparte. It may actually be a folk collage of clichés from the late 1800s, appealing to lovers of Chinese animal mythology and Europeans curious about a mysterious land (Tian 2014). Despite its historical inaccuracy, however, President Xi Jinping, in a 2014 state speech in Paris, used the Napoleon "quote" before adding, "The lion is now awake, but it is a peaceful, affable, and civilized lion" (Xi 2014).

Even as the world encounters rising China, the awakened lion seems unwilling to acknowledge its own fearsomeness. As China embarks on ever more ambitious undertakings with bilateral partners on the global stage and in outer space, Chinese state officials adopt a determinedly apolitical framing of their activities. A rare-earth embargo is good for the environment, we are told, just as we are told that big Earth data are good for humanity. As the cases in this and the preceding chapters illustrate, the non-environmental consequences of China's "green" interventions are many. Yet China's official narrative ignores these programs' non-environmental ambitions, knock-on effects, and unintended impacts. In a near-Orwellian reluctance to acknowledge the lion as others see her, Chinese state spokespersons routinely dismiss even the slightest intimation that China is a threat. In response, they regurgitate the official line that China is peaceful, friendly, and civilized.

With respect to the green technologies China deploys and spreads on a global scale, China seeks to envelop them in the matter-of-fact frame of scientific progress. In so doing, it seeks to reassure a wary global audience. State scientists and engineers present technologies, from the most personally invasive to the most potentially earth-shattering, in a singularly positive light. No politics. No ideology. No agenda. No strings attached. All is for the pragmatic betterment of the earth and humanity through the use of innocent technologies.

"[T]he interesting puzzle in our times," wrote philosopher of science Langdon Winner (1986), "is that we so willingly sleepwalk through the process of reconstituting the conditions of human existence" – a problem he calls "technological somnambulism." Winner's admonition was timely in the context of the rapid technological advances of the 1980s but is no less relevant in the current age of global China, when high modernism has become a defining experience of our planet. As we celebrate the convenience and efficiency brought by big (and bigger) data, smart technologies, cloud computing and the internet of things, technological innovation can feel mesmerizing. But high-tech transformations may usher in new forms of authoritarian control. In the case of an increasingly ambitious China, command of technological methods is enveloped in high-minded values that seem impossible to reject: sustainability, productivity, prosperity, connectivity, co-benefits, and so on. Hungry for condition-free investments and low-cost technologies, some countries have already opened their doors to "green" China as others remain suspicious and vigilant. Yet as the awakened lion paces the globe, China's "green" technology blandishments may become harder and harder to resist.

As we have seen in this chapter, the emergence of global "green" China is placing other countries at China's beck and call with respect to the trade in waste, rare earths, and biodiversity. It is making the very air subject to China's local and regional needs for clear skies and precipitation. And it is bringing the global infrastructure of outer space, which is widely regarded as belonging to all humankind, under the command and control of the longest-lasting authoritarian regime on the planet.

5

Environmental Authoritarianism on a Troubled Planet

In the introductory chapter of this book, we suggested that the global failure to deal with climate change and other transboundary environmental challenges has revived a conversation about whether the planet needs a green autocracy. With the arrival of the Anthropocene, it appears that radically new forms of governance are required. There is no time to dilly-dally with messy consultative processes. Decisive, top-down measures led by an authoritarian, technocratically inclined leadership may save the planet when all else has failed. That, at least, is the tempting logic. We raised the possibility that China may have something to teach the world in this regard.

We then showed how in the more developed parts of China, campaigns, crackdowns, targets, and behavioral modifications have been core tools of a state anxious to maintain legitimacy while struggling to curb pollution and infectious disease and tamp down corruption and post-Mao cynicism. For many Chinese citizens, the constantly shifting political climate, growing inequality, and uncertainty about whether there will be a chance to make money in the future have promoted a rush to get rich quickly. That can mean using illegal production methods, falsifying figures, using banned additives, cutting corners, dumping chemicals and toxic waste-water, hiding dangerous materials, and creating pyramid investment schemes. It is easy to see why an insecure state would turn to environmental campaigns and crackdowns as a way to compensate for the ineffec-tiveness of the legal system, even as these methods perpetuate a cycle of mistrust and evasion.

In chapter 2, we turned to the less-developed parts of China. Cookie-cutter policymaking, green-grabbing, and forcible relocations in the name of afforestation, renewable energy production, and biodiversity conser-vation have furthered the state's goals to pacify the borderlands even as they secure hydropower energy sources and provide the state with new revenue from ecotourism. By contrast, we saw how, when state planners considered local conditions and were open to civil society groups and the input of citizens and activists, there was more support for the state's initia-tives. But when the state applied projects in a uniform and unilateral fashion and when it heavy-handedly forced people to give up traditional livelihoods and cultures and move into settlements in the name of environmental protection, ecological and social outcomes were poor and the potential for long-term dissatisfaction became that much greater.

Moving beyond China's borders, we then showed how the Belt and Road Initiative relies on a framing of win-win green development, soft-power projection, and the export of technologies that can be used for surveillance as well as for environmental "goods." We explored the deep ambivalence of recipient countries and communities who see the arrival of China as both an opportunity and a threat. We noted the enormous environmental impacts of infrastructure projects that fragment biodiversity habitat and destroy human liveli-hoods, even as Chinese policy makers and investors seem singularly deaf to the risks of intensified globalization of trade and the "connectivity" that they tout in soft-power propaganda and on-the-ground technologies. These technologies, we saw, can be used to strengthen state control over individuals and communities even as they gather data about environmental change.

Finally, we explored China's adoption of additional tools to further global goals: dictating trade rules on "green" issues, manipulating the weather at the earth's surface, and researching space engineering in the name of mitigating climate change. While full deployment of many of these technologies may lie in the future, and while China is articulating a generally cautious, precau-tionary approach, we saw that China is positioning itself to be a major player in geoengineering, space mining, and the colonization of outer space. Given China's poor record on consultation and transparency, it would be wise for all parties to tread carefully in the age of global China.

Many Chinese citizens describe themselves as proud of the achievements of the 40 years since the reform and opening policies started to salve the wounds of the Mao years. Indeed, the struggling China of 1979 when paramount leader Deng Xiaoping implemented the Four Modernizations policy is all but unrecognizable compared with today's powerhouse, especially in the wealthier East. But the current government suppresses information and deliberation about the very tragedies on which, by contrast, it has built its own legitimacy. Post-Mao reformers offered capitalism as opposed to collectivism, wealth accumulation as opposed to equality in the face of famine, shopping and consumption as opposed to endless hardship and self-sacrifice. At its core, however, the post-Mao Communist Party is not so very different from that of the Mao era. It is still afraid of real and imagined enemies, still intent on reorganizing society in its name, and still keen to concentrate as much power as possible in the hands of Beijing. At the same time, some of the environmental externalities inherent to a quasi-capitalist economic system have raised a host of new challenges for a state feeling its way in a globalized world.

The examples and cases presented in the preceding chapters have shown how China's style of authoritarian environmentalism collects political, economic, legal, and scientific power within the central leadership. By simultaneously expanding the regulatory scope of the state to encompass a growing range of environmental issues and co-opting non-state actors into the state's environmental agenda, the Chinese state uses the appearance of going green to consolidate its power over territory and over the individual. Environmental concerns are linked to other goals of an increasingly totalitarian regime, not least because citizen dissatisfaction with pollution is a source of unrest. While many aspects of China's environmental leadership are praiseworthy, other aspects are deeply troubling and should cause us to rethink the wisdom of imagining that a green autocrat can save the planet.

These observations have led us to question whether the term "authoritarian environmentalism" best characterizes contemporary China. The term suggests that authoritarianism is merely a means to the laudable goal of sustainability. As we suggested in the Introduction, however, our investigation has yielded an inverted picture, whereby authoritarianism is the goal and environmentalism is the means for achieving it. Common to almost all of the "green" initiatives we have chronicled is the consolidation of state power and its deeper reach across space and into the individual. As we have shown in the preceding chapters, a more accurate term than "authoritarian environmentalism" is thus "environmental authoritarianism."

Just as we have come to see the "authoritarian environmentalism" formulation as less accurate for what is occurring in China than "environmental authoritarianism," we see China's model as less beneficial "for" a troubled planet than simply "on" it, as is reflected in this chapter's title. The ecological civilization that China is projecting internationally and globally is less a salve for the planet's wounds than an intensification of them. "Coercive environmentalism on a troubled planet" is a sad but accurate description rather than a prescription for success.

Environmental Fix

In his classic analysis of globalization, David Harvey deploys the concept of the "spatial fix" to explain the expansionist tendency of late capitalism. To Harvey, the "fix" has a double meaning: the physical fixity of capital investments on land and a metaphor for the need of capital to resolve, or "fix," the problem of overaccumulation and resource depletion. The spatial fix temporarily displaces the inevitability of capitalist crises that result from contradictions within capitalism itself such as overaccumulation and underconsumption. It does so by finding new resources and markets. Harvey writes that the material meaning of fixity contradicts the metaphorical one: capital is fixed in material assets and territorial spaces, but at the same time it requires endless expansion and mobility. Herein lies the inherent contradiction of capitalist globalization (Harvey 1985; 2003). The contradiction of late capitalism is experienced as both overproduction, upon which Marx expounded extensively, and the systematic tendency to undermine and even destroy the material and ecological conditions of capitalist production, which sociologist James O'Connor defined as the "second contradiction of capitalism" (O'Connor 1988; 1991).

The ecological conditions of the earth are thus increasingly caused by capitalism's "fixing" of its second contradiction. In Jason Moore's words, "capitalism does not have an ecological regime; it is an ecological regime" (Moore 2011). To clarify capitalism's entanglements with the environment, Karen Bakker has developed the notion of "environmental fix" in her study of water privatization. She argues that the environmental fix entails specific capitalist strategies to displace environmental externalities and secondary impacts onto others and to exploit these externalities as profit-making opportunities (Bakker 2004). Noel Castree advances an even broader notion of environmental fix, seeking to understand capital's tendency to profiteer from conservation, dispossession, and even degradation (Castree 2008). The state stands front and center in the global deployment of environmental fixes for the second contradiction by maintaining property regimes, investing in physical infrastructures, dispensing scientific knowledge, and managing environmental hazards (Rome 2002; Parenti 2015).

China's practice of coercive environmentalism brings to light a different kind of environmental fix in action. This environmental fix has a double meaning similar to that described by Harvey. Literally, through the exercise of coercive environmentalism, China is affixing manifestations of state power on the surface of the planet: in the monocultural poplar forests of Inner Mongolia, in dams along major waterways in China and beyond, in ports and coal-fired power plants in Djibouti and Sri Lanka, in a satellite station within the Arctic Circle, and in the dent on the far side of the moon made by the Chang'e-4 lander. Authoritarian China has planted material embodiments of its power everywhere – they are a tangible expression of China's sprawling authority.

Coercive environmentalism also constitutes a metaphorical fix for the authoritarian state. The green initiatives at home help state power penetrate into the everyday lives of citizens, from the industrial East to the borderlands. They thus aim to "fix" many of the state's problems, including dwindling political legitimacy in the eyes of an affluent urban citizenry, local government officials' non-compliance with central orders, and unrest in ethnic minority regions that are resisting assimilation. By the same token, overseas green initiatives help China project its growing power onto the world and even beyond the globe while also resolving China's many self-imposed problems on the global stage, such as its appetite for soft power and "face," the need for a global market for China-made products and technologies, and what China sees as its undervalued position in international markets. China's efforts to "fix" these problems are accomplished by deploying an astonishingly diverse range of green governmental tools, techniques and technologies, from community morality banks to big Earth data. The "fixing" of these varied political problems of the Chinese state comes alongside the familiar "fixing" of the nominally socialist but essentially capitalist China's need for domestic and global procurement of natural resources like minerals, fossil fuels, and grain, and the international transfer of environmental externalities. This is the second contradiction of capitalism with Chinese characteristics.

Unlike Harvey's fix, however, the literal and metaphorical meanings of China's environmental fix do not contradict each other. In fact, they cross-fertilize. The physical manifestation of China's ecological civilization is a core strategy for the Chinese state to address homegrown and international challenges to its rising power. The physical actuality of the Three Gorges and other dams, for example, helps the Chinese state monopolize the lucrative hydropower business and impose its will upon minority peoples. Similarly, the physical actuality of Chinese technological infrastructure along the Belt and Road enables China to make a universal case for its state-of-the-art surveillance technologies. The environmental "fix" may well be the hidden recipe for successful authoritarian resilience – in the Chinese style.

Authoritarian Resilience

Our findings offer new insights into the Chinese state's longevity. Already the longest-lasting authoritarian regime on the planet, the People's Republic of China has demonstrated impressive adaptability and staying power during the seven decades of its existence since 1949. Many scholars have sought to understand the secret of its endurance by examining how the regime manages criticism and dissent to avoid eruption into a large-scale collective challenge to the Communist Party. Such defensive management takes the form of institutional control of channels for public expression (Shi 1997; Nathan 2003), piecemeal strategic tolerance of vitriolic criticisms of the government on social media (King et al. 2013), and permission for investigative reporting on low-level officialdom (Lorentzen 2014). Taken together, past research points to a subtle and calculated approach in the Chinese state's effort to defend itself from challenges to its power (Roberts 2018), prompting one analyst to consider China "a cautious bully" (K. Zhang 2019).

By contrast, our investigation suggests that the state has stepped up its strategies for self-preservation by turning from the defensive to the offensive, now adopting a far more assertive stance in its claims to power. The environment has moved to the forefront of China's escalated power plays. For example, Shanghai's mandate to recycle applies to all residents in an indiscriminate fashion, even as the city's overworked middle class struggles to comply with the counter-intuitive categorization system, restrictive hours of trash disposal, and uninvited and intrusive inspections of household trash bags. Despite the undue hardship to which Shanghai citizens are now subjected, the city government is proud to pronounce the new rules as the beginning of an "era of coercion." The conundrum for those on the receiving end of such offensive moves is that the planet's ecological condition is cited as a justification.

Internationally, China's charm offensives also enlist the natural environment. By envisaging the "green" Belt and Road for a planet on the brink of ecological collapse, China projects itself as a confident global power that is capable of leading humanity toward ecological civilization. Such confidence is even codified into President Xi Jinping's much-regurgitated theory of "Four Confidences" or *sige zixin* 四个自信, which conveys nationalistic confidence in China's "paths, theories, institutions, and cultures." Indeed, developmental agencies that are rife with Chinese characteristics now present an alternative institutional universe that purports to be greener and better, as underlined by claims of allegiance to ecological civilization in mission statements and strategic plans. These include the Asian Infrastructure Investment Bank, New Development Bank, China Development Bank, Shanghai Cooperation Organization, and Silk Road Fund.

Taken together, by appearing to be on the side of the earth, the Chinese state and its escalated power plays seem impossible for partner countries to resist. Perhaps the Chinese state's maneuvers exemplify the adage that "the best defense is a good offense." Armed with "paths, theories, institutions, and cultures" with Chinese characteristics, the Middle Kingdom's authoritarianism has become stronger and more resilient than ever.

Techno-political Underpinnings

We cannot aspire to understand Chinese authoritarian resilience without appreciating the state's technocratic support system. In much of the existing literature on authoritarian environmentalism in China, the focus is on the environmental competence and technological literacy of state officials (Beeson 2010; Gilley 2012), the bureaucratic shortcuts for implementing swift cures for environmental "bads" (Ahlers and Shen 2018; Geall 2018; Zhu and Chertow 2019), and the rollout of environmental targets, plans, and laws (Mol and Carter 2006; Qi and Wu 2013). Seen in these lights, China appears to be an exemplar of state-led environmental stewardship, replete with benevolent officials and adaptive institutions that, together, produce regulatory and legislative interventions in the service of sustainability.

While we have also observed some of these features, they are only part of the overall exercise of environmental power in authoritarian China. In fact, after consideration of the case studies and examples, it becomes increasingly clear that these environmental qualities of the state are subsumed under a host of non-environmental agendas, many of which are techno-political in nature.

We see a state enamored of a high-modernist vision of a polity whose highly "legible" citizens are monitored, evaluated, scored, rewarded, and punished in accordance with their acquiescence in the state's decisions on their behalf. At the same time, natural elements from trees to rivers and minerals to the atmosphere itself are subject to ever-harsher technological contrivances, controls, and conquests. Emboldened by domestic successes in the deployment of green tools, techniques, and technologies, Chinese state officials eye the rest of the world for new spaces for subjugation. "Our ready-made approach could be applied elsewhere in the world," as an unnamed Chinese forestry expert is quoted about afforestation knowledge in China (Hao 2019).

"No idea is more provocative in controversies about technology and society than the notion that technical things have political qualities," wrote philosopher of science Langdon Winner (1986) more than three decades ago. What our investigation makes abundantly clear is that technologies not only embody a full suite of political qualities, but also expand the scope of political control and intensify the penetration of state into society. The techno-political complex thus constitutes an indispensable element in the state's pursuit and realization of its political ambitions at home and overseas. Yet the state poses as an "anti-politics machine," to borrow a term from James Ferguson (1990). It presents itself as a value-neutral bearer of world-bettering technologies. Its maneuvers encapsulate the notion that the world's problems can be solved through continuously advancing technologies.

Transactional Logic

In such a context, the transactional nature of China's dealings in the environmental realm is clearly on display. In transacting with the urban middle class, for example, the state offers access to a desired commodity that it monopolizes – license plates – in exchange for citizens' purchases of specific types of vehicles. The transactional relationship between the state and the buyer ends with the delivery of the car: there is a win for both and no liability for either. In transacting with the nomadic people in the borderlands, the state desires the ancestral lands of the citizens and therefore builds new, more "modern," and supposedly nicer settlements. Resistance from ecological migrants is shrugged off as ingratitude, despite plentiful examples of forced relocation leading to cultural destruction and despair. In interactions with China's partners on the Belt and Road, the transactional logic is even more pronounced. Roads, railways, and ports are delivered by Chinese SOEs and lending institutions in exchange for oil, minerals, timber, grain, fish, and other raw materials and resources. Globally, in its tit-for-tat trade war with the United States, China does not hesitate to deploy environmental measures like so many playing cards.

One might argue that transactions are common in modern politics and that the Chinese state cannot be faulted for adopting a realist position in its approach to political affairs. China is by no means the only country that has kept allies and foes off balance with unexpected policy shifts, particularly in recent years when there has been chaos in long-standing Western geopolitical loyalties and enmities. However, China's transactional logic is remarkably oblivious of the cornerstones of the modern political enterprise. Absent is room for building durable institutions and rules that guide transactions for the long term. At will, the Chinese state rewrites the code of conduct for its citizens, the conditions of cooperation for its partners, and the terms of trade for global commerce. No transaction is reliably indicative of the rules to be followed in the next. China's compliance with the 2014 WTO ruling against its restrictions on rare-earth exports to Japan, for example, bore no hint that it would threaten to play the rare-earth card against the US a mere five years later.

Also absent is genuine commitment to core environmental and social values such as sustainability and human wellbeing. "Green" China proffers no shortage of high-minded declarations and great-hearted slogans. From ecological civilization to low-carbon urbanism, these admirable terms frame the overall discursive landscape of Chinese state-led environmentalism. Yet, beyond their discursive qualities and propaganda functions, they offer little guide to the workings of the Chinese state. The rhetorical devices have a tenuous connection to the unfolding of programs that have profound environmental impacts, as can be seen most clearly in the case of "win-win development" in the Belt and Road Initiative. Likewise, at home, citizens were left literally in the cold when the state launched a single-minded pursuit of coal reduction in indoor heating systems, despite the Communist Party's constitutional commitment to serve the people. Ecological civilization became a hollow concept when the imperative to assert global leverage outweighed other countries' need for rare earths, although some were essential to produce environmentally friendly products such as electric car batteries and solar panels. Only transactional concerns of cost and benefit tilt the calculus of the Chinese state.

Indispensable Civil Society

The most striking reality of China's brand of coercive environmentalism is the jarring gap between the high-minded narratives of green development and ecological civilization on the one hand, and the matter-of-fact pursuits of bureaucratic self-interest and nationalistic objectives on the other. Such a gap enables the state to maintain its claim to legitimacy even as the nation is plagued with environmental atrocities at home and denounced for resource-grabbing abroad. The blame, if it emerges at all, is shifted to low-level officialdom, technical glitches, regulatory misinterpretation, or minor hiccups in an otherwise sound system. Benevolence on the part of the authoritarian throne is framed as absolute.

This gap, however, opens structural opportunities for non-state social forces to hold the Chinese state to account. After all, the state's hyperbolic framings and unfulfilled pledges have become its largest political liability. Non-state groups have taken advantage of the gap to position their research and advocacy efforts. Signs of hope emerge from the preceding chapters. We saw how the state turned to Ma Jun and the IPE for help with its "Black and Smelly Water" app: by empowering citizens to report polluters, the state allows evidence-gatherers and enforcers to work together to identify and resolve problems. We also saw the power of citizen–state collaboration in the Tiger Leaping Gorge dam and shark fin cases. Environmental journalists and anthropologists are at the forefront of challenging environmental injustice, exposing the harsh realities of cancer villages and hazardous dump sites, and warning of the cultural damage wrought by ecological migration. Independent-minded scientists continue to produce rigorous research to challenge the state's rosy discourses about hydropower dams and artificial affor- estation. International and domestic filmmakers and advocacy groups are drawing sustained global attention to the most outrageous violations of citizens' basic rights to a healthy environment. There is pressure on Chinese Belt and Road investors to do a better job of consulting with recipient communities, if only because they are learning the hard way that not doing so means trouble ahead. During the coronavirus outbreak in 2020, scientists fought state officials' bogus claims that the new virus "could not transmit from human to human" and that the epidemic was "completely under control." They circumvented the state censorship apparatus by publishing clear contrary evidence in top international medical journals such as the *Lancet* and the *New England Journal of Medicine*. The gap between the rosy official story and the scientists' grim findings embarrassed the state so much that the Ministry of Science and Technology ordered on January 30 that all domestic scientists refrain from publishing new information before the virus was eradicated. In all, these non-state groups refuse to pretend that the transaction is closed whenever environmental justice has not been served, or when genuine environmental information has not been cleared, thereby providing an essential public service that mitigates some of the worst excesses of the authoritarian state.

Domestically, the state produces better policy outcomes when its regulatory efforts are complemented by non-state inputs. On the global stage, the state is demonstrating environmental effectiveness where it engages with local communities and activists, but it is stirring resistance and animosity when it single-mindedly pursues government-to-government negotiations in the expectation that partner states will exert the same control over citizens that it is accustomed to wield at home.

The bureaucratic institutions of the Chinese state are complex and do not always pursue the same agenda with the same intensity. At times, policy makers in the Ministry of Ecology and Environment have demonstrated a keen awareness of the darker sides of coercive environmentalism. For example, there have been apparently well-meaning efforts to stave off local authorities' overreactions to the *yidaoqie* (cutting everything with the same knife) approach to pollution mitigation. In response to criticism from scholars and resistance from local communities, some state agencies and semi-governmental think tanks have proposed to reform plans for the enormous national protected area of Sanjiangyuan so as to make it more porous and less fortress-like. There are also internal efforts to expose the falsification of environmental data that is so common because officials fear the consequences of failing to meet targets. However, these measures generally seek to offset the overreach of state power with even more state interventions. As a result, Chinese state-led environmentalism has grown into a bewildering patchwork of international commitments, leadership pledges, ministerial mandates, local action plans, central crackdowns, local workarounds, and "extra urgent" communiqués from the Center. Such a patchwork reflects the often-conflicting lines of authority that fragment the Chinese state, and they are integrated into its environmental governance. This system leaves private citizens and businesses perpetually at risk of being punished in the next wave of state power incursion or environmental impositions. As a result, environmental compliance is ad hoc and short-lived, rendering genuine sustainability an elusive concept.

At the international and global levels, we have seen China confronted by both state and non-state actors who do not take for granted that China's arrival on the scene brings the promised mutual benefits. National governments like those in Malaysia and Myanmar have demanded to renegotiate Belt and Road deals in light of the experience of neighbors with debt and environmental and social damage. Communities deeply affected by Chinese dams, roads, and ports have mobilized in waves of anti-Chinese sentiment. Worldwide, there is widespread ambivalence about China's new role. With the cancelation of an airport and mining projects in Sierra Leone and a court challenge to a coal mine in Kenya among multiple projects that have been put on hold, China is discovering that not all intended beneficiaries are willing to receive China's largesse. That said, it appears that China has learned that cloaking investments and partnerships in "green" is an effective technique to buy acceptance.

At the same time, China's endeavors are not mere greenwashing of its top-down political system.

Environmental achievements are evident in cases such as the blue sky campaigns, the switch from coal to natural gas, the crackdown on food waste, the phase-in of electric cars, the ecological restoration in protected areas, and the enhancement of domestic recycling after the waste import ban. In these regards, the greening of China has indeed materialized. However, the green achievements have not been consistent, nor lasting in practice. Some were one-off fads. Others tightened and loosened abruptly as political winds changed. Yet others were rolled back as the state reconsidered. The green cloak of Chinese authoritarianism is therefore more ornamental than functional.

Counterintuitively, then, the success of state-led environmentalism for both ecological wellbeing and good governance hinges not on a strong state but on mechanisms that place state power in check. A closed-door, mandate-driven state undermines its own power, but an open, collaborative, and adaptive state shows real promise. The Chinese state under the leadership of the Communist Party is no monolith. Consistent with past research, we have discovered that the fragmented nature of Chinese state institutions, with their often-conflicting lines of authority and tensions between the Party and the state, has permitted *de facto* checks and balances (Mertha 2009; Spires 2011; Teets 2018). This is evident, for example, when Chinese SOEs investing overseas seek to understand and even adopt international environmental and human rights safeguards above and beyond their supervising agencies' directives merely to comply with host-country laws. Similarly, China's move to curb the endangered species trade came about because progressive voices in the National People's Congress prevailed against the medical and trade establishments. These and other examples in this book demonstrate the imperative for the exercise of state power to be premised on a broad base of knowledge, perspectives, expertise, participation, and, ultimately, support.

Consultation under State Leadership

Ironically, the indispensability of a broad base of support was fully recognized at the founding of the People's Republic of China seven decades ago. Mao Zedong proposed in May 1948 to establish a formal mechanism for political consultation as a check on the power of the Communist Party. In his opening speech to the First Political Consultative Conference in September 1949, Mao remarked, "It is imperative to summon a conference that is inclusive of democratic parties, people's associations, representatives from all fields, ethnic minorities, and members of the Chinese diaspora" (Mao 1950). In fact, even a decade before that, when Mao developed his "mass line" at the Communist base in Yan'an, consultative mechanisms had been an integral part of the Party's political theory and practice.

Despite its orthodox origins, political consultation became a marginal institutional mechanism in subsequent waves of development and reform of the Chinese state. Even when civil society groups carved out new space for political participation, the state's imperative to control grew in tandem (Teets 2013). The state routinely seeks inputs only from semi-governmental bodies such as the Chinese Academy of Sciences, the Chinese Academy of Social Sciences, and the China Council for International Cooperation on Environment and Development. In fact, it has been shown that individuals with robust political connections are more likely to communicate criticisms of the government (Tsai and Xu 2018). For ordinary citizens, there are few safety valves, although the state has set up dedicated complaint hotlines for specific types of citizen grievances. Each level of the government also has a "letters and visits office" to collect citizen feedback. But these fall short of genuine public participation and Chinese scholars continue to advocate for deeper political consultation through better institutional and legal mechanisms.

In fact, the prospect for genuine political consultation on environmental challenges is in peril. The exercise of environmental authoritarianism has produced a prevailing public sentiment of apathy toward environmental problems. This is despite the Chinese public's high level of awareness of the risks of intensive daily exposure to environmental harms like breathing toxic air, drinking unsafe water, and consuming contaminated foods. Unlike in the United States, where climate change denial is produced by misinformation campaigns organized by the fossil fuel industry and its hired-gun "experts" (Oreskes and Conway 2011), or in Norway, where residents avoid the uncomfortable topic of their national dependence on fossil fuel extraction despite their personal commitments to environmental protection (Norgaard 2011), Chinese residents are keenly aware of China's major environmental challenges and their causes. This awareness has been on a steady upswing since the 1990s (Yan et al. 2010; Ouyang et al. 2015). But although few in China deny the gravity of climate change and other environmental challenges, few see the need for individual political action (Chang et al. 2012). In fact, an overwhelming majority of respondents consider environmental protection to be the responsibility of the government, and the government alone (Yu et al. 2013).

This apparent contradiction of high environmental awareness and low propensity to act underscores the perils of life under authoritarianism. Acute awareness has not translated into robust environmental action, at least in part because independent, grassroots citizen action seems like a distant dream. Isolated instances of not-in-my-backyard resistance to certain projects have erupted in some cities, but citizens' low sense of political efficacy has prevented them from pursuing action beyond obvious immediate threats. As the Chinese proverb goes, they are sweeping the snow on their own doorstep, or *zisao menqian xue* 自扫门前雪.

To be fair, the waves of coercive campaigns from the government have kept urban Chinese residents busy with a plateful of government-mandated environmental actions: leave no leftovers on the dinner table, bring your own shopping bags, correctly sort household garbage, plant trees in the desert, and even buy an electric vehicle. If you are unlucky enough to live in a less developed area, the actions might include: accept relocation if you live upriver from a dam, substitute cows for sharp-hooved sheep and goats and put them in corrals to keep them away from the grasslands, move out of the national park, and so on. On the receiving end of wave after wave of environmental campaigns, the people of China have adopted a passive, apathetic frame of mind toward environmental problems, even in the midst of unprecedented levels of pollution in their immediate surroundings (Lora-Wainwright 2017). At most, citizens translate their environmental awareness into the purchase of protective gear such as masks and purifiers; individual consumerism reigns supreme in the midst of environmental catastrophe (Tu et al. 2020). Any further individual initiatives seem redundant or even politically risky in light of the constant stream of mandates, bans, and orders from capricious state officials who supposedly know best. Under the shadow of "green" authoritarianism, then, apathy provides a pragmatic coping mechanism for the subjects of the state. Reopening and reviving consultative channels is perhaps the only "fix" for environmental apathy, and ultimately for the interlocking political and ecological challenges of China.

In the Anthropocene, China has an opportunity to play a leadership role if it lives up to the potential of its official model of mutual benefit, consultation, win-win development, and public participation. Political consultation, formalized through robust institutions, could provide the state with valuable inputs from multiple social sectors while permitting the Party to retain power. Consultative mechanisms are therefore key to the authoritarian state's political effectiveness and legitimacy. At this historic moment, as environmental challenges become increasingly interconnected and environmental harms increasingly unevenly distributed, the Chinese state is badly in need of reviving and empowering the consultative process. This is by no means only a domestic issue. The weight of China's global impacts means that the ecological future of the planet hinges on China's ability to address its environmental problems both at home and overseas. China must truly "go green."

References

Ahlers, Anna L. and Yongdong Shen. 2018. "Breathe Easy? Local Nuances of Authoritarian Environmentalism in China's Battle against Air Pollution." *China Quarterly* 234: 299–319.

Albert, Eleanor. 2018. "China's Big Bet on Soft Power." *Council on Foreign Relations*, February 9.

Areddy, James T. 2019. "Xi Flexes Trade Muscle with Tech Metals." *Wall Street Journal*, May 22, A9.

Bai, Chaoyang (白朝阳) and Wei Zhang (张伟). 2012. "War on Shark Fins (鱼翅的'战争')." *China Economic Weekly (中国经济周刊)* (35): 28–35.

Baile, Sibao Cairen (百乐·司宝才仁) and Zhaoqing Han (韩昭庆). 2007. "On Cultural Changes of the Ecological Emigrants from the Three-river Source (试论三江源生态移民的文化变迁)." *Fudan Journal (Social Science) (复旦学报(社会科学版))* (03): 134–40.

Bakker, Karen J. 2004. *An Uncooperative Commodity: Privatizing Water in England and Wales*. Oxford University Press.

Balmer, Crispian. 2019. "China's Belt and Road Plan Could Be Good for Italy: Italian PM." *Reuters*, March 9.

Barboza, David. 2007. "Virus Spreading Alarm and Pig Disease in China." *New York Times*, August 16.

Beck, Ulrich. 1992. *Risk Society: Towards a New Modernity*. Sage Publications.

Beeson, Mark. 2010. "The Coming of Environmental Authoritarianism." *Environmental Politics* 19(2): 276–94.

Bloomberg. 2018. "China Steps Up Its Push into Clean Energy." *Bloomberg News*, September 26.

Borras, Saturnino M., Ruth Hall, Ian Scoones, Ben White, and Wendy Wolford. 2011. "Towards a Better Understanding of Global Land Grabbing: An Editorial Introduction." *Journal of Peasant Studies* 38(2): 209–16.

Bradsher, Keith and Hiroko Tabuchi. 2010. "China Is Said to Halt Trade in Rare-Earth Minerals with Japan." *International Herald Tribune*, September 25.

Brewster, David. 2017. "Silk Roads and Strings of Pearls: The Strategic Geography of China's New Pathways in the Indian Ocean." *Geopolitics* 22(2): 269–91.

Brooks, Amy L., Shunli Wang, and Jenna R. Jambeck. 2018. "The Chinese Import Ban and Its Impact on Global Plastic Waste Trade." *Science Advances* 4(6): eaat0131.

Burtynsky, Edward. 2007. *Manufactured Landscapes: The Photographs of Edward Burtynsky*. Yale University Press.

Cai, Fang. 2010. "Demographic Transition, Demographic Dividend, and Lewis Turning Point in China." *China Economic Journal* 3(2): 107–19.

Cai, Jane. 2017. "How Will China's Sweeping Pollution Crackdown Affect Its Economy?" *South China Morning Post*, September 14.

Cao, Jilu (曹冀鲁) and Jing Li (李竞). 2008. "No Rain Tonight at the Bird's Nest: Report of Artificial Rain Reduction for the Olympic Games Opening Ceremony ('鸟巢'今夜无雨——人工消（减）雨保障北京奥运会开幕式纪实)." *China Meteorological News Press* (中国气象报), August 11.

Cao, Shixiong, Li Chen, Chenguang Xu, and Zhande Liu. 2007. "Impact of Three Soil Types on Afforestation in China's Loess Plateau: Growth and Survival of Six Tree Species and Their Effects on Soil Properties." *Landscape and Urban Planning* 83(2): 208–17.

Carrington, Damian. 2019. "MPs Warn Post-Brexit Environment Plans Fall 'Woefully Short.'" *Guardian*, April 25.

Castree, Noel. 2008. "Neoliberalising Nature: The Logics of Deregulation and Reregulation." *Environment and Planning A: Economy and Space* 40(1): 131–52.

CCICED (China Council for International Cooperation on Environment and Development). 2019. "Special Policy Study on Green Belt and Road and 2030 Agenda for Sustainable Development."

CDB (China Development Bank), UNDP (United Nations Development Programme), and SEPKU (The School of Economics, Peking University). 2017. "The Economic Development along the Belt and Road 2017."

Chamberlain, Heath B. 1987. "Party-Management Relations in Chinese Industries: Some Political Dimensions of Economic Reform." *China Quarterly* 112: 631–61.

Chang, Genying (常跟应), Fupeng Huang (黄夫朋), Man Li (李曼), and Guojing Li (李国敬). 2012. "Public Perception of Climate Change and Their Support of Climate Policy in China: Based on Global Surveys and in Comparison with USA (中国公众对全球气候变化认知与支持减缓气候变化政策研究——基于全球调查数据和与美国比较视角)." *Scientia Geographica Sinica (*地理科学*)* 32(12): 1481–7.

Chen, Chi, Taejin Park, Xuhui Wang, Shilong Piao, Baodong Xu, Rajiv K. Chaturvedi, Richard Fuchs, Victor Brovkin, Philippe Ciais, Rasmus Fensholt, Hans Tømmervik, Govindasamy Bala, Zaichun Zhu,

Ramakrishna R. Nemani, and Ranga B. Myneni. 2019. "China and India Lead in Greening of the World through Land-Use Management." *Nature Sustainability* 2(2): 122–9.

Chen, Geoffrey C. and Charles Lees. 2018. "The New, Green, Urbanization in China: Between Authoritarian Environmentalism and Decentralization." *Chinese Political Science Review* 3(2): 212–31.

Chen, Meiling. 2017. "Determined Entrepreneur Turns Desert Home into Lush Garden." *China Daily*, September 6.

Chen, Stephen. 2018. "China's Building a Rain-Making Network Three Times the Size of Spain." *South China Morning Post*, March 26.

China-ASEAN Environmental Cooperation Center (中国-东盟环境保护合作中心). 2013. *China-ASEAN Green Envoys Program (*中国-东盟绿色使者计划*).* China Environmental Science Publishing House (中国环境出版社).

Chinese Academy of Sciences. 2016a. "Beijing Declaration on Earth Observation for Belt and Road." *Bulletin of the Chinese Academy of Sciences* 30(02): 106–7.

Chinese Academy of Sciences. 2016b. "China's First Overseas Land Satellite Receiving Station Put into Operation." *Newsroom*, December 16.

Clapp, Jennifer and Peter Dauvergne. 2011. *Paths to a Green World: The Political Economy of the Global Environment.* Second edition. MIT Press.

Conrad, Björn. 2012. "China in Copenhagen: Reconciling the 'Beijing Climate Revolution' and the 'Copenhagen Climate Obstinacy.'" *China Quarterly* 210: 435–55.

Couldry, Nick and Ulises A. Mejias. 2019. *The Costs of Connection: How Data Is Colonizing Human Life and Appropriating It for Capitalism.* Stanford University Press.

Cui, Tiankai. 2019. "Why the U.S. Shouldn't Sit Out the Belt and Road Initiative." *Fortune*, April 23.

Dauvergne, Peter. 1997. *Shadows in the Forest: Japan and the Politics of Timber in Southeast Asia*. MIT Press.

Deng, Jianping (邓建平). 2019. "Deng Jianping, Party Secretary and Director of the Shanghai Landscaping & City Appearance Bureau, Appears at the Summer Hotline Desk This Morning (上海市绿化和市容管理局党组书记、局长邓建平上午走进本报夏令热线)." *Green Shanghai (绿色上海)*, August 6.

Ding, Shineng (丁士能) and Feng Shi (石峰). 2017. "Implementing the Green Silk Road Messenger Program to Tell the Story of China's Environmental Protection (实施绿色丝路使者计划 讲述中国环保故事)." *China Ecological Civilization (中国生态文明)* (03): 47–50.

Du, Fachun. 2012. "Ecological Resettlement of Tibetan Herders in the Sanjiangyuan: A Case Study in Madoi County of Qinghai." *Nomadic Peoples* 16(1): 116–33.

Du, Haitao (杜海涛). 2018. "866.8 Thousand Tons of 'Foreign Garbage' Verified Last Year (去年查证'洋垃圾'86.68万吨)." *People's Daily (人民日报)*, February 7, 14.

Du, Yue. 2019. "Urbanizing the Periphery: Infrastructure Funding and Local Growth Coalition in China's Peasant Relocation Programs." *Urban Geography* 40(9): 1231–50.

Dutta, Tanushree, Ki-Hyun Kim, Minori Uchimiya, Eilhann E. Kwon, Byong-Hun Jeon, Akash Deep, and Seong-Taek Yun. 2016. "Global Demand for Rare Earth Resources and Strategies for Green Mining." *Environmental Research* 150: 182–90.

Eaton, Sarah and Genia Kostka. 2014. "Authoritarian Environmentalism Undermined? Local Leaders' Time Horizons and Environmental Policy Implementation in China." *China Quarterly* 218: 359–80.

Eaton, Sarah and Genia Kostka. 2017. "Central Protectionism in China: The 'Central SOE Problem' in Environmental Governance." *China Quarterly* 231: 685–704.

Elmer, Keegan. 2019. "Swedish Agency Warns Satellite Station Could Be Serving Chinese Military." *South China Morning Post*, January 14.

Eriksson, Hampus and Shelley Clarke. 2015. "Chinese Market Responses to Overexploitation of Sharks and Sea Cucumbers." *Biological Conservation* 184: 163–73.

European Chamber. 2019. *The Digital Hand: How China's Corporate Social Credit System Conditions Market Actors.* European Union Chamber of Commerce in China.

Eyler, Brian. 2019. *Last Days of the Mighty Mekong.* Zed Books.

Fairhead, James, Melissa Leach, and Ian Scoones. 2012. "Green Grabbing: A New Appropriation of Nature?" *Journal of Peasant Studies* 39(2): 237–61.

Feng, Weilin (冯伟林), Shuzhuo Li (李树茁), and Cong Li (李聪). 2016. "Study on the Failure of Human Capital and Social Capital in Economic Recovery of the Ecological Migrants: A Survey of Ecological Migrants in Southern Shaanxi (生态移民经济恢复中的人力资本与社会资本失灵——基于对陕南生态移民的调查)." *Population & Economics (人口与经济)* (01): 98–107.

Feng, Xiaoming, Bojie Fu, Shilong Piao, Shuai Wang, Philippe Ciais, Zhenzhong Zeng, Yihe Lü, Yuan Zeng, Yue Li, Xiaohui Jiang, and Bingfang Wu. 2016. "Revegetation in China's Loess Plateau Is Approaching Sustainable Water Resource Limits." *Nature Climate Change* 6(11): 1019–22.

Ferguson, James. 1990. *The Anti-Politics Machine: Development, Depoliticization, and Bureaucratic Power in Lesotho.* University of Minnesota Press.

Fialka, John. 2016. "Why China Is Dominating the Solar Industry." *Scientific American*, December 19.

Finamore, Barbara. 2018. *Will China Save the Planet?* Polity.

Flower, John. 2009. "Ecological Engineering on the Sichuan Frontier: Socialism as Development Policy, Local Practice, and Contested Ideology." *Social Anthropology* 17(1): 40–55.

French, Howard W. 2017. *Everything under the Heavens: How the Past Helps Shape China's Push for Global Power*. Knopf Doubleday.

Fu, Bojie, Shuai Wang, Yu Liu, Jianbo Liu, Wei Liang, and Chiyuan Miao. 2017. "Hydrogeomorphic Ecosystem Responses to Natural and Anthropogenic Changes in the Loess Plateau of China." *Annual Review of Earth and Planetary Sciences* 45(1): 223–43.

Gallagher, Kelly Sims and Qi Qi. 2018. *Policies Governing China's Overseas Development Finance Implications for Climate Change*. Center for International Environment and Resource Policy, Fletcher School, Tufts University.

Gardiner, Stephen M. 2011. *A Perfect Moral Storm: The Ethical Tragedy of Climate Change*. Oxford University Press.

Gare, Arran. 2016. *The Philosophical Foundations of Ecological Civilization: A Manifesto for the Future*. Routledge.

Ge, Chazhong (葛察忠), Jinnan Wang (王金南), Yong Zhang (张勇), and Wenhu Ye (叶文虎). 2003. "Evaluating Chinese Water Pollution Mitigation Policies through an Innovative Framework (中国水污染防治政策评估与创新框架)." *Environmental Policy Research Series (*中国环境政策*)* 4(7): 1–17.

Ge, Jiangtao (葛江涛). 2008. "Two New Criminal Charges from 600 Metric Tons of Foreign Garbage (600吨洋垃圾'熏出'两项新罪名)." *New Beijing News (*新京报*)*, May 2.

Ge, Lingyan (葛玲燕). 2018. "In Jiande Yangqiao Village, Why the Race to Do Good? (在建德杨桥村，为什么大家都争着做好事?)." *Daily Business* (每日商报), December 19, 1–17.

Geall, Sam. 2018. "Climate-Change Journalism and 'Edgeball' Politics in Contemporary China." *Society & Natural Resources* 31(5): 541–55.

Geall, Sam and Adrian Ely. 2018. "Narratives and Pathways towards an Ecological Civilization in Contemporary China." *China Quarterly* 236: 1175–96.

Gegen, Gaowa (葛根高娃) and Batu Uyun (乌云巴图). 2003. "The Concept, Problems and Countermeasures of Ecological Immigration in Inner Mongolia Pastoral Areas (内蒙古牧区生态移民的概念、问题与对策)." *Inner Mongolia Social Science (*内蒙古社会科学 (汉文版)*)* 24(2): 118–22.

Gilley, Bruce. 2012. "Authoritarian Environmentalism and China's Response to Climate Change." *Environmental Politics* 21(2): 287–307.

Gladney, Dru C. 2004. *Dislocating China: Muslims, Minorities, and Other Subaltern Subjects.* University of Chicago Press.

Gong, Baihua (龚柏华). 2011. "Review on the Practice of China's Participation in the WTO Dispute Settlement Mechanism during Its Ten Years as WTO Member (中国入世十年主动参与WTO争端解决机制实践述评)." *World Trade Organization Focus (*世界贸易组织动态与研究*)* 18(05): 9–18.

Greenhalgh, Susan. 2008. *Just One Child: Science and Policy in Deng's China.* University of California Press.

Greenpeace. 2019a. "Chinese Equity Investments in Energy Reshape South and Southeast Asia." Press release, July 29.

Greenpeace. 2019b. "Research on Sewage Treatment Management of China's Industrial Parks (中国工业园区污水处理管理研究)."

Greenstone, Michael. 2018. "Four Years after Declaring War on Pollution, China Is Winning." *New York Times*, March 12.

Guha, Ramachandra. 1989. "Radical American Environmentalism and Wilderness Preservation." *Environmental Ethics* 11(1): 71–83.

Guo, Huadong. 2018. "Steps to the Digital Silk Road." *Nature* 554(7690): 25–7.

Guo, Huadong, Gang Liu, Dong Liang, Lu Zhang, and Han Xiao. 2018. "Progress of Earth Observation in China." *China Journal of Space Science (空间科学学报)* 38(05): 797–809.

Guttman, Dan, Oran Young, Yijia Jing, Barbara Bramble, Maoliang Bu, Carmen Chen, Kathinka Furst, Tao Hu, Yifei Li, Kate Logan, Lingxuan Liu, Lydia Price, Michael Spencer, Sangwon Suh, Xiaopu Sun, Bowen Tan, Harold Wang, Xin Wang, Juan Zhang, Xinxin Zhang, and Rodrigo Zeidan. 2018. "Environmental Governance in China: Interactions between the State and 'Nonstate Actors.'" *Journal of Environmental Management* 220: 126–35.

Habich, Sabrina. 2016. *Dams, Migration and Authoritarianism in China: The Local State in Yunnan*. Routledge.

Hafeez, Muhammad, Yuan Chunhui, David Strohmaier, Manzoor Ahmed, and Liu Jie. 2018. "Does Finance Affect Environmental Degradation: Evidence from One Belt and One Road Initiative Region?" *Environmental Science and Pollution Research* 25(10): 9579–92.

Hao, Feng. 2019. "Can China's Afforestation Knowledge Green the World?" *China Dialogue*, August 30.

Hardin, Garrett. 1968. "The Tragedy of the Commons." *Science* 162(3859): 1243–8.

Harrell, Stevan. 1995. *Cultural Encounters on China's Ethnic Frontiers*. University of Washington Press.

Harrell, Stevan. 2002. *Ways of Being Ethnic in Southwest China*. University of Washington Press.

Harvey, David. 1985. "The Geopolitics of Capitalism." In D. Gregory and J. Urry (eds.) *Social Relations and Spatial Structures*. Macmillan Education, pp. 128–63.

Harvey, David. 2003. *The New Imperialism*. Oxford University Press.

Hauenstein, Severin, Mrigesh Kshatriya, Julian Blanc, Carsten F. Dormann, and Colin M. Beale. 2019. "African Elephant Poaching Rates Correlate with Local Poverty, National Corruption and Global Ivory Price." *Nature Communications* 10(1): 1–9.

Hayes-Labruto, Leslie, Simon J. D. Schillebeeckx, Mark Workman, and Nilay Shah. 2013. "Contrasting Perspectives on China's Rare Earths Policies: Reframing the Debate through a Stakeholder Lens." *Energy Policy* 63: 55–68.

Hebei Province Metallurgical Industry Association. 2019. "Letter Regarding Member Companies' Concerns over Crackdowns and Closures for Environmental Protection (关于报送钢铁企业停对限产和环保相关问题意见的函)."

Hilton, Isabel. 2017. "Guidance and Transgression: The Contest for Narratives of Environment and Pollution in China – Commentary." *International Journal of Communication* 11: 1323–41.

Hilton, Isabel and Oliver Kerr. 2017. "The Paris Agreement: China's 'New Normal' Role in International Climate Negotiations." *Climate Policy* 17(1): 48–58.

Hong, Pingfan. 2017. "Integrated Policy Approaches to the Implementation of the 2030 Agenda." United Nations Department of Economic and Social Affairs.

Hook, Leslie. 2019. "Climate Change: How China Moved from Leader to Laggard." *Financial Times*, November 25.

Hsieh, Pasha L. 2010. "China's Development of International Economic Law and WTO Legal Capacity

Building." *Journal of International Economic Law* 13(4): 997–1036.

Hsu, Angel, Zhi Yi Yeo, and Amy Weinfurter. 2020. "Emerging Digital Environmental Governance in China: The Case of Black and Smelly Waters in China." *Journal of Environmental Planning and Management* 63(1): 14–31.

Hua, Chunying. 2018a. "Foreign Ministry Spokesperson Hua Chunying's Regular Press Conference on April 18, 2018."

Hua, Chunying. 2018b. "Foreign Ministry Spokesperson Hua Chunying's Regular Press Conference on March 26, 2018."

Huang, Echo and Isabella Steger. 2017. "Norway Wants China to Forget about the Human Rights Thing and Eat Salmon Instead." *Quartz*, June 15.

Huang, Yanzhong. 2020. *Toxic Politics: China's Environmental Health Crisis and Its Challenge to the Chinese State.* Cambridge University Press.

Huntington, Samuel P. 1968. "The Bases of Accommodation." *Foreign Affairs* 46(4): 642–56.

International Hydropower Association. 2019. *Hydropower Status Report 2019: Sector Trends and Insights.* IHA Central Office.

Jahiel, Abigail R. 1997. "The Contradictory Impact of Reform on Environmental Protection in China." *China Quarterly* 149: 81–103.

Jia, Xiaoxu, Ming'an Shao, Yuanjun Zhu, and Yi Luo. 2017. "Soil Moisture Decline Due to Afforestation across the Loess Plateau, China." *Journal of Hydrology* 546: 113–22.

Jiang, Hong. 2004. "Cooperation, Land Use, and the Environment in Uxin Ju: The Changing Landscape of a Mongolian-Chinese Borderland in China." *Annals of the Association of American Geographers* 94(1): 117–39.

Jiang, Hong. 2005. "Grassland Management and Views

of Nature in China since 1949: Regional Policies and Local Changes in Uxin Ju, Inner Mongolia." *Geoforum* 36(5): 641–53.

Jiang, Hong. 2006a. "Decentralization, Ecological Construction, and the Environment in Post-Reform China: Case Study from Uxin Banner, Inner Mongolia." *World Development* 34(11): 1907–21.

Jiang, Hong. 2006b. "Fences, Ecologies, and Changes in Pastoral Life: Sandy Land Reclamation in Inner Mongolia, China." In K. S. Zimmerer (ed.) *Globalization and New Geographies of Conservation.* University of Chicago Press, pp. 296–314.

Jiang, Huanhuan (姜欢欢), Qingdan Yuan (原庆丹), Liping Li (李丽平), Bing Zhang (张彬), Yuanyuan Li (李媛媛), and Xinhao Huang (黄新皓). 2018. "From Participants to Leaders – Review of China's Environmental Protection Development (从参与者 贡献者到引领者——我国环保事业发展回顾)." *Ziguangge (*紫光阁*)* (11): 49–50.

Jiangsu Provincial Government (江苏省人民政府). 2018. "Interpretation of the 'Implementation Plan for the Fight against Black and Stinky Water in Jiangsu Province' (《江苏省城市黑臭水体治理攻坚战实施方案》解读)."

Jin, Ling. 2018. "Synergies between the Belt and Road Initiative and the 2030 SDGs: From the Perspective of Development." *Economic and Political Studies* 6(3): 278–92.

Jin, Xu (金旭). 2010. "Congratulations on the 30th Anniversary of the Establishment of the Academy for International Business Officials (热烈祝贺商务部国际商务官员研修学院建院30周年)." *Intertrade (*国际贸易*)* (04): 73.

Johnson, Michael P. 2001. "Environmental Impacts of Urban Sprawl: A Survey of the Literature and Proposed Research Agenda." *Environment and Planning A* 33(4): 717–35.

Kalantzakos, Sophia. 2018. *China and the Geopolitics of Rare Earths*. Oxford University Press.

Khagram, Sanjeev. 2004. *Dams and Development: Transnational Struggles for Water and Power*. Cornell University Press.

Khan, Yasir Habib. 2019. "Beijing: Where Innovation Drives Development." *The Nation*, September 1.

Kim, Sung-Young, Elizabeth Thurbon, Hao Tan, and John Mathews. 2019. "China Succeeds in Greening Its Economy Not Because, but in Spite of, Its Authoritarian Government." *The Conversation*, May 28.

King, Gary, Jennifer Pan, and Margaret E. Roberts. 2013. "How Censorship in China Allows Government Criticism but Silences Collective Expression." *American Political Science Review* 107(2): 326–43.

Klein, Julia A., Emily Yeh, Joseph Bump, Yonten Nyima, and Kelly Hopping. 2011. "Coordinating Environmental Protection and Climate Change Adaptation Policy in Resource-Dependent Communities: A Case Study from the Tibetan Plateau." In J. D. Ford and L. Berrang-Ford (eds.) *Climate Change Adaptation in Developed Nations: From Theory to Practice, Advances in Global Change Research*. Springer Netherlands, pp. 423–38.

Klein, Naomi. 2010. *The Shock Doctrine: The Rise of Disaster Capitalism*. Henry Holt and Company.

Kliman, Daniel and Abigail Grace. 2018. *Power Play: Addressing China's Belt and Road Strategy*. Center for a New American Security.

Klinger, Julie Michelle. 2018. *Rare Earth Frontiers: From Terrestrial Subsoils to Lunar Landscapes*. Cornell University Press.

Kostka, Genia. 2016. "Command without Control: The Case of China's Environmental Target System." *Regulation & Governance* 10(1): 58–74.

Kostka, Genia and Jonas Nahm. 2017. "Central-Local

Relations: Recentralization and Environmental Governance in China." *China Quarterly* 231: 567–82.

Kostka, Genia and Chunman Zhang. 2018. "Tightening the Grip: Environmental Governance under Xi Jinping." *Environmental Politics* 27(5): 769–81.

Kou, Jiangze (寇江泽). 2019. "Four Ministries to Adjust Waste Import Control List (四部门调整进口废物管理目录)." *People's Daily (*人民日报*)*, January 3.

Krugman, Paul. 2010. "Rare and Foolish." *New York Times*, October 17.

LaFraniere, Sharon. 2009. "Possible Link between Dam and China Quake." *New York Times*, February 6.

Lam, Long T., Lee Branstetter, and Inês M. L. Azevedo. 2017. "China's Wind Industry: Leading in Deployment, Lagging in Innovation." *Energy Policy* 106: 588–99.

Larson, Christina and Emily Wang. 2019. "Yellowstone in Tibet: China Designs New National Park System." *Associated Press*, November 12.

Lee, Ching Kwan. 2018. *The Specter of Global China: Politics, Labor, and Foreign Investment in Africa*. University of Chicago Press.

Lei, Tu. 2019. "Chinese Authorities Rush to Tame Rising Pork Prices." *Global Times*, September 1.

Lei, Yanchao (雷燕超) and Haonan Liu (刘浩南). 2019. "Farmers Required to Hand-Harvest Crops to Avoid Dust in Shangcai, Henan; Environmental Harvesters Dispatched (担心扬尘要求农户手割麦田 河南上蔡：已派环保型收割机)." *New Beijing News (*新京报*)*, June 7.

Leslie, Jacques. 2005. *Deep Water: The Epic Struggle over Dams, Displaced People, and the Environment*. Picador.

Levien, Michael. 2018. *Dispossession without Development: Land Grabs in Neoliberal India*. Oxford University Press.

Lewis, Joanna I. 2013. *Green Innovation in China: China's Wind Power Industry and the Global Transition to a Low-Carbon Economy.* Columbia University Press.

Li, Guangshou (黎光寿). 2010. "Rare-Earth Pollution from Baogang Leaves 66 Dead of Cancer (包钢稀土污染66人因癌死)." *National Business Daily (*每日经济新闻*)*, December 2.

Li, Peilin (李培林) and Xiaoyi Wang (王晓毅). 2013. "Immigration, Poverty Alleviation and Ecological Civilization Construction: Investigative Report of Ningxia Ecological Immigration (移民、扶贫与生态文明建设——宁夏生态移民调研报告)." *Social Sciences in Ningxia (*宁夏社会科学*)* (03): 52–60.

Li, Shengyong (李生勇), Songyong Feng (封松林), Guangwei Liu (刘广卫), Xiaoyu Hou (侯晓宇), and Huaiyu Xu (徐怀宇). 2017. "Reinforcing the Construction of Xiongan Smart City by Information Technology (以信息技术深化雄安智慧城市建设)." *Bulletin of the Chinese Academy of Sciences (*中国科学院院刊*)* 32(11): 1237–42.

Li, Vic and Graeme Lang. 2010. "China's 'Green GDP' Experiment and the Struggle for Ecological Modernisation." *Journal of Contemporary Asia* 40(1): 44–62.

Li, Yifei. 2019. "Bureaucracies Count: Environmental Governance through Goal-Setting and Mandate-Making in Contemporary China." *Environmental Sociology* 5(1): 12–22.

Li, You. 2019. "City Slammed over Stopgap Solutions for Meeting Pollution Goals." *Sixth Tone*, September 5.

Liao, Wulin (廖武林), Lifen Zhang (张丽芬), and Yunsheng Yao (姚运生). 2009. "Characteristics of Seismicity in the Three Gorges Reservoir Area (三峡水库地震活动特征研究)." *Seismology and Geology (*地震地质*)* 31(4): 707–14.

Lim, Louisa and Julia Bergin. 2018. "Inside China's

Audacious Global Propaganda Campaign." *Guardian*, December 7.

Lin, Liza and Laura Stevens. 2017. "Alibaba's Jack Ma Heads to Detroit to Impress Entrepreneurs – and Trump." *Wall Street Journal*, June 19.

Lin, Xu. 2019. "China Takes Extraordinary Initiatives in South-South Cooperation." *United Nations Office for South-South Cooperation Country Highlight*, April 30.

Linzner, Roland and Stefan Salhofer. 2014. "Municipal Solid Waste Recycling and the Significance of Informal Sector in Urban China." *Waste Management & Research* 32(9): 896–907.

Liu, Hongqiao. 2016. *Rare Earths: Shades of Grey – Can China Continue to Fuel Our Clean and Smart Future?* China Water Risk.

Liu, Jianqiang. 2013. "Defending Tiger Leaping Gorge." In S. Geall (ed.) *China and the Environment: The Green Revolution*. Zed Books, pp. 203–35.

Lo, Kwai-Cheung and Jessica Yeung. 2019. *Chinese Shock of the Anthropocene: Image, Music and Text in the Age of Climate Change*. Springer.

Lora-Wainwright, Anna. 2017. *Resigned Activism: Living with Pollution in Rural China*. MIT Press.

Lorentzen, Peter. 2014. "China's Strategic Censorship." *American Journal of Political Science* 58(2): 402–14.

Lu, Chenxi, Tingyang Zhao, Xiaoliang Shi, and Shixiong Cao. 2018. "Ecological Restoration by Afforestation May Increase Groundwater Depth and Create Potentially Large Ecological and Water Opportunity Costs in Arid and Semiarid China." *Journal of Cleaner Production* 176: 1213–22.

Lynas, Mark. 2009. "How Do I Know China Wrecked the Copenhagen Deal? I Was in the Room." *Guardian*, December 22.

Ma, Tianjie. 2015. "Put China's Tough New Law to Protect the Environment to the Test." *South China Morning Post*, January 14.

Magee, Darrin. 2014. "Dams in East Asia: Controlling Water but Creating Problems." In P. G. Harris and G. Lang (eds.) *Routledge Handbook of Environment and Society in Asia*. Routledge, pp. 216–36.

Manuel, Anja. 2017. "China Is Quietly Reshaping the World." *The Atlantic*, October 17.

Mao, KuoRay and Qian Zhang. 2018. "Dilemmas of State-Led Environmental Conservation in China: Environmental Target Enforcement and Public Participation in Minqin County." *Society & Natural Resources* 31(5): 615–31.

Mao, Zedong (毛澤東). 1950. "Speech (講話)." In Secretariat (秘書處) (ed.) *Commemoration Publication of First Plenary Session of the Chinese People's Political Consultative Conference (*中國人民政治協商會議第一屆全體會議紀念刊*)*. Xinhua Bookstore (新華書店), pp. 6–7.

Marcuse, Gary. 2011. *Waking the Green Tiger: Rise of a Green Movement in China*. Face to Face Media.

Maughan, Tim. 2015. "The Dystopian Lake Filled by the World's Tech Lust." *BBC Future*, April 2.

MEE (Ministry of Ecology and Environment 生态环境部). 2018. "MEE to Explicitly Ban 'Yidaoqie' in Environmental Enforcement (生态环境部明确禁止环保'一刀切'行为)."

MEE (Ministry of Ecology and Environment 生态环境部). 2019a. "Block-unblock Linkage in Transforming the 'E-Waste Capital': The Comprehensive Rectification of 'Scattered Pollution' in Guiyu Township, Shantou City, Guangdong Province (疏堵结合 '电子垃圾之都'转型跨越——广东汕头市贵屿镇'散乱污'综合整治实践)."

MEE (Ministry of Ecology and Environment 生态环境部). 2019b. "Green Belt and Road Facilitates Sustainable Development (绿色'一带一路'推动可持续发展)."

MEE (Ministry of Ecology and Environment 生态环

境部), Central Commission for Guiding Cultural and Ethical Progress (中央精神文明建设指导委员会办公室), Ministry of Education (教育部), Central Committee of the Communist Youth League (中国共产主义青年团中央委员会), and All-China Women's Federation (中华全国妇女联合会). 2018. "Announcement on the Publication of 'Citizen Ecological Environmental Behavioral Code of Conduct (for Trial Implementation)' (关于公布《公民生态环境行为规范（试行）》的公告)."

MEP (Ministry of Environmental Protection 环保部). 1997. "China's Environmental Yearbook for 1996 (1996年中国环境状况公报)."

MEP (Ministry of Environmental Protection 环保部). 2016. "Technical Guide for Zero-Livestock Zoning (Draft for Soliciting Opinions) 畜禽养殖禁养区划定技术指南（征求意见稿）."

MEP (Ministry of Environmental Protection 环保部). 2017. "Letter from the Ministry of Environmental Protection on the Special Supervision of Guaranteeing the 2017 Winter Heating for the '2+26' Cities in Beijing-Tianjin-Hebei and Surrounding Areas (环境保护部关于开展京津冀及周边地区'2+26'城市2017年冬季供暖保障工作专项督查的函)."

MEP (Ministry of Environmental Protection 环保部), MFA (Ministry of Foreign Affairs 外交部), NDRC (National Development and Reform Commission 国家发展和改革委员会), and MOFCOM (Ministry of Commerce 商务部). 2017. "Guidance on Promoting Green Belt and Road (关于推进绿色'一带一路'建设的指导意见)."

MEP (Ministry of Environmental Protection 环保部), NDRC (National Development and Reform Commission 国家发展和改革委员会), Ministry of Finance (财政部), National Energy Administration (国家能源局), Beijing Municipal Government (北京市人民政府), Tianjin Municipal Government (天津

市人民政府), Hebei Provincial Government (河北省人民政府), Shanxi Provincial Government (山西省人民政府), Shandong Provincial Government (山东省人民政府), and Henan Provincial Government (河南省人民政府). 2017. "Notice on Printing and Distributing 'The Work Plan for the Prevention and Control of Air Pollution in Beijing-Tianjin-Hebei and the Surrounding Areas in 2017' (关于印发《京津冀及周边地区2017年大气污染防治工作方案》的通知)."

Mertha, Andrew. 2008. *China's Water Warriors: Citizen Action and Policy Change*. Cornell University Press.

Mertha, Andrew. 2009. "'Fragmented Authoritarianism 2.0': Political Pluralization in the Chinese Policy Process." *China Quarterly* 200: 995–1012.

Miehe, Georg, Sabine Miehe, Knut Kaiser, Christoph Reudenbach, Lena Behrendes, La Duo, and Frank Schlütz. 2009. "How Old Is Pastoralism in Tibet? An Ecological Approach to the Making of a Tibetan Landscape." *Palaeogeography, Palaeoclimatology, Palaeoecology* 276(1): 130–47.

Miles, Tom. 2018. "U.S. Asks China Not to Implement Ban on Foreign Garbage." *Reuters*, March 24.

MoHURD (Ministry of Housing and Urban-Rural Development 住房和城乡建设部). 2004. "Opinions on Strengthening Supervision of Urban Wastewater Treatment Plants (建设部关于加强城镇污水处理厂运行监管的意见)."

MoHURD (Ministry of Housing and Urban-Rural Development 住房和城乡建设部). 2006. "Notice on Organizing the Investigation and Verification of Urban Wastewater Treatment (关于组织开展城镇污水处理情况调研核查工作的通知)."

Mol, Arthur P. J. and Neil T. Carter. 2006. "China's Environmental Governance in Transition." *Environmental Politics* 15(2): 149–70.

Moore, Jason W. 2011. "Transcending the Metabolic

Rift: A Theory of Crises in the Capitalist World-Ecology." *Journal of Peasant Studies* 38(1): 1–46.

Morris, William and Alison Schonberg. 2017. *Sustainability Insights: Shanghai Informal Waste Management*. Collective Responsibility.

Mozur, Paul, Jonah M. Kessel, and Melissa Chan. 2019. "Made in China, Exported to the World: The Surveillance State." *New York Times*, April 24.

Nathan, Andrew J. 2003. "China's Changing of the Guard: Authoritarian Resilience." *Journal of Democracy* 14(1): 6–17.

NDRC (National Development and Reform Commission 国家发展和改革委员会). 2016. "Development Plan for Rare Earth Industry (2016–2020) (稀土行业发展规划（2016－2020年）."

NDRC (National Development and Reform Commission 国家发展和改革委员会). 2018. "Notice from the National Development and Reform Commission on Printing and Distributing the Overall Plan of Sanjiangyuan National Park (国家发展改革委关于印发三江源国家公园总体规划的通知)."

NDRC (National Development and Reform Commission 国家发展和改革委员会). 2019. "Overall Action Plan for Launching Green Living (绿色生活创建行动总体方案)."

NDRC (National Development and Reform Commission) and MEE (Ministry of Ecology and Environment). 2020. "Opinions on Further Tightening of the Regulation of Plastic Pollution (关于进一步加强塑料污染治理的意见)."

NDRC (National Development and Reform Commission 国家发展和改革委员会), Ministry of Foreign Affairs (外交部), and MOFCOM (Ministry of Commerce 商务部). 2015. "Vision and Actions on Jointly Building Silk Road Economic Belt and 21st-Century Maritime Silk Road (推动共建丝绸之路经济带和21世纪海上丝绸之路的愿景与行动)."

NDRC (National Development and Reform Commission 国家发展和改革委员会), Ministry of Science and Technology (科技部), Ministry of Industry and Information Technology (工业和信息化部), Ministry of Finance (财政部), Ministry of Land and Resources (国土资源部), Ministry of Environmental Protection (环境保护部), Ministry of Housing and Urban-Rural Development (住房和城乡建设部), Ministry of Transportation (交通运输部), Ministry of Commerce (商务部), State-owned Assets Supervision and Administration Commission (国资委), General Bureau of Taxation (税务总局), General Administration of Quality Supervision, Inspection and Quarantine (质检总局), and National Energy Administration (国家能源局). 2017. "Notice on Printing and Distributing the 'Opinions on Accelerating the Use of Natural Gas' (关于印发《加快推进天然气利用的意见》的通知)."

Nijhuis, Michelle. 2006. "In China, Yu Xiaogang Is Helping Locals Fight Back against Dams." *Grist*, April 26.

Nixon, Rob. 2011. *Slow Violence and the Environmentalism of the Poor*. Harvard University Press.

Norgaard, Kari Marie. 2011. *Living in Denial: Climate Change, Emotions, and Everyday Life*. MIT Press.

Normile, Dennis. 2007. "Getting at the Roots of Killer Dust Storms." *Science* 317(5836): 314–16.

O'Connor, James. 1988. "Capitalism, Nature, Socialism a Theoretical Introduction." *Capitalism Nature Socialism* 1(1): 11–38.

O'Connor, James. 1991. "On the Two Contradictions of Capitalism." *Capitalism Nature Socialism* 2(3): 107–9.

Oreskes, Naomi and Erik M. Conway. 2011. *Merchants of Doubt: How a Handful of Scientists Obscured the Truth on Issues from Tobacco Smoke to Global Warming*. Bloomsbury Publishing.

Oreskes, Naomi and Erik M. Conway. 2014. *The Collapse of Western Civilization: A View from the Future.* Columbia University Press.

Ostrom, Elinor. 1990. *Governing the Commons: The Evolution of Institutions for Collective Action.* Cambridge University Press.

Ouyang, Bing (欧阳斌), Zheng Yuan (袁正), and Jingsi Chen (陈静思). 2015. "Environmental Awareness and Environmental Behavior of City Residents in China (我国城市居民环境意识、环保行为测量及影响因素分析)." *Economic Geography (经济地理)* 35(11): 179–83.

Pan, Yue (潘岳). 2004. "Environmental Indicators and Official Performance Evaluation (环保指标与官员政绩考核)." *Scientific Decision Making (科学决策)* (6): 13–16.

Parenti, Christian. 2015. "The 2013 *Antipode* AAG Lecture The Environment Making State: Territory, Nature, and Value." *Antipode* 47(4): 829–48.

Pellow, David N. 2007. *Resisting Global Toxics: Transnational Movements for Environmental Justice.* MIT Press.

Peng, Hui (蓬慧). 2019. "Can China Take the Risk of 'If's'? (中国能吞下'如果'带来的苦果吗？)." *People's Daily (人民日报)*, June 19.

Peng, Pingan (彭平安), Guoying Sheng (盛国英), and Jiamo Fu (傅家谟). 2009. "Overview of Pollution by Electronic and Electric Wastes (电子垃圾的污染问题)." *Progress in Chemistry (化学进展)* 21(Z1): 550–7.

Petrzelka, Peggy and Michael M. Bell. 2000. "Rationality and Solidarities: The Social Organization of Common Property Resources in the Imdrhas Valley of Morocco." *Human Organization* 59(3): 343–52.

Power, Marcus, Giles Mohan, and May Tan-Mullins. 2012. *China's Resource Diplomacy in Africa: Powering Development?* Palgrave Macmillan.

Puckett, Jim. 2002. *Exporting Harm: The High-Tech Trashing of Asia*. Basel Action Network.

Qi, Ye and Tong Wu. 2013. "The Politics of Climate Change in China." *Wiley Interdisciplinary Reviews: Climate Change* 4(4): 301–13.

Qu, Geping and Jinchang Li. 1994. *Population and the Environment in China*. Lynne Rienner.

Ran, Ran. 2013. "Perverse Incentive Structure and Policy Implementation Gap in China's Local Environmental Politics." *Journal of Environmental Policy & Planning* 15(1): 17–39.

Reed, John. 2018. "Thailand to Ban Foreign Plastic Waste from 2021." *Financial Times*, October 14.

Ren, Peng, Chang Liu, and Liwen Zhang. 2017. *China's Involvement in Coal-Fired Power Projects along the Belt and Road*. Global Environmental Institute.

Roberts, Margaret E. 2018. *Censored: Distraction and Diversion inside China's Great Firewall*. Princeton University Press.

Rome, Adam. 2002. "What Really Matters in History: Environmental Perspectives in Modern America." *Environmental History* 7(2): 303–18.

Rousseau, Jean-François. 2020. "When Land, Water and Green-Grabbing Cumulate: Hydropower Expansion, Livelihood Resource Reallocation and Legitimisation in Southwest China." *Asia Pacific Viewpoint*, 61(1): 134–46.

Sawyer, Jon (ed.). 2015. *Ecological Civilization*. Pulitzer Center on Crisis Reporting.

Schmitz, Rob. 2017. "China Shuts Down Tens of Thousands of Factories in Unprecedented Pollution Crackdown." *National Public Radio, Morning Edition*, October 23.

Schnaiberg, Allan. 1980. *Environment: From Surplus to Scarcity*. Oxford University Press.

Scott, James C. 1998. *Seeing like a State: How Certain*

Schemes to Improve the Human Condition Have Failed. Yale University Press.

Shahar, Dan Coby. 2015. "Rejecting Eco-Authoritarianism, Again." *Environmental Values* 24(3): 345–66.

Shambaugh, David. 2016. *China's Future.* Polity.

Shan, Renping (单仁平). 2017. "Switching from Coal to Gas – the Country Is Not to Let People Freeze (煤改气，国家不是要让部分群众冻着)." *Global Times (*环球时报), December 4.

Shapiro, Judith. 2001. *Mao's War against Nature: Politics and the Environment in Revolutionary China.* Cambridge University Press.

Shapiro, Judith. 2015. *China's Environmental Challenges.* Second edition. Polity.

Shapiro, Judith and Heng Liang. 1986. *Cold Winds, Warm Winds: Intellectual Freedom in China Today.* Wesleyan University Press.

Shearer, Christine, Aiqun Yu, and Ted Nace. 2019. *Out of Step: China Is Driving the Continued Growth of the Global Coal Fleet.* Global Energy Monitor.

Shi, Tianjian. 1997. *Political Participation in Beijing.* Harvard University Press.

Simons, Craig. 2013. *The Devouring Dragon: How China's Rise Threatens Our Natural World.* St. Martin's Press.

Sneath, David. 2000. *Changing Inner Mongolia: Pastoral Mongolian Society and the Chinese State.* Oxford University Press.

Solly, Meilan. 2019. "China's National Panda Park Will Be Three Times the Size of Yellowstone." *Smithsonian,* May 13.

Song, Jianlan. 2016. "DBAR Initiative: Big Earth Data for 'Belt and Road' Development." *Bulletin of the Chinese Academy of Sciences* 30(02): 99–105.

Spires, Anthony J. 2011. "Contingent Symbiosis and Civil Society in an Authoritarian State: Understanding the Survival of China's Grassroots NGOs." *American Journal of Sociology* 117(1): 1–45.

Stanway, David, Philip Wen, and Stella Qiu. 2019. "A Pollution Crackdown Compounds Slowdown Woes in China's Heartland." *Reuters*, May 24.

State Council (国务院). 1993. "Major Events China's Rare Earth Industry in 1992 (1992 年中国稀土十件大事)." *Rare Earth Information (*稀土信息*)* (01): 2–4.

State Council (国务院). 2007. "Wu Yi: Special Rectification Campaign for Product Quality and Food Safety (吴仪：打好产品质量和食品安全专项整治特殊战役)."

State Council (国务院). 2012. "State of China's Rare Earths Policies (中国的稀土状况与政策)."

State Council (国务院). 2013a. "Notice from the State Council on Printing and Distributing the Air Pollution Prevention and Control Action Plan (国务院关于印发大气污染防治行动计划的通知)."

State Council (国务院). 2013b. "Pollution Control Regulations for Livestock Farms (畜禽规模养殖污染防治条例)."

State Council (国务院). 2014. "Strategic Action Plan for Energy Development (2014–2020) (能源发展战略行动计划 (2014–2020年))."

State Council (国务院). 2016. "Thirteenth Five-Year Plan for Ecological Environmental Protection ('十三五'生态环境保护规划)."

Stewart, Ashleigh. 2019. "The Online Silk Road: China's Growing Influence on Tech in the UAE." *The National*, February 4.

Sun, Chao (孙超). 2018. "How to Secure a Livelihood When the Pig Farms Are Gone (拆了养猪场，生计咋保障)." *People's Daily*, January 11.

Sun, Lichao (孙丽朝). 2019. "'Bubbles' on the China–Europe Freight Trains (中欧班列挤'泡沫')." *China Business Journal (*中国经营报*)*, July 26.

Sun, Lingli (孙伶俐), Yunsheng Yao (姚运生), Lingxia

Jiang (蒋玲霞), Guichun Wei (魏贵春), Hui Wang (王慧), and Junqiu Luo (罗俊秋). 2015. "Effect of Water Load Variation in the Three Gorge Reservoir on the Crustal Deformation (三峡水库水体荷载变化对地壳形变的影响)." *Journal of Yangtze River Scientific Research Institute (*长江科学院院报*)* 32(12): 46–50.

Sun, Weizeng (孙伟增), Danglun Luo (罗党论), Siqi Zheng (郑思齐), and Guanghua Wan (万广华). 2014. "Environmental Assessment, Local Official Promotion and Environmental Management: Evidence from 86 Main Cities of China (2004–2009) (环保考核、地方官员晋升与环境治理——基于2004—2009年中国86个重点城市的经验证据)." *Journal of Tsinghua University (Philosophy and Social Sciences) (*清华大学学报*(*哲学社会科学版*))* 29(04): 49–62, 171.

Tang, Jiaxuan (唐家璇). 2012. *The Glorious Course of China's Diplomacy at the Turn of the Century (*中国跨世纪外交的光辉历程*)*. Ministry of Foreign Affairs.

Teets, Jessica. 2013. "Let Many Civil Societies Bloom: The Rise of Consultative Authoritarianism in China." *China Quarterly* 213: 19–38.

Teets, Jessica. 2018. "The Power of Policy Networks in Authoritarian Regimes: Changing Environmental Policy in China." *Governance* 31(1): 125–41.

Thorne, Devin and Ben Spevack. 2017. *Harbored Ambitions: How China's Port Investments Are Strategically Reshaping the Indo-Pacific*. C4ADS.

Tian, Fangmeng (田方萌). 2014. "Was Napoleon the First to Advance the Sleeping-Lion Theory of China? (拿破仑最早提出中国睡狮论吗?)." *New York Times – Chinese Edition (*纽约时报中文网*)*, April 3.

Tian, Jiexiong (田杰雄). 2019. "Widespread Drought Affects Anhui (安徽沿江地区出现30至50年一遇特大干旱)." *New Beijing News (*新京报*)*, October 31.

Tilt, Bryan. 2014. *Dams and Development in China: The Moral Economy of Water and Power*. Columbia University Press.

Tilt, Bryan. 2019. "China's Air Pollution Crisis: Science and Policy Perspectives." *Environmental Science & Policy* 92: 275–80.

Tracy, Elena F., Evgeny Shvarts, Eugene Simonov, and Mikhail Babenko. 2017. "China's New Eurasian Ambitions: The Environmental Risks of the Silk Road Economic Belt." *Eurasian Geography and Economics* 58(1): 56–88.

Trevithick, Joseph. 2019. "China's Historic Mission to the Dark Side of the Moon Is about More Than Science." *The Drive*, January 3.

Tsai, Lily L. and Yiqing Xu. 2018. "Outspoken Insiders: Political Connections and Citizen Participation in Authoritarian China." *Political Behavior* 40(3): 629–57.

Tu, Meng, Bing Zhang, Jianhua Xu, and Fangwen Lu. 2020. "Mass Media, Information and Demand for Environmental Quality: Evidence from 'Under the Dome.'" *Journal of Development Economics* 143: 102402.

UN (United Nations). 2019. "At China's Belt and Road Forum, Guterres Calls for 'Inclusive, Sustainable and Durable' Development." *UN News*, April 26.

UN ESCAP (United Nations Economic and Social Commission for Asia and the Pacific). 2017. "A Study of ICT Connectivity for the Belt and Road Initiative (BRI): Enhancing the Collaboration in China-Central Asia Corridor."

UNEP (United Nations Environment Programme). 2018. "Green Belt and Road Strategy."

Uxin Banner (乌审旗). 2019. *Forestry Gazetteer of Uxin Banner* (乌审旗林业志). Shaanxi People's Publishing House (陕西人民出版社).

van der Kamp, Denise. 2017. "Clean Air at What Cost? The Rise of Blunt Force Pollution Regulation in China." PhD dissertation, UC Berkeley.

van Rooij, Benjamin. 2006. "Implementation of

Chinese Environmental Law: Regular Enforcement and Political Campaigns." *Development and Change* 37(1): 57–74.

van Rooij, Benjamin, Rachel E. Stern, and Kathinka Fürst. 2016. "The Authoritarian Logic of Regulatory Pluralism: Understanding China's New Environmental Actors." *Regulation & Governance* 10(1): 3–13.

WAM (Emirates News Agency). 2019. "'UAE to Become a Shining Pearl along Belt and Road,' Says Chinese Foreign Minister." *Gulf News*, July 21.

Wan, Jun (万军), Huiyuan Zhang (张惠远), Jinnan Wang (王金南), Chazhong Ge (葛察忠), Shuting Gao (高树婷), and Sheng Rao (饶胜). 2005. "Policy Evaluation and Framework Discussion of the Ecological Compensation Mechanism in China (中国生态补偿政策评估与框架初探)." *Research of Environmental Sciences (*环境科学研究*)* 18(2): 1–8.

Wang, Guangyu, John L. Innes, Jiafu Lei, Shuanyou Dai, and Sara W. Wu. 2007. "China's Forestry Reforms." *Science* 318(5856): 1556–7.

Wang, Haikun, Xi Lu, Yu Deng, Yaoguang Sun, Chris P. Nielsen, Yifan Liu, Ge Zhu, Maoliang Bu, Jun Bi, and Michael B. McElroy. 2019. "China's CO_2 Peak before 2030 Implied from Characteristics and Growth of Cities." *Nature Sustainability* 2(8): 748–54.

Wang, Jiuliang. 2017. *Plastic China*. Journeyman Pictures.

Wang, Keju. 2018. "Nation Plans to Phase Out Gasoline-Fueled Vehicles in Near Future." *China Daily*, June 5.

Wang, Lixin (王立新), Huamin Liu (刘华民), Jie Yang (杨劼), Cunzhu Liang (梁存柱), Wei Wang (王炜), and Jien Zhang (张继恩). 2010. "Climate Change of Mu Us Sandy Land and Its Influence on Vegetation Coverage (毛乌素沙地气候变化及其对植被覆盖的影响)." *Journal of Natural Resources (*自然资源学报*)* 25(12): 2030–9.

Wang, Qiang (王强). 2013. "Why Officials Valuing Environmental Protection Find It Difficult to be Promoted? (重视环保的官员因何升迁难?)." *New York Times – Chinese Edition (*纽约时报中文网*)*, April 15.

Wang, Qingkai (王庆凯). 2019. "Five State Council Measures to Balance Pork Price (国务院出五招让你吃上便宜肉)." *National Affairs Express (*国是直通车*)*, August 22.

Wang, Xiaoyi. 2007. *Undermining Grassland Management through Centralized Environmental Policies in Inner Mongolia*. Working Paper #29. World Resources Institute.

Wang, Xunming, C. X. Zhang, Eerdun Hasi, and Zhibao Dong. 2010. "Has the Three Norths Forest Shelterbelt Program Solved the Desertification and Dust Storm Problems in Arid and Semiarid China?" *Journal of Arid Environments* 74(1): 13–22.

Wang, Yifeng (王义凤), Shipeng Yong (雍世鹏), and Zhongling Liu (刘钟龄). 1979. "Characteristics of Vegetation Zone in Inner Mongolia Autonomous Region (内蒙古自治区的植被地带特征)." *Journal of Integrative Plant Biology (*植物学报*)* 21(3): 274–84.

Wang, Yinan (王亦楠). 2014. "How to Resolve Environmental Mass Incidents? (如何化解环境类群体性事件?)." *21st Century Business Herald (*21世纪经济报道*)*, May 13.

Wang, Yu (王钰). 2019. "The 38-Year Journey of National Voluntary Tree Planting (全民义务植树38年)." *China Green Times (*中国绿色时报*)*, March 12.

Wang, Zheng (王振), Fuchun Zhao (赵付春), and Yingbo Wang (王滢波). 2017. "Developing Digital Economy, Brightening the Road to Innovation (发展数字经济点亮创新之路)." *People's Daily (*人民日报*)*, May 22, 22.

Wang, Zhengxu and Jinghan Zeng. 2016. "Xi Jinping: The Game Changer of Chinese Elite Politics?" *Contemporary Politics* 22(4): 469–86.

Wang, Zhihe, Huili He, and Meijun Fan. 2014. "The Ecological Civilization Debate in China: The Role of Ecological Marxism and Constructive Postmodernism – Beyond the Predicament of Legislation." *Monthly Review* 66(6): 37–59.

Wang, Zipei (王梓佩). 2019. "'Strictest Village Code' Goes Awry ('最严村规'好心办错事)." *Nanfang Daily (南方日报)*, October 10.

Wang, Zongming, Kaishan Song, and Liangjun Hu. 2010. "China's Largest Scale Ecological Migration in the Three-River Headwater Region." *Ambio* 39(5–6): 443–6.

Wei, Tianfei (魏天飞) and Yufei Zhang (张羽飞). 2014. "China's Plastic Waste Recycling Industry Starts a Revolutionary Transformation: Entering the 'Post-Green Fence Era' (中国废塑料再生产业开始革命性转型——中国废塑料产业进入'后绿篱时代')." *China Packaging Industry (中国包装工业)* (09): 46–55.

Wilson, Scott. 2016. "Environmental Participation in the Shadow of the Chinese State." *Economic and Political Studies* 4(3): 211–37.

Winner, Langdon. 1986. *The Whale and the Reactor: A Search of Limits in an Age of High Technology.* University of Chicago Press.

WTO (World Trade Organization). 2012. "DS431: China – Measures Related to the Exportation of Rare Earths, Tungsten and Molybdenum."

WTO (World Trade Organization). 2017. "Notification G/TBT/N/CHN/1211."

Wu, Yuehe (五月荷). 2019. "America: Do Not Underestimate China's Ability to Strike Back (美方不要低估中方反制能力)." *People's Daily (人民日报)*, May 29, 3.

Wübbeke, Jost. 2013. "Rare Earth Elements in China: Policies and Narratives of Reinventing an Industry." *Resources Policy* 38(3): 384–94.

WWF. 2017. *The Belt and Road Initiative: WWF Recommendations and Spatial Analysis*. WWF.

WWF. 2018. *Greening the Belt and Road Initiative: WWF's Recommendations for the Finance Sector*. WWF.

WWF. 2019. *Demand under the Ban: China Ivory Consumption Research 2019*. WWF and GlobeScan.

Xi, Jinping (习近平). 2014. "Xi's Speech at the 50th Anniversary of the Establishment of Sino-France Diplomatic Relations (习近平在中法建交50周年纪念大会上的讲话)."

Xi, Jinping (习近平). 2017. *Why I Proposed the Belt and Road* (《国家相册》 "一带一路"特别节目：大道之行). CGTN, May 12.

Xi, Jinping (习近平). 2019. "Together Envision Green Life, Together Build a Beautiful Home: Speech at the Opening Ceremony of the International Horticultural Exhibition 2019, Beijing, China (共谋绿色生活，共建美丽家园——在二〇一九年中国北京世界园艺博览会开幕式上的讲话)."

Xia, Ying. 2019. "Wealth from Waste? Chinese Investments and Technology Transfer in the Tanzanian Plastic Recycling Industry." *China Africa Research Initiative Policy Brief Series* (35).

Xiao, Yinong (肖亦农). 2016. *Green Great Wall* (毛乌素绿色传奇). China Translation & Publishing House.

Xinhua. 2012. "Commentary: Promoting the Sustainable Development of the Rare Earth Industry (述评：促进稀土行业可持续发展)." May 8.

Xinhua. 2015. "The Difficult Transformation of the 'E-Waste Capital': Investigation into the Rectification of the Electronic Dismantling Industry in Guiyu Township, Guangdong Province ('电子垃圾之都'艰难转型记——广东贵屿电子拆解业整治追踪调查)." December 15.

Xinhua. 2016. "Exploiting Earth-Moon Space: China's Ambition after Space Station." March 8.

Xinhua. 2017a. "'Belt and Road' Incorporated into CPC Constitution." October 24.

Xinhua. 2017b. "China's Cloud Seeding in Past Five Years Produced Enough Rain to Fill Three Qinhai Lakes (我国五年人工降雨'洒'下 3 个青海湖)." September 20.

Xinhua. 2018. "Belt and Road Initiative China's Gift to World: UAE Minister." July 21.

Xinhua. 2019a. "China Holds 130 Officials Accountable in Latest Environment Inspection." August 9.

Xinhua. 2019b. "China Launches Three New Satellites." September 12.

Xinhua. 2019c. "Exemplary Dream Chasers: Background of State-of-the-Art Planning Blueprint for Xiongan New Area, Hebei (追梦典范——河北雄安新区高质量规划蓝图出炉的背后)." April 3.

Xinhua. 2019d. "MV: 'Two Sessions': To the World, from China."

Xinhua. 2019e. "The Belt and Road Initiative: Progress, Contributions and Prospects (共建'一带一路'倡议：进展、贡献与展望)." April 22.

Xinhua. 2019f. "Xi Highlights Sustainable Development as 'Golden Key' to Solving Global Problems at SPIEF." June 8.

Xu, Muyu and David Stanway. 2019. "China CO2 Emission Targets at Risk from U.S. Trade War – Official." *Reuters*, August 30.

Xu, Yili (许一力). 2013. "How to Hide Our Strength and Bide Our Time on the Issue of Chinese Rare Earths? (中国稀土该如何韬光养晦?)." *Ministry of Natural Resources (自然资源部)*, April 11.

Yan, Guodong (闫国东), Jiancheng Kang (康建成), Xiaojing Xie (谢小进), Guodong Wang (王国栋), Jianping Zhang (张建平), and Wenwu Zhu (朱文武). 2010. "Trends of Chinese Environmental Awareness (中国公众环境意识的变化趋势)." *China Population,*

*Resources, and Environment (*中国人口·资源与环境*)* 20(10): 55–60.

Yan, Sophia. 2019. "The Sleepy Village Testing China's Social Credit System." *South China Morning Post*, June 2.

Yang, Junfeng (杨俊峰). 2018. *Let's Sing a Song Called "I'd Like to Build the World a Road."* People's Daily Online Publishing.

Yang, Ruby and Thomas Lennon. 2010. *Warriors of Qiugang.* Cinema Guild.

Yang, Ye (杨烨). 2014. "The Ministry of Environmental Protection: Wastewater Treatment Plant Turned into a Pollution Source, the Last Defensive Line Broken (环保部：污水处理厂反成污染源　最后一道关卡失守)." *Economic Information Daily (*经济参考报*)*, July 25.

Yeh, Emily T. 2005. "Green Governmentality and Pastoralism in Western China: 'Converting Pastures to Grasslands.'" *Nomadic Peoples* 9(1/2): 9–30.

Yeh, Emily T. 2009. "Greening Western China: A Critical View." *Geoforum* 40(5): 884–94.

Yeh, Emily T. 2013. *Taming Tibet: Landscape Transformation and the Gift of Chinese Development.* Cornell University Press.

Yong, Huang. 2019. "Construction of Digital Silk Road Lights Up BRI Cooperation." *People's Daily*, April 24.

Young, Oran R. 1994. *International Governance: Protecting the Environment in a Stateless Society.* Cornell University Press.

Young, Oran R. 2017. *Governing Complex Systems: Social Capital for the Anthropocene.* MIT Press.

Yu, Hao, Bing Wang, Yue-Jun Zhang, Shouyang Wang, and Yi-Ming Wei. 2013. "Public Perception of Climate Change in China: Results from the Questionnaire Survey." *Natural Hazards* 69(1): 459–72.

Yue, Jiachen (岳家琛). 2015. "The Secret 'Karate' in Trading Environmental Assessment Qualifications, the First Line of Defense in Pollution Mitigation (第一道污染防线上的'空手道'环评资质倒卖经)." *Southern Weekly (南方周末)*, March 26.

Zhang, Ketian. 2019. "Cautious Bully: Reputation, Resolve, and Beijing's Use of Coercion in the South China Sea." *International Security* 44(1): 117–59.

Zhang, Zhihao. 2019. "Databank Puts Info at World's Fingertips." *China Daily*, January 16.

Zhao, G., X. Mu, Z. Wen, F. Wang, and P. Gao. 2013. "Soil Erosion, Conservation, and Eco-environment Changes in the Loess Plateau of China." *Land Degradation & Development* 24(5): 499–510.

Zhao, Siwei (赵思维) and Xiaomei Zhong (钟笑玫). 2019. "Henan Officials: We Shouldn't Defame Environmental Protection in the Name of Environmental Protection; Banning Harvesters next to the Monitoring Station Is Misconduct (豫官方：反对以抓环保之名黑环保，监测站旁禁收割机是乱作为)." *The Paper (澎湃新闻)*, June 7.

Zhao, Yinping (赵银平). 2019. "Xi Jinping Proposed China's Solution for Win-Win Human and Nature Development (人类与自然共生共赢 习近平提出中国方案)." *Xinhua News Agency – Learning Xi Jinping Thought (新华社 学习进行时)*, April 29.

Zhao, Yusha. 2018. "Raising a Stink." *Global Times*, May 28.

Zheng, Yongnian. 2009. *The Chinese Communist Party as Organizational Emperor: Culture, Reproduction, and Transformation.* Routledge.

Zhou, Huakun (周华坤), Xinquan Zhao (赵新全), Chaoyuan Zhang (张超远), Xiaofang Xing (邢小方), Baowen Zhu (朱宝文), and Fachun Du (杜发春). 2010. "The Predicament of Ecological Migrants and Sustainable Development Strategy in Sanjiangyuan (三江源区生态移民的困境与可持续发展策略)." *China Population, Resources and Environment (中国人口·资源与环境)* 20(3): 185–8.

Zhou, Xuehong, Qiang Wang, Wei Zhang, Yu Jin, Zhen Wang, Zheng Chai, Zhiqiang Zhou, Xiaofeng Cui, and Douglas C. MacMillan. 2018. "Elephant Poaching and the Ivory Trade: The Impact of Demand Reduction and Enforcement Efforts by China from 2005–2017." *Global Ecology and Conservation* 16: e00486.

Zhu, Junming and Marian R. Chertow. 2019. "Authoritarian but Responsive: Local Regulation of Industrial Energy Efficiency in Jiangsu, China." *Regulation & Governance* 13(3): 384–404.

Zinda, John Aloysius. 2012. "Hazards of Collaboration: Local State Co-optation of a New Protected-Area Model in Southwest China." *Society & Natural Resources* 25(4): 384–99.

Zinda, John Aloysius, Yifei Li, and John Chung-En Liu. 2018. "China's Summons for Environmental Sociology." *Current Sociology* 66(6): 867–85.

Zweig, David. 2002. *Internationalizing China: Domestic Interests and Global Linkages*. Cornell University Press.

Index